Metaphors of Masculinity

Metaphors

Stanley Brandes

Publications of the American Folklore Society
New Series
General Editor, Marta Weigle
Volume I

# of Masculinity

Sex and Status in Andalusian Folklore

University of Pennsylvania Press / 1980

Library of Congress Cataloging in Publication Data

Brandes, Stanley
    Metaphors of masculinity.

    Bibliography: p. 215
    Includes index.
    1. Folk-lore—Spain—Andalusia. 2. Andalusia—Social life and customs.
3. Men—Spain—Andalusia.
I. Title.
GR237.A52B7   398'.353'09468   79-5258
ISBN O-8122-7776-7 (cloth)
        O-8122-1105-7 (paper)

For Judy

Contents

Acknowledgments

I am happy for this opportunity to express my gratitude to everyone who assisted me, whether directly or indirectly, to produce this book. Two granting agencies awarded me the financial means to carry out my research: the National Institute of Child Health and Human Development supported fieldwork from July 1975 through August 1976 and provided three months' write-up time during winter 1977; and the American Council of Learned Societies funded a second visit to Spain in summer 1977, when I was able to evaluate and refine the ideas that I had originally worked out. The material contained in this volume represents only a portion of the total research that I was able to accomplish with the generous support of these agencies.

Fieldwork in Andalusia would have been impossible for me without the companionship and spirited adventuresomeness of my wife, Judy. She and my two daughters, Nina and Naomi, participated fully in rural Andalusian life and quickly established a reputation for being goodnatured and trustworthy. Largely as a result of their personal sacrifices and cultural adaptability, I earned the rapport that enabled me to collect much of the sensitive data contained in this volume. Judy provided me emotional support and an intelligent, perceptive, and sympathetic ear while we were in the field. She also read and commented critically on various drafts of chapters in progress. Because the field experience inseparably combines personal and professional life, Judy's contribution to this volume has been inestimably great.

I also owe a large debt of gratitude to my friend and colleague Alan Dundes. He wisely encouraged me to develop my natural inclination toward the psychological and symbolic interpretation of folkloristic material. With specific regard to the present volume, he selflessly gave of his time to listen to my ideas, critique my interpretations, and suggest fruitful directions for research. As anyone who knows him can attest, his energy and enthusiasm are as boundless as his bibliographic knowledge and scholarly insights.

A number of other people have given me enthusiastic support and constructive suggestions of one type or another during the several years that this volume has been in preparation. For their assistance and encouragement, I wish to thank George M. Foster, Mary LeCron Foster, Howard Gardner, Richard Herr, David Ringrose, Tom Davies, John Polt, Stanley Chojnacki, Percy Cohen, Gail Kligman, David Gilmore, Jan de Vries, Lee Davis, and, in Spain, Carmelo Lisón Tolosana, Claudio Esteva Fabregat, Honorio Valesco, Luis López Guerra, Becky de López, and María Jesús Buxó. As series editor, Marta Weigle offered valuable bibliographic advice and helped me to clarify concepts that otherwise might have remained vague and undeveloped in the finished manuscript. This book has benefited substantially from her guidance. It has also benefited from having been copyedited by Michael Stoner and by Grace Buzaljko, who is well known in the Bay Area for her fine sensitivity to literary style. The office staff of the Department of Anthropology at Berkeley, especially Toni Cord and Jane Taylorson, must be thanked for adhering to a pressured typing schedule on my behalf.

Finally, my greatest debt of all is to the people of Monteros, without whose warmth, openness, and friendly cooperation this study could never have been accomplished. My family and I, even after several years of absence from Spain, feel nearly as much a part of their society as we do our own. In the way they have treated us as much as in their willingness to reveal to us their considerable insights into the human condition, they have transformed my work into a fascinating and pleasurable enterprise. For this, I shall never cease to be thankful to them.

Berkeley, California
May 1979

Metaphors of Masculinity

The Study of Male Folklore in Andalusia

1

This tendency of the Andalusians to represent themselves and mimic themselves reveals a surprising collective narcissism. Only the person who can imitate himself to himself is capable of being spectator to his own person, and the only individual who is capable of this is he who has become accustomed to look at himself, contemplate himself, and give pleasure to himself through his own form and being.

José Ortega y Gasset,
Teoría de Andalucía (1944)

Stereotypes, though often misleading, may sometimes embody some profound truths. Throughout Spain, Andalusia—comprising the nation's eight southernmost provinces—is famous both for what it is and for what it is not. It is said to be backward, and yet it contains some of the richest agricultural land in the Iberian peninsula and has one of the most flourishing tourist industries in Europe. It is said to be poor and misery-ridden, and yet it boasts enormous concentrations of wealth and a general populace that enjoys all the conveniences of modern life, including television, washing machines, refrigerators, and automobiles. Its inhabitants are perceived to be innocent and unsophisticated, and yet, more so than in any other major region within Spain, they have lived for centuries in predominantly urban conglomerations of rich social and cultural variety. The origin of all these stereotypes can be explained historically as the result of Andalusia's long-term cultural and economic domination by the nation's center, Castile. If these stereotypes at one time bore some resemblance to reality, they are certainly in the late 1970s no longer valid.

There is one other stereotype, however, that seems as accurate as any crude generalization about a people can possibly be. I refer to the portrait of Andalusians as poetic, musical, and artistic—in short, as highly capable of and given to demonstrating their innermost sentiments through the major expressive media. In part, this image derives from the enormous cultural achievements of world-famous figures whose lives and work are intimately associated with their Andalusian background. In music, one has only to mention Falla, in poetry Alberti, Góngora, Lorca, and the Machado brothers, and in painting Murillo, Valázguez, Zurbarán, Zabaleta, and, of course, Picasso, who was born and spent his early childhood in Málaga. All these men, and numerous others of their stature, have added to the overall picture of an Andalusia in which the arts flourish.

The tendency for Andalusians to express themselves artistically manifests itself not only at the level of high culture but also at the popular level, among the common people, many of them still illiterate. Andalusians love to sing and dance their native flamenco, one of the few regional musical forms in Spain that still truly thrives and that has extended its area of influence. Among the upper classes, painting and drawing are common pastimes. But this artistic temperament emerges perhaps more consistently in speech than in any other medium. Andalusians, scorned and ridiculed throughout the rest of the country for their distinctive accent, are masters of their tongue. They are given to inventing poetry, everything ranging from simple but elegant four-line coplas to much longer, more complex works elaborating the gamut of topics from love to politics. They are born storytellers and spend endless hours entertaining each other with jokes and riddles. And, as the ultimate test of their poetic nature, they sprinkle their speech liberally with metaphor. They rarely miss an opportunity to illustrate an idea or to explain situations and sentiments through vivid comparison.

This book concerns the symbolic folklore of the men of Monteros, the pseudonym of a township (municipio) in eastern Andalusia with a population of about ten thousand. My goal is to demonstrate the rich variety of folkloristic genres through which the men of this town both express and define their identity. What intrigues me most is that the same cultural themes manifest themselves over and over, whether in pranks or skits, in jokes or slang, in riddles or pageants. The very repetition of these themes in such diverse expressive forms—representing the wide panoply of conversational, play, and fictive media, as analyzed by Abrahams (1976)—is itself a confirmation of the central position of these themes in the lives of the men who constitute the subject of this study.

Monteros (partial view) and olive groves.

The men of Monteros show themselves to be concerned above all with two problems of identity: their place in the social hierarchy and their relationship to women. We may take the first problem to concern the general domain of social status, in which each man comes to rank himself as high or low relative to other men in the society. The day laborer, the large landowner, the schoolteacher, the shopkeeper—each of these, as well as those of numerous other occupational groups—has his *categoría social*, or social rank, which groups him with some members of his society, just as it places him in contrast to others. This basic economic criterion of rank is, under some circumstances, tempered by considerations of education and family background. For this reason, whenever I refer in the text to people of the lower class, working class, upper class, or the like, the word *class* indicates the preeminence of a materialist basis to the classification. In using other words to denote status groups I imply a ranking based on more diverse criteria, all of which are discussed in chapter 3. I have adopted the term *social status* simply as a convenience to cover all types of ranked levels (except those of gender, which are accorded full, separate treatment throughout the volume).

The term *status*, as used here, is also designed to include ranking based on ethnicity. In Monteros, as shall be indicated in chapter 4, there exists a relatively small though highly visible community of Gypsies. Gypsies in this town, as throughout Andalusia, figure prominently in folklore. By examining this folklore, particularly the jokes that are told about Gypsies, it is evident that the contrast between this group and other Spaniards constitutes a critical component of the masculine self-image. For our purposes, therefore, status identity in part means ethnic identity.

Aside from questions of status, the major identity problem that the men of Monteros face concerns gender. Each man in Monteros, as elsewhere in the world, has to determine in what ways he is different from or similar to women. Townsmen, it is fair to say, vastly emphasize the differences between the sexes and believe that these differences are fundamentally biological rather than social in origin. Men are preoccupied with behaving in a masculine manner and with determining in whatever new situation might arise how their reactions should vary from women's. The theme of sexual identity is so consistently and emphatically revealed in male behavior and conversation that no one living in Monteros for any length of time can help but notice it. No wonder, then, that this theme, like that of social status, predominates in male folklore.

It is these cultural themes, rather than the folkloristic genres through which they are expressed, that form the basis of the book's organization. The volume is framed by an analysis of two rituals—the pageant of Giants and Big-Heads (chapter 2) and the procession in honor of the Señor del Consuelo (chapter 10)—which taken individually and together provide a highly condensed, dramatic metaphor of both the sex and the status considerations of Monteros men. They are ceremonial manifestations of practically the entire male experience. In chapter 3 on "Titles, Names, and Pronouns" and chapter 4 on "Gypsy Jokes and the Andalusian Self-Image" I discuss the ways in which folklore reflects and reinforces status divisions in Monteros. Chapter 5 on "Masculine Metaphors in Folk Speech" and chapter 6 on "Jokes and the Male Identity" above all concern the split between the sexes as revealed in folklore, and the reasons why men feel threatened by and isolated from women. Finally, chapter 7 on "Pranks and Riddles," chapter 8 on "Space and Speech at the Olive Harvest," and chapter 9 on "Skits and Society" all demonstrate a variety of means through which folklore helps men to overcome, however temporarily, the divisions that isolate them from their fellow men as well as from women.

Roughly, then, the first half of the book focuses on social and sexual divisions, in that order, while the second half analyzes situations in which interpersonal hostilities can be ameliorated. I have tried to ensure that each chapter when read in sequence contains the necessary background information on Monteros economy, society, and polity, for a full understanding of the folkloristic material under consideration. Indeed, because each item of folklore can only be interpreted through the wider context in which it is manifested, I would commit a scholarly injustice if I analyzed folklore and context separately.

I wish to demonstrate throughout this volume how the various folkloristic genres operate in two distinct ways to assist men to know who they are as sexual and social beings. First, these expressive forms reflect shared assumptions about masculinity and give these assumptions a concrete reality. When men listen to a joke or watch a parade, they are confronted with an image of themselves. Even if only momentarily, the uncertain becomes sure, the ambiguous becomes obvious. I can best explain these transformations by referring to an instance in which a Monteros man and I climbed to the second-story balcony of his apartment, from which we peered down at the throng of Sunday evening strollers below. We remained speechless for perhaps ten minutes, after which he said, "This is the perfect spot. We can see them, but they can't see us. I love to look at the people promenade, because when I look at them I see myself. I see how I look to them, and how I should look, if it's different from the way I actually do look." Just as the passersby are transformed for this man into a mirror of himself, so too do skits, jokes, pranks, riddles, and other items of folklore function generally among Monteros men to demonstrate who they are or who they should be.

Probably the single most important projective mechanism for establishing one's own identity in Monteros is the metaphor. In his influential "Mission of Metaphor," James Fernandez wrote, "In general, the semantic movement accomplished by metaphor is from the abstract and inchoate in the subject to the more concrete, ostensive, and easily graspable in the metaphoric predicate" (Fernandez 1974, p. 123). Fernandez and others (see, for example, the essays in Sapir and Crocker 1977) have correctly pointed to the fact that metaphors serve both cognitive and affective functions. Metaphors explain an item that, by itself, would be unclear, but they do so by evoking certain associated emotions as well.

To illustrate, I can refer to a popular legend that circulates among the working-class segments of Monteros society. It is said that a wealthy landowner and his young son were seated in the dining room of their country estate, where they were surrounded by fine furniture, linens, and silver. The son casually asked his father, "Papá, when we die will we go to heaven or hell?" To this the father replied, "Son, when we die, we are buried in the ground, and that's that. Heaven and hell are right here before us. Do you see that man out there in the field with the hoe in his hand? That's hell. And can you observe us in this room, with servants at our beck and call and all the ham we can eat? This is heaven."

This legend demonstrates the way cognitive and affective functions may be served simultaneously through metaphor. The father teaches his son to equate abstract entities like heaven and hell with the concrete realities of daily existence; he thereby instructs his son about the meaning of these terms. At the same time, the positive and negative emotions invariably associated with heaven and hell are applied to the mundane circumstances of daily existence. Through the employment of metaphor, the legend links two otherwise distinct domains, thereby both informing the child and influencing his feelings. The legend shows us in microcosm how the general use of metaphor in folklore functions on a wider scale for the men of Monteros.

Another way in which the folklore operates is to provide men a culturally acceptable outlet for the frustrations, tensions, and other feelings that cannot be expressed directly. As we shall observe throughout this volume, Monteros men, in the process of retaining their sexual and social identities, assume a combined posture of aggressiveness and defensiveness. [As men, they have to protect themselves against the continual threat of being physically and morally undermined by women.] As occupants of a particular social rank, they must guard themselves and their families from a host of injustices to which they believe themselves constantly subject by the covert scheming of those from other segments of society. [The best overall protective device is to assume an aggressive stance in all social relationships; this strategy, more than anything, helps to preserve one's position in the world and by extension to consolidate one's masculine identity.] The simultaneous aggressiveness and defensiveness of the male mentality is nowhere given a better outlet than in jokes, pranks, riddles, and other items of folklore. All these genres provide for the relatively innocuous yet satisfying expression of potentially dangerous and hurtful sentiments. They operate as culturally sanctioned safety valves.

An understanding of this psychological function of folklore is grounded partly in the assumption that ritual, narrative, play, and various speech acts should to one degree or another be perceived as performances in Bauman's sense (1975). From this point of view, the actual content of any given item of expressive culture is inseparable from the way it is employed and the entire social context in which it is articulated. Hence, as we shall see in chapter 7, the men of Monteros distinguish among a variety of types of pranks, but none of them are identifiable without some knowledge of the presumed or actual intention of the prankster or of the concrete situation in which a prank occurs. At the same time—drawing again on Bauman's perspective—the performance of a cultural item itself has the power to influence the social structure or an individual's position in it. Thus, it is the performance of particular riddles that imparts prestige and comparative advantage to a competent riddler, just as a deft prankster has the ability to reduce others, albeit temporarily, to a submissive posture.

At this point, I wish to make explicit several other aspects of my own theoretical stance. First, I make no claim that the psychological processes that I describe in this volume are unique either to the men of Monteros or to Andalusian men generally. On the contrary, I believe that Andalusian men are fundamentally like men everywhere else in the world. It is not their psychological dynamics that are unique, but rather the specific manner in which these dynamics are expressed through their folklore. It is not even that the particular items of folklore presented in these pages are to be found only in Monteros and Andalusia; many of them—probably most of them—have counterparts elsewhere in Europe and the Mediterranean world, from where they no doubt derive. But I would claim that at least in Monteros, and probably throughout most of Andalusia as well, widely diverse genres of male folklore give an especially coherent expression to the issue of male sexual and status identity. It is the specific syndrome of folkloristic items found in Monteros, not the items themselves or the underlying psychological processes they express, that is characteristic of this part of the world. To my knowledge this syndrome, in all its richness and variety, has yet to receive the scholarly treatment it deserves.

But precisely what part of the world do I claim as my unit of analysis? All the folklore I discuss in this volume was collected in the town of Monteros; strictly speaking, then, I cannot hold that my research findings are valid for any wider area, especially because my treatment of the material is grounded so deeply in a consideration of Monteros society and economy. Yet Monteros is in many ways an archetypical Andalusian agro-town, characterized by rigid social ranking and conflict between the sexes. Its economy is rooted in the land, and yet in its occupational diversity, ethnic heterogeneity, and overall ambiance it is urban. And, despite many recent changes in attitude among the youth, it is still a place where female chastity and masculine displays of sexual prowess and aggression are of paramount concern. To judge by the literature, Monteros is, in fact, not unlike agro-towns throughout the Mediterranean, particularly throughout southern Italy, Sicily, and southern Iberia, where settlements with similar traits have been described by anthropologists in varying detail. Rather than make a potentially extravagant claim for the representativeness of Monteros, however, I have chosen the more conservative route of speaking about the town itself while citing comparative evidence from elsewhere whenever relevant.

Considering the social heterogeneity of Monteros, I must address the issue of intracultural variation as it relates to the folklore in this volume. Problems of social status and sexual identity are, on the one hand, individual problems that each man has to work out for himself. Doubtless, there are as many distinctive ways in which men come to define themselves to themselves as there are male human beings in the world. On the other hand, men who are immersed from childhood in the same cultural milieu learn to think and act on the basis of shared assumptions. Each culture provides men with the means to express their sexual and social identities, and through constant reliance on these means, men consolidate and affirm their self-image. It is these culturally shared assumptions and expressions of masculinity with which we are concerned, not the idiosyncratic variations that are part of every man's personal experience.

Nonetheless, in a community as large and diverse as Monteros there inevitably exists patterned variation in the way men from different social strata think about themselves. I have tried to take this variation into account in several ways. First, many of the chapters contain explicit analyses of why a particular folkloristic medium appeals to one segment of male society rather than another. Thus, I try to explain why the pageant of Giants and Big-Heads appeals to workers rather than to adult members of the town elite, and why workers, too, seem to know and enjoy riddles to a greater extent than do men of the upper social stratum. The chapters on titles and names, on skits and religious ritual, and on behavior at the olive harvest all embody the same types of consideration. Second, I have tried to indicate variation by citing the specific source of my information. Hence, in directly quoting either an item of folklore or personal interpretation of the folklore, I state that the source of my data was a large landowner, a butcher, a schoolteacher, a shepherd, or whoever. Third, I have attempted to relate the frequency with which certain folkloristic items can be encountered. In the case of skits and folk medical beliefs, the analysis is accompanied by an explanation of their current rarity; I also point out the segments of society among which they were most widely distributed in the past. Likewise, in speaking of nicknames, religious ritual, and other expressive media, I indicate the relative degrees to which they are embraced and accepted among different social sectors.

Inevitably, there are people who conform neither in their beliefs nor in their behavior to the general patterns described by the folklorist with a social scientific orientation. The community under discussion is no exception in this regard, so that when, for the sake of stylistic smoothness, I speak of "the men of Monteros," I cannot claim that *every single individual* knows the joke or riddle that I recount nor that he would agree with the interpretation that one informant or another places on a particular folkloristic item. Yet the reader can be assured that when I phrase my analysis in general terms I have taken careful note of such phrasing and sincerely believe that my analysis represents the *prevailing* or *most highly-valued* beliefs, behavior, or knowledge among townsmen. Always, too, we must keep in mind that both the folklore and the society of Andalusia are in rapid flux. My analysis pertains specifically to the period in which I resided in Monteros. It also applies particularly to the adults in town, for social norms among people under the ages of twenty or twenty-five years seem to be departing abruptly from those held by their parents.

I must emphasize this point, especially because economic and political developments in rural Spain are influencing the countryside at an unimaginably fast pace. The fabric of Monteros society, in only two or three years, has begun to change to a point where some of my material—I must confess—is already obsolete. For instance, the term "middle class" has become a commonly heard descriptive category, whereas in the period I carried out research it was rarely uttered. Recent governmental price and wage regulations for olive-growing have assured that large-scale proprietors will henceforth abdicate the privileged social and economic position to which they were accustomed even as few years back as 1975–76, when my primary data-collecting took place. In addition, members of the *Partido Socialista Obrero Español*, or Spanish Socialist Workers' Party, now hold control of the mayorship and town council, a situation that has imparted to the working class an entirely different image of itself from that which prevailed when I did the research reported herein. Thus, this volume must be read as representing the ethnographic present, specifically the years 1975–76. These years, of course, were the end of the Franco era and the end of policies that in many ways encouraged extreme social and sexual stratification.

This brings me to the critical issue of folk versus social scientific explanations of folklore. I make no claim that the men of Monteros would agree in all respects with the analysis that I bring to bear on their expressive culture. I have unfortunately been unable to test every one of my symbolic interpretations by systematically presenting them to a large sample of male informants. But I have discussed my interpretations in enough detail and with enough men to know that in many cases informants immediately confirm their validity, while in other (and fewer) instances they disagree.

To explain the latter circumstance, I might only state here my own theoretical bias: the folkloristic items under discussion are psychological projections, and as such, they may well disguise some of the underlying attitudes and emotions they represent. Expressive media thereby protect individuals from the direct articulation of sentiments that might prove threatening or otherwise hurtful. Dundes has defended this point cogently:

> It is my contention that much of the meaning of folkloristic fantasy is unconscious. Indeed, it would have to be unconscious—in the Freudian sense—for folklore to function as it does. Among its functions, folklore provides a socially sanctioned outlet for the expression of what cannot be articulated in the more usual, direct, way. It is precisely in jokes, folktales, folksongs, proverbs, children's games, gestures, etc. that anxieties can be vented. If a person knew exactly what he was do-

ing when he told a joke to his boss or to his spouse (or if the boss
or spouse knew what he was doing), the joke would probably
cease to be an escape mechanism (Dundes 1976, pp. 1503–4).

There is thus no reason to believe that the folk themselves are any
more capable of penetrating the folkloristic facade than is the outside observer. On the other hand, it is clear that in some of the instances we shall be discussing—including anticlerical humor and
cross-sex banter at the olive harvest—people are well aware of the
psychological implications of what they are saying. We could claim
that the underlying meaning of most of the folklore we shall be examining is largely unconscious, but that it is not necessarily wholly
unconscious or, in some cases, unconscious at all.

Finally, I should like to explain my virtually exclusive concentration on male folklore, as opposed to the folklore of Monteros in
general. In Monteros, as throughout most of Andalusia, there exists—at least among the adult generation—a rigid separation between the sexes. The separation is not nearly great enough to prevent the male folklorist or anthropologist from interviewing women
or even from making in-depth observations of female behavior. It is
sufficiently great, however, to ensure that I would be considered a
normal human being and thereby be incorporated in Monteros
society only if I spent many hours in the exclusive company of men.
Folklore is best collected in its natural context as it emerges spontaneously from the mouths of the folk, rather than as it is elicited in
formal interviews. Because I spent an enormous amount of time
among men, I was able to record their folklore in the manner I consider best. This I was not able to accomplish for women, just as I was
not able to accomplish it for Gypsies of either sex. To have been too
closely associated with women or with Gypsies would have essentially cut me off from the element of Monteros society with which I
have most in common and to which therefore I have the most
ready-made access: the "Castilian" (i.e., European, non-Gypsy)
man. For obvious reaons, I was classified as belonging to this majority group of men and found my closest friends, informants, and
associates among them. I would have been foolish to pass up the opportunity to make them the subject of special investigation.

Readers may be curious enough about my field situation and
methods of data collection to warrant a brief discussion. In 1969 and
1970 and again in 1972, my wife and I lived in a small peasant
village of northern Spain, about which I subsequently published a
number of ethnographic and folkloristic accounts. On the basis of
our rewarding experiences in that community we decided to con-

tinue research in Spain, this time in a medium-sized rural town in Andalusia. We knew that in the south the contour of society would provide an instructive contrast to the one with which we were already familiar, and yet we would still be able to operate in Spanish, which would not be the case in some of the more ethnically distinctive regions of Iberia. We chose Monteros for several reasons. It seemed, even upon superficial observation, to conform to our image of the ideal Andalusian agro-town: large enough to contain the social heterogeneity that we were looking for, but small and compact enough to be studied thoroughly through participant observation. Monteros was also appealing because it is located in a region that up to that point had been relatively underinvestigated by anthropologists and folklorists; we could thus share in the excitement of ethnographic and folkloristic discovery. We found a good furnished house to rent, and there were decent schools for my two daughters, who were seven and four years old at the time. Of the fifteen or twenty site possibilities we considered, we predicted that Monteros would suit our needs—both intellectual and familial—the best, and so we settled there.

Within several months of settling in Monteros we had completely adopted the town routine. Our most important social contacts initially were with neighbors, who were mostly laborers. With several of these households we formed close friendships, and could visit these homes regularly; their menfolk periodically invited me to accompany them to the fields as well. Gradually, by hanging around shops and the marketplace, I was able to broaden my social network and establish relationships with butchers, teachers, and storekeepers. I was invited to the home of a large landowner only after residing in town for about six months, but after that my contacts within that stratum of society broadened widely. On balance, I believe that by the time I had completed my first year of field research in Monteros, I had about an equal number of friends from each of the diverse social strata, and could count bankers, bureaucrats, plumbers, olive pickers, shepherds, masons, owners of large estates, and others among those who could act for me as reliable informants. In retrospect, I realize that it was my status as a foreigner—and, at that, a foreigner who would only reside in the community temporarily—that enabled me to maintain close friendships among such a wide variety of people. There might have been considerably more pressure on a Spaniard to "declare," so to speak, for one social stratum or another.[1]

---

[1]Gerald Berreman (1962) provides a sensitive, insightful account of the difficulties of carrying out fieldwork in a rigidly stratified society.

The folklore presented in this volume was collected mainly through participant observation and interviews. On two occasions, in 1975 and 1977, I was able to observe the pageant of Giants and Big-Heads and the procession of the Señor del Consuelo; it is mainly the personal scrutiny of these events that forms the basis for my analysis of them. To learn about skits, however, I had to rely (as is explained fully in chapter 9) almost exclusively on interviews. For jokes and riddles, the methodology falls somewhere in between these two extremes. After listening to a spontaneous joke- or riddle-telling session, usually in the bars but sometimes in homes as well, I jotted down the items (always noting the social context and order in which they appeared) and only later asked informants to record them for me by tape. Pranks, speech forms, and the behavior that accompanied the olive harvest were all observed entirely in the course of daily life.

As far as the total bulk of folkloristic data is concerned, the material presented here represents only a portion of my observations and collection. Elsewhere (Brandes 1977) I have analyzed political folklore that pertains only marginally to the topic under discussion. In addition, there are dozens of jokes, riddles, and other expressive items that might have been included if I had designed this book as a collection—which I have not—but that I have decided to omit on the grounds that they would do nothing to deepen my interpretations.

My wife, who is currently a bilingual teacher, provided me access to the world of Monteros women. Not only did her friends willingly act as informants for me, but also her mere presence in town automatically converted me into a much more trustworthy figure than if I had been on my own. Still, given the social system in which I was operating, there were relatively few women, as compared with men, who could be completely at ease in my company. In fact, Monteros men and women are well aware of the fact that they generally feel most comfortable, and that their conversation flows most smoothly, when those of the opposite sex are absent. Since much of the female folkloristic repertoire is expressed in sex-exclusive groups, there was no way I could achieve a complete balance in male and female data.[2] Under the circumstances, I naturally came to understand the male mentality much better than the female.

In any case, as a man, coming from a society in which sex roles

[2]A folklorist like Kay Cothran, who was able to collect rich examples of male folk speech from rural Georgia (Cothran 1974), must be admired for her ability to transcend the sexual barrier. We must, of course, also take note of recent articles (Farrer 1975; Weigle 1978) defining issues in the study of female folklore.

and identities have recently become subject to particular scrutiny, my scholarly investigation was perhaps more a natural outgrowth than I originally realized of my interest in my own identity. Given that Monteros men have similar interests about themselves—albeit interests that are traditional rather than the product of contemporary political developments—it was perhaps inevitable that my study should have taken the turn it has. It was perhaps inevitable, too, that I should come to empathize with these men, who—from the contemporary American point of view and from the perspective of many Monteros youth themselves—unquestionably dominate and exploit women unjustly. I neither deny nor condone this domination and exploitation. But I also reject the idea that it confers unmitigated advantages, either material or psychological, on the oppressors. Any system of severe inequality is bound to have at least some negative effect on all the participants within it, and the system, in Monteros, with its rigid divisions of sex and status, is no exception.

Giants and Big-Heads

2

The play-concept as such is of a higher order than is seriousness. For seriousness seeks to exclude play, whereas play can very well include seriousness.

Johan Huizinga, *Homo Ludens* (1955)

Every year on 16 September in Monteros there occurs a brief parade of costumed figures known as Giants (*Gigantes*) and Big-Heads (*Cabezudos*). When I first witnessed the event I had resided less than a month in the community and thus was ill-prepared to evaluate its full symbolic significance. But I never doubted that it had a highly charged significance. Anybody would have been struck, as I was, by the sharp contrast between the overbearingly tall, stiff, austere, royally clothed Giants and the short, foolish, garishly garbed Big-Heads. At once, the town seemed transformed into a Renaissance court with its monarchs and jesters (Willeford 1969), or into a circus ring with straightmen and clowns (Bouissac 1976). The parade, while taking place in a specific Andalusian town and at a particular point in time, nonetheless seemed to embody some universal meaning.

The parade lasts barely an hour, and is only one of several components of the most important celebration of the town's ritual calendar: the festival in honor of the Santísimo Señor del Consuelo, the Most Holy Lord of Consolation, a miraculous image that is the object of deep and widespread devotion in the town and surrounding countryside. Throughout four days of festivities, Monteros swells with outsiders and pulses with activity, including an impressive evening fireworks display, a solemn religious procession, and a steady flow of dances and entertainment. When compared with the truly grand ritual spectacles, the parade of Giants and Big-Heads initially seems rather inconsequential because of its relative brevity and small attendance. Yet I shall show how this event can be viewed as a metaphor, a concrete expression and projection of critical aspects of Monteros society and culture, as well as of the emotional concerns of the town youth. Like the Balinese cockfight described by Geertz (1973), the parade of Giants and Big-Heads is, at least to certain segments of the Monteros populace, "a story they tell about themselves" (ibid., p. 448). It is an interpretive, humanistic display of both collective and personal experience.[1]

If we were to apply the language of symbolic anthropology to Giants and Big-Heads, we might say that they are, above all, "elaborating" symbols, in Sherry Ortner's use of the term (1973, p. 1340). In and of themselves, these figures are in no sense objects of reverence or deep emotion as the flag, the cross, or other "summarizing" symbols are. Rather, they are best seen as unconscious vehicles that the people of Monteros draw upon "for sorting out complex feelings and ideas" (ibid., p. 1340). As elaborating symbols, Giants and Big-Heads not only enable the people themselves to express some of the most salient features of their society but also provide us—students of folk culture—with a key to the native conceptualization of experience. In Monteros, the outside observer, unlike the townspeople under investigation, may hope to ascertain in what way the parade of Giants and Big-Heads provides a reenactment of the most psychologically and socially important aspects of town life. For, if we judge by informant statements alone, the parade simply occasions an enjoyable, mirthful break from ordinary routine.

As a concrete projection of feelings and experience, the parade of Giants and Big-Heads is probably best understood as representing the issue of social domination and control, with which the people of Monteros are clearly preoccupied. I intend to demonstrate that the

---

[1]An earlier version of this chapter was presented to the Symposium on Fundamentals of Symbolism, sponsored by the Wenner-Gren Foundation for Anthropological Research, and held at Burg Wartenstein, Austria, 16–24 July 1977. In revising the chapter, I have benefited from the comments of conference participants, who of course bear no responsibility for the accuracy of data or interpretations.

A slightly different version of the chapter appears in *Symbol as Sense*, edited by Mary LeCron Foster and myself and scheduled for publication by Academic Press.

Giants operate as an unconscious metaphor for parents, that the Big-Heads act as metaphoric children, and that the entire parade is a dramatic enactment of power relationships not only within the nuclear family, but also within society generally. The costumed figures, in both form and behavior, suggest a collective, vicarious rebellion against authority and control. The rebellion is most graphically portrayed at the family level, with the children displaying unharnessed aggression. But there is evidence, too, that this hostility becomes generalized, so that it is directed against all the major forces of control and containment with which people, both as individuals and as members of groups, have to contend.

To develop my thesis, I wish first to give a stark description of the parade. I shall go on to provide relevant ethnographic background, and then conclude with an analysis of the parade's symbolic significance. I should caution that the present study refers specifically to Giants and Big-Heads in contemporary Monteros. These figures, particularly the Giants, have a long history and widespread distribution throughout western Europe. René Meurant (1960, 1967, 1969) and Klaus Beitl (1961) have devoted years of investigation to the enormously variegated manifestations of Giant figures, past and present. It seems that bona fide processional Giants first appeared in early fifteenth-century Flanders (Meurant 1967, p. 123), and shortly thereafter diffused to the Iberian peninsula (Gennep 1935, 1, p. 168). We know that Giants and Big-Heads have existed in Spain throughout the past four hundred years, during which they have usually been associated with Corpus Cristi and pre-Lenten *Carnaval* celebrations (Almerich 1944; Caro Baroja 1965; Gómez-Tabanera 1968b, pp. 188–93; Plá Cargol 1947, pp. 291–96). What we lack in virtually all accounts, however, is the combination of detailed description and extensive local ethnography that might explain the phenomenon from a symbolic, structural, or other point of view.

Belgian folklorist Albert Marinus is the one investigator to have posited more than merely a historical or diffusionist explanation for the existence of processional Giants. He suggests that these figures "must be considered as manifestations of the need for the masses to translate in a concrete and conspicuous fashion their ideas or abstract feelings, particularly in the domain of the supernatural and the extraordinary" (Marinus 1951, 3, p. 281; my translation). Elsewhere, he indicates that the Giants reveal a sort of "collective conscience" (ibid., 2, p. 232). These universalistic statements may point in the right direction, but they fail to account for variations in the types and numbers of Giants, or for the persistence of these

figures in some regions and not others. Nor can such analyses explain
the absence or presence of Big-Heads or other similar masked
characters. These are all complex issues for which adequate comparative data are presently unavailable. The most we can hope for
at this stage is a thorough examination of a single occurrence of
Giants and Big-Heads whose meaning may be interpreted in terms
of the immediate social environment in which they appear.

The Parade of Giants and Big-Heads

We may begin our analysis with a simple description of the
parade of Giants and Big-Heads. At noon, amidst the loud, incessant
ringing of churchbells, the Giants emerge from the Town Hall,
located just off the main square. There are two of them, a man and a
woman, known as the King and the Queen, dressed in crowns and
simple tunics reminiscent of the garb of medieval monarchs. Each
figure is about twelve feet tall, its clothing and molded pâpier-
maché head suspended from a wooden frame that is borne by a man.
The man remains anonymous, for his entire body from the knees up
is enveloped and hidden by the flowing gown of the towering image.

Immediately following the Giants appear fourteen Big-Heads,

Giants and a Big-Head.

whose oversized pâpier-maché heads and necks rest directly on the shoulders of young townsmen. In the case of the Big-Heads, the human body becomes part of the figure itself. However, because of the baggy, flamboyant costumes and especially the false heads themselves, the actors' identities remain completely disguised. No two Big-Heads are the same. Some, like Popeye, the Devil, a Witch, a Chinese, and a Black African, are easily recognizable. Others, like the Ape and Cow-Goat, two anthropomorphic figures, are the grotesque products of fantasy. A number of the Big-Heads obviously represent men, both young and old, but there is one with clean-shaven face and medium long hair whose sex is ambiguous. The Witch, Devil, and Ape wear specially designed costumes appropriate to their images. The others wear the loud, brightly colored garb of jesters or clowns. Aside from the Witch with her broom and the Devil with his blunt wooden spear, the Big-Heads all carry white, sausage-shaped cloths, about a foot long, stuffed stiff with sawdust and attached loosely to a short stick.

For about forty-five minutes the Giants and Big-Heads wind their way through the most important, centrally located streets and plazas of Monteros, with a crowd of children following. The Giants, tall and domineering, walk together at a slow, even, dignified pace.

Big-Heads emerge from the Town Hall.
(Note the frightened child at lower left corner.)

Big-Heads.

The Big-Heads swarm around them, skipping, running, and jumping erratically; they seem intrusive and disruptive, a chaotic element compared with the stately Giants. The Big-Heads pause at the several plazas where townspeople are gathered and rush around in unpredictable directions, bopping people with their stuffed cloths. The Devil and Witch use their spear and broom for the same purpose. Adults and teenagers find the scene amusing and laugh, but young children become frightened and cling to their older brothers and sisters. And no wonder, for in many Monteros homes, children are scared into eating or going to sleep with the threat that otherwise the Big-Heads will come to take them away.

Meanwhile, a large crowd has gathered in the main plaza, which is known as the Corredera. From a second-story window of the Town Hall small skyrockets laden with candy and miniature toys are sent up and out over the Corredera. The rockets explode in midair with a loud crack, causing the candy and toys to shower down on the people below. Explosions take place at intervals of two or three minutes, and with every blast the spectators compete furiously for the spoils. Teenaged boys, because of their size and aggressiveness as much as because they attend the event in the greatest numbers, catch most of the flying objects. But they are usually con-

The Big-Head witch.

tent merely to win the contest, and distribute the goods to the unsuccessful girls and young children who would otherwise remain disappointed. The skyrockets make the Corredera the center of action, and it is here, too, that the Giants and Big-Heads stop for fifteen minutes at the end of their tour. By 1:00 P.M. the churchbells and cannonfire cease, the Giants and Big-Heads reenter the Town Hall, and the crowds disperse.

To understand the metaphoric imagery of this parade, more information is needed about who participates in it as actors and audience. This will tell us for whom the parade is designed, to whom its symbolism would most likely appeal, and consequently of which social entity—the town as a whole or only certain segments of it—the event may be said to supply an inside view. The performers can be described easily enough; they are all young working-class men, selected on a first-come, first-served basis. Since there is competition for the posts, many sign up several days in advance to assure themselves of a part. Informants claim that no woman, regardless of age or social background, has ever acted in the parade. It is said that the Giants' frames are too heavy and awkward for a woman to carry and that the Big-Heads play a role that would be shameful for any female to assume. The people of Monteros find it impossible even to imagine how a woman might act in the parade. Similarly, no upper-class man would taint his own or his family's dignified image by dressing up in a silly costume and behaving like a fool. The roles of Giants and Big-Heads are set aside for male working-class youth.

To define the audience is more difficult, because even though some townspeople claim that "everyone" attends, it is clear that certain segments of the community are more heavily represented than others. The spectators are overwhelmingly children and teenagers,[2] with perhaps a quarter of the onlookers—a third at most—being mature or elderly adults. Males of all ages vastly outnumber females. This disproportion is especially evident among young children because many little girls voluntarily avoid the event or are prevented by their parents from attending. Small girls tend to be afraid of the costumed figures and, if they are incautious, they can be trampled in the scramble for toys that occurs in the Corredera.

[2]That the parade of Giants and Big-Heads is of special significance to young people is substantiated, too, by the fact that these same figures inaugurate the sporadically held Fiestas de la Juventud, or Youth Festivals. The Youth Festivals are held in some years in late spring, at no fixed date, and consist largely of dances and sports events. Most recently they were given in 1974 and 1977. In 1976, the only year in which I spent the spring in Monteros, they were suspended, and so I have never witnessed them and therefore know little about them.

Of the females in attendance, most are teenagers, with a smattering of young mothers accompanying their children. There is, finally, a status component to the audience. Young people from all socio-economic segments of the populace come to watch the parade. But of those spectators past the teenaged years, virtually all come from among the workers. Members of the elite consider themselves too sophisticated to waste their time on a frivolous, rowdy event like the parade of Giants and Big-Heads.

It is on the basis of the social composition of performers and audience alike that I shall claim that the parade is of paramount importance to the following segments of the Monteros populace: children of all ages and socio-economic strata and men of the working class. The social composition of the actors, in particular, gives the parade a distinctly male, lower-class aspect. This, by the way, is why an outsider like myself, witnessing the pageant for the first time, views it as rather poorly attended and insignificant compared with other festival occasions. For purposes of discussion, we may assume that those who participate and attend are the people for whom the parade has meaning. It is from their point of view that we shall analyze Giant and Big-Head imagery. First, however, we should introduce some critical features of society in Monteros.

Dominance and Submission in Monteros

To understand the parade of Giants and Big-Heads, it is necessary to realize that Monteros is a typical Andalusian agro-town. Unlike the small, egalitarian, corporate communities of northern Spain (see, e.g., Aceves 1971; Brandes 1975a; Freeman 1970; Kenny 1966), the agro-towns of the south are deeply divided by conflict between classes as well as between sexes. In Monteros, as in most such communities (e.g., Gilmore 1975, 1976; Moreno Navarro 1972), power relationships are uppermost in people's minds, and provide one of the most pervasive themes of interaction. No matter what a person's status, the tendency is to feel dominated and controlled by those of the opposing group. In everyone, from all segments of society, there is a perpetual yearning for personal autonomy, which is perceived as being somehow seriously limited or threatened. The hatred and fear of allegedly powerful elements in society can only be described as immediate and pressing.

To these specific features of Andalusian society, we must add the ubiquitous conflict between the generations. In Monteros, as everywhere else in the world, children must learn to develop mechanisms of self-control. During this process, parents are the initial agents of suppression and domination; later, of course, their role is incorporated within the self, so that each person gradually becomes master or mistress of his or her own behavior, and in this sense becomes his or her own parent. In Monteros, whether we speak of class, sex, or generational conflict, it is the concern with restrictions on personal freedom that dominates people's thoughts and emotions. The class and generational dimensions, in particular, emerge in the parade of Giants and Big-Heads; they therefore merit brief discussion.

Let us turn first to class. People frequently distinguish between two prominent socio-economic groups in Monteros: a small, landed, educated elite, and the mass of illiterate or semiliterate workers who earn their living by daily wage labor. Workers deeply resent the landed elite, upon whom they depend for their livelihood. They claim that the elite exploits and cheats them by taking advantage of their economically precarious position, and that the elite controls the town government so as to divert public funds to its own benefit. Above all, workers are convinced that the elite has done and will do everything possible to prevent the economic advancement of the poorer segment of the community. The elite, they state bitterly, is accustomed to having "slaves" at its disposal, and wants nothing less than to suppress the poor completely, thereby keeping them at the continual mercy of the rich.

Members of the elite themselves, however, feel far from omnipotent. They remember the Civil War years (1936–39), when the Communists overturned the town government and workers' committees seized their land, converted the churches into granaries, and distributed the harvest to all families equally. They recall that extensive and valuable family libraries were burned as fuel, and that landowners were imprisoned, executed, or put to work building roads. And they desperately fear the resurgence of these events. The hatred and distrust between the classes in Monteros is intense. And the single greatest source of class conflict is the real or presumed threat of domination. Each group believes that the other has more power than it deserves and that this power had been and will be used as a tool of exploitation and destruction.

An even deeper, and certainly more universal, point of conflict represented in Monteros is the opposition between the generations. We know from psychoanalytic research that young children develop a profound resentment and hostility toward their parents as a reaction to restrictions placed on their freedom of action and bodily function. In Monteros, as in other parts of the Hispanic world

(Brandes 1974), the youngest child in a family is lavishly indulged; but once a new infant is born, the displaced child becomes subject to severe ridicule and at times corporal punishment in case of misbehavior, accidents of bowel or bladder, or other transgressions. Even teenagers expect an occasional thrashing, especially when their misconduct is carried out in public and might endanger the family's reputation. Children naturally develop a strong emotional attachment to and dependence on their parents, but this dependence in no way negates the anger and resentment they simultaneously feel toward them.

At least for the men of Monteros, submission to an older generation persists throughout life and becomes a nagging source of anxiety. Increasingly throughout the middle years and into old age, a man's wife becomes like a mother to him. The wife, in addition to feeding and clothing her husband, just as his mother did, chides him for drinking too much or staying out too late. She controls the purse and doles out money. In short, she is a source of maternal-like security, but also a cause of irritating restrictions on personal freedom. In Monteros the role of child—whether enacted in chronological childhood or in adulthood—requires submission to a dominant powerholder, whose rules and regulations seem irrational and unnecessarily confining. The child, in this context, feels as threatened and oppressed as do members of the two classes in their relations with one another.

Giants and Big-Heads as Social Metaphors

To place the parade in its social context, let us begin by simply listing the formal characteristics of Giants and Big-Heads, as revealed in their appearance and demeanor during the pageant. Here we are struck by a series of binary oppositions that also characterize contrasting dyads of generation and class in Monteros.

Giants	Big-Heads
few	many
tall	short
dignified	foolish
haughty	familiar
graceful	clumsy
unified	disorganized
controlled	spontaneous
dominant	subordinate

Other contrasting features also come to mind, but even this short list presents for each of our costumed figures seemingly inconsistent traits which will have to be explained; the list certainly provides an adequate basis for discussion.

Drawing upon these binary oppositions, and keeping the perspective of performers and audience in mind, we may postulate an association between Giants and Big-Heads, on the one hand, and particular groups in Monteros society, on the other. The evidence for the generational analogy is clear. The two Giants, crowned male and female figures, stand tall and erect and move smoothly through the crowds, exhibiting complete bodily control, a self-control that to anthropologist Mary Douglas would indicate conformity to the demands imposed by the wider society (Douglas 1973, pp. 99–100). Within the family, of course, it is the parents who exhibit this type of behavior, while the children, still incompletely socialized, manifest spontaneous, unpredictable, and clumsy movements, which are characteristic also of the Big-Heads. There could be no clearer example of Douglas's contention that "the social body constrains the way the physical body is perceived" (ibid. p. 93). "Socialization," she says (ibid. p. 101), "teaches the child to bring organic processes under control." In our case, it is the graceful Giants of this parade who have already grown up, while the erratic, playful Big-Heads are still immature.

Of course, the appearance and number of Giants in relation to Big-Heads also conforms to their images as parents and children. First there is the matter of relative height; though the Big-Heads' costumes make them some seven feet tall, they are still a good deal shorter than the Giants, who loom upwards of twelve or thirteen feet. Then, too, the Big-Heads, like children, have heads that are much larger in proportion to their bodies than are those of adults.[3] It is in this aspect that the Big-Heads contrast with the Giants, whose heads and bodies are proportionately like those of adult humans. And finally, Big-Heads, like the children in most families of traditional Monteros, are considerably more numerous than their Giant/parent counterparts.

More than anything, however, it is the following drawing—reproduced from the official program notes for the 1975

---

[3]Philippe Ariès' influential historical study of family life (1962) points out that in Western society children were until recently considered as little adults. Perhaps this is why their heads were represented artistically as small in proportion to their bodies. It was no doubt after children came to be thought of as different from adults that their heads were drawn true to size. I am indebted to Howard Gardner for reminding me of Ariès' analysis.

Día 16

A las 12, Inauguración Oficial de Festejos con disparo de cohetes y fuegos japoneses, repique general de campanas y desfile de

GIGANTES Y CABEZUDOS

acompañados por la Banda Local de Música.

A las 12 de la noche en la Plaza de Santa María, se quemará una vistosa colección de

Fuegos Artificiales

confeccionados por la Pirotécnica «Ntra. Sra. de Fátima», de Martos, y subvencionados por el Excmo. Ayuntamiento.

*Printed announcement of Giant
and Big-Head pageant.*

parade—that demonstrates the popular conception of Giants and Big-Heads as representing a human family. The drawing is all the more striking if we consider that I have never heard anyone in Monteros articulate conscious recognition of these figures as family symbols. Here, there is significant distortion from the actual figures; in reality, the two Giant figures are of about equal height, while the drawing shows the female markedly shorter than the male. In the drawing, too, the Big-Heads are much smaller proportionate to the Giants than they should be. The relative size of the figures in the drawing suggests strongly that people conceive of Giants and Big-Heads as parents and children. And in the drawing, as in the parade itself, the stiff, controlled, dignified bearing of the parents contrasts markedly with the free-flowing, unbridled spirit of the children.

The element of self-control is also essential to an understanding of Giants and Big-Heads as symbols of social class. Here once again we can turn to Mary Douglas for assistance in interpretation:

> A complex social system devises for itself ways of behaving that suggest that human intercourse is disembodied compared with that of animal creation. It uses different degrees of disembodiment to express the social hierarchy. The more refinement, the less smacking of the lips when eating, the less mastication, the less the sound of breathing and walking, the more carefully modulated the laughter, the more controlled the signs of anger, the clearer comes the priestly-aristocratic image (Douglas 1973, pp. 101–2).

Thus, in Monteros we may compare the relatively hushed, sedate atmosphere that prevails in the bars most heavily frequented by upper-class members of the community with the noisy, boisterous, and fully demonstrative setting characteristic of lower-class bars. Upper-class people claim that they can identify lower-class people by their awkward, gawky posture and gait. At the same time, those of the lower class assume a certain defensive pride in the fact that they are unfettered by the excess *etiqueta* of the elite; unlike those of the upper class, these commoners claim, they can use the same utensils throughout several courses of a meal or even on occasion eat with their hands or share a single platter or bowl among all members of the family. In reality, of course, lower-class people have internalized the image that the upper class holds of them. They feel awkward and graceless, loud and crass, and generally untutored in the social amenities as practiced by the elite. They perceive themselves, in other words, as imperfectly or only partially socialized.

The Giant figures, of course, specifically represent King and Queen, the supreme rulers. Their aloof, dignified bearing accords perfectly with the lower-class image of monarchs as well as of the social elite. As with the most graphic representations, however, the Giants are an exaggerated portrayal. The Giant as a social being is so divorced from and independent of the Giant as physical being that the Giant's body is actually invisible, for it will be recalled that the figure's simple garb reaches to the feet of the human bearer, obscuring him completely. This cloaking may be construed as an indication that the Giants, like the elite, are fully socialized, free from the chaotic passions and whims of the human organism.[4]

Not so with the Big-Heads, whose entirely human bodies bounce and twist as if purposefully to mimic the awkward, foolish, uncontrolled demeanor of the workers. The Giants stand taut and rigid, their faces peering out from a great height over and away

[4]One of the Monteros priests, upon hearing my interpretation of Giants and Big-Heads as representing parents and children, agreed with me, and then spontaneously offered the suggestion that the figures symbolize social classes as well. I had already come to this conclusion on my own, but decided, before telling him so, to listen to his reasoning. In Torrendonjimeno, the town where he grew up, Giants and Big-Heads are also part of an annual festival. There, however, the Giants are actually given names: Don Jimeno and Doña Leonor. The titles *Don* and *Doña* are awarded to the social elite in Andalusian agro-towns, a circumstance that evoked for this priest the class dimension to the costumed figures.

It is apparently not uncommon for age distinctions to operate as a metaphor for social hierarchy. Renato Rosaldo (1968) has analyzed a comparable situation in Mayan ritual.

from the Big-Heads and the human crowd below. The Big-Heads interact closely with that crowd, mingling with it, standing level with it, and relating to it by touch. "Greater space means more formality, nearness means intimacy," Douglas reminds us (1973, p. 101). By this measure, too, Giants and Big-Heads conform to the social images of elite and worker.

There are other, more obvious, but equally important ways in which the socio-economic division is represented by our figures. Again, the relative size and number of Giants and Big-Heads have to be taken into account. To the people of Monteros, economic position is associated with physical size, so that the elite is often referred to collectively as *los grandes*, "the large ones." With this sort of conceptual correlation between the economic and the organic spheres, it is understandable that the relatively huge Giants should symbolize the elite and the Big-Heads the workers. Like the Giants, the elite are relatively few in number. "Our land is superabundant and rich," say the workers. "The only problem is that it is divided among only a handful of people (*cuatro personas*). The rest of us have nothing."

The Giants and Big-Heads also undoubtedly speak to the specific fears of dominance and submission characteristic of the workers. It is likely that Big-Heads, from the workers' point of view, reflect their own individualism and disorganization. Strength comes from unity, say the workers, who chastise themselves for their inability to organize and cooperate with each other. The Giants, who march at a slow, even pace alongside each other, convey an impression of indestructible cohesion, a cohesion that the workers in Monteros attribute to the elite.

The metaphoric relationship between Giants and Big-Heads and social classes is certainly not as explicit as is the relationship between these costumed figures and their generational counterparts. But the class analogy is still strikingly evident. Moreover, if we accept Percy Cohen's analysis (1977), it is likely that human beings tend to think of dominance relationships within society in terms that derive from their own childhood experiences (which, as he points out, is not the same as saying that these relationships actually derive from those experiences). Cohen argues that we tend to represent or symbolize social class distinctions as if they were differences between parents and children. One of the major generational distinctions is that adults are not only invariably much taller than infants, but continue to be taller than children at least until these children reach adolescence. From this obvious but all too ignored fact, Cohen believes, we can explain the linguistic reference in English to "high" and "low" classes. He concludes that the uses of these terms to refer to rank are not only metaphoric but symbolic, in that they represent the unconscious, adult reference to visual and other forms of childhood experience of power and advantage.

In Monteros, we may say, Giants and Big-Heads are fundamentally a visual representation of powerful, large people in juxtaposition with weak, small ones. Like the English usage of the terms "high" and "low," the Andalusian costumed figures, while referring to all sorts of societal distinctions, are fundamentally modeled on childhood perceptions of power relationships within the family. It is no wonder, then, that the parade has a special appeal to children, for it effectively communicates its wider social message by couching its representations of status in generational terms. The parade not only symbolizes critical social divisions within Monteros but also through subtle means teaches children about these divisions. It is an effective agent of socialization.

The Parade as Fantasy

We have seen how the parade of Giants and Big-Heads juxtaposes a dominant, organized, emotionally controlled group against one characterized by subordination, disorganization, and emotional abandon. Now it remains to explain the activity, the performance, of the Giants and Big-Heads. Here I am particularly interested in exploring two aspects of the parade: Big-Head clowning, and the skyrockets.

Big-Heads, as we already know, spend the entire course of the parade in typical clowning behavior. Perhaps the most essential part of their act is the wielding of the sausage-shaped stuffed cloth, known in Spanish as a *porra*, or "club." Aside from this object's physical similarity to the penis, there is the fact that the term *porra* and its derivatives are used colloquially in Monteros to refer to the male organ.[5] The phallic symbolism of the object is inescapable. When Big-Heads attack the crowd with the *porra*, they are not only

---

[5]The term *porra* is not among the most commonly used words to refer to penis in Monteros. But *porra*, meaning "club," is the name for a baton-type toy that men occasionally fashion from wild grasses in the surrounding hills and that they say could be put to good use by widows and other "needy" women. The phallic symbolism of the object does not escape them. Moreover, in every religious procession in Monteros there are two men who are dressed in Renaissance garb and armed with large wooden maces. Irreverently, the people of Monteros refer to these men as *momporros*, a word obviously derived from the term *porra*, and one that refers specifically to the workers in horse-breeding farms who are charged with guiding the stallion's exhausted phallus into the desired location.

symbolically exposing the penis but are also asserting their masculinity through the penis's aggressive activity.

This is evident not only in the way Big-Heads use the *porra*, but also in their general antics, their skipping, hopping, jumping, and sliding. The Big-Heads are essentially clowns, and as Martha Wolfenstein has pointed out

> most clowns and comic characters are male. . . . What is funny in the man is the unpredictable behavior of the penis. This is functional rather than structural, and so readily translatable into comic action. Thus we get the characteristic gambits of the clown or comedian with his unexpected movements, his alternate collapses and surprising hyperactivity (Wolfenstein 1954, pp. 136–37).

In Monteros the word *cabeza* ("head") is associated linguistically with the male organ. The foreskin, for example, is called the "head of the penis" (*cabeza del pijo*). And men also jokingly state that "We men have two heads; when the lower one gets erect, you lose the one above!" ("*Cuando se endurece la de abajo ¡se pierde la de arriba!*") One cannot help but postulate that the Big-Heads represent the "heads" in this saying who are trying to become erect and assert their potency.

This genital imagery is reinforced by the fact that it is the young unmarried men, and not those from other segments of society, who play and (unlike the Giants) actually enjoy the role of Big-Heads. Teenaged boys are sexually aware and potent but their sexuality has not yet been harnessed and brought under control through the bond of marriage. Big-Head clowning may be viewed as a means by which Monteros society at once highlights the chaotic impulses of these men and permits these impulses to be expressed safely on a symbolic plane. Both actors and audience experience a libidinal release through the representational enactment of aggressive and sexual feelings; at the same time the social order remains stable and unthreatened because the parade is a regular, predictable event in which all participants behave in a fully expectable manner. Big-Head antics are thus no mere reversal of behavioral norms, as some analysts would say. Clowning enables young men to act out an exaggerated version of their normal, legitimate social role as the sexually rampant members of town.

But the parade speaks not only to adolescent men but also to the dominant segment of the audience, the young children. The parade refers, in this respect, to each child's battle to incorporate within

himself all the rules which his parents lay down for him, as much his
efforts to control bladder and bowels as his efforts to conform to appropriate regulations of social interaction. The child, like the Big-
Head, wants to burst out of the straitjacket of conformity, and,
watching the parade, he can identify with his costumed counterparts and do just that. The parade provides an occasion when
children can vicariously express aggression toward and release from
constricting rules. And to the extent that people of both sexes and all
ages are engaged in the constant battle to overcome the surging irrational passions within them, Big-Head behavior can provide the
same cathartic release for adults as it does for children. In the
parade, we are presented with almost a classic visual representation
of the struggle of the forces of emotional release against those of con-
straint and containment.

The skyrockets set off over the Corredera might be seen as a symbolic representation of one way in which society deals with potential
chaos. The skyrockets, of course, produce small toys and packages of
candy, which, like the skyrockets themselves, are paid for by the
Monteros government. Significantly, the place from which these
items are distributed is the Town Hall, the locus of municipal
authority, which is in the hands of officeholders drawn predomi-

*The crowd scramble for falling objects
in the Corredera.*

nantly from the social elite. It is tempting to speculate that this scenario is a symbolic means by which governing powerholders provide both children and commoners of their town with a sop. A sop, as George Foster reminds us, "is a token item given to assuage the disappointment of someone who has lost in a competition, or who has not had success comparable to others. . . . In other words, the sop is a device to buy off the possible envy of the loser" (Foster 1972, p. 177). In a general sense, Foster continues, "Symbolic sharing, and the symbolic offer to share, can thus be described as 'sop behavior' " (ibid.).

The dispersal of small gifts in the Corredera fits this definition well. In the eyes of the elite, who have ultimate control over the pageant, children in general and people of the working class in particular create—in their own respective ways—a threat to social and political stability. It is precisely children and working-class members of the community who attend the pageant of Giants and Big-Heads in the greatest numbers. The distribution of toys and candy that takes place at that time may be seen as an attempt to placate these potentially disruptive elements of society through the token sharing of wealth. To the extent that this unconscious tactic works by keeping a potentially chaotic crowd under control, the pageant of Giants and Big-Heads reinforces the hierarchies of generation and status by demonstrating the power of the town elite.

In the final analysis, I expect, the parade is a metaphoric statement of potential social chaos, of the threat to both the individual and society if the forces of order and control are not permitted to prevail. Paradoxically, by institutionalizing an annual occasion like this, during which disorder reigns under controlled conditions, the people of Monteros demonstrate to themselves the advantages of predictability in social life and some of the ways in which predictability can be attained.

The parade is emotionally charged largely because the costumed figures are able simultaneously to represent contrasting features of society and the individual. Thus, a man observing or enacting the pageant of Giants and Big-Heads may easily identify with both types of figures, for each of them embodies an essential aspect of himself. Even working-class men are powerholders to some extent, if only in their role as family leader; in this capacity, they may identify with the Giants. To the degree that they feel powerless and oppressed, however, they may project themselves into the Big-Heads, who lash out in a hostile, assertive burst of activity, as if to protest against their subordinate position.

Further, a young boy observing the Big-Heads might invest

these figures with at least two distinct meanings: they may seem to embody an ideal of physical and sexual aggressiveness, or they may appear to represent the unsocialized, immature state of childhood that is best outgrown. It is no doubt this sort of multiple imagery—an imagery that Victor Turner has called *polysemy* (1967, p. 50)—that keeps the parade alive in an epoch when local customs such as this are being progressively eroded throughout Spain.

Titles, Names, and Pronouns

Tu honra en ti no está, sino en los demas.
Your reputation is not up to you, but to others.

3

Spanish proverb

In Monteros, as I have said, a man's identity depends in large measure upon his estimation of his social rank, including his overall notion both of the social hierarchy in which he finds himself and of his place within the scheme. Unlike the small farming villages of northern Spain, described, for example, by Aceves (1971), Brandes (1975a), Freeman (1970), and Kenny (1966), the agro-towns of the south are socially heterogeneous and are divided into ranked groups, based upon a host of criteria. It is the issue of social category, particularly as reflected in speech, that I wish to analyze in this chapter.

I shall begin with the question of labeling, for it is the denotation of certain classes by particular terms that in effect determines the social reality of rank. I then wish to discuss titles and the pronoun usages to which they correspond; these aspects of speech are carefully manipulated by all the people of Monteros to achieve definite social ends. There is, finally, the important question of naming, particularly the use of nicknames and diminutives, and the implications of this practice for the formation of personal and social identity.

The Denotation of Social Rank

In Monteros, it is safe to say, there is no single, definitive ranking system that everyone agrees upon. Rather, there exists a variety of systems, each reflecting a different point of view and emphasizing distinctive elements of the social environment.

Most members of the wealthy, landed elite tend to emphasize differential education or sophistication in their classificatory schemes. Hence, they distinguish between the *gente culta* ("cultured people") and *gente humilde* ("humble people"), or, alternatively, between the *sector culto* ("cultured sector") and the *sector popular* ("common sector"). The categorization is presented simply as an objective description, devoid of value judgments. It is clear, however, that individuals are placed in one camp or the other according to a range of criteria—family background, demeanor, speech, taste in clothing, and friends—that extends considerably beyond the number of years of formal schooling. Even students at the University of Madrid who have earned their way through college by dint of academic excellence and hard-earned scholarships are lumped with the "humble" or "common" people if their fathers are laborers. Those, on the other hand, who have never attended college are nonetheless considered to be of the *gente culta* if they happen to have inherited a large estate.

Some upper-class people in Monteros refer to a highly elite segment of the populace as *sociedad*, or "society," in the sense of high society. This label, which is nearly obsolete and which is today used as a term of social rank only by the people to whom it refers, denotes the old, landed families of town. Members of this group can be clearly identified by any of eighteen surnames, and family trees indicate nearly exclusive endogamy among the people who bear them. The criterion for membership in *sociedad* is unabashedly genealogical: either you are born into such a family or you are not. Membership in *sociedad*, regardless of wealth or formal education, immediately implies being among the "cultured people." Not all the "cultured people," however, are in *sociedad*.

There is a single, primary criterion for distinguishing between the *gente culta* and *gente humilde*, on the one hand, and those who are of *sociedad* as opposed to those who are not, on the other: family background. In the first instance, the distinction refers to what we might call the quality of breeding, to which formal schooling certainly contributes, but for which it alone is insufficient. To be "cultured," one must additionally receive informal training from a family that knows how to comport itself in a sophisticated, worldly manner. In the second instance, family background is the sole and sufficient criterion for membership in or exclusion from the group. Though the boundary line between "cultured" and "humble" people often is vague and subject to controversy, membership in "society" is indisputable. In either instance, however, the populace is divided into two opposing groups.

When we turn to opinions of the majority of the town populace, we discover a different set of ranking criteria. According to many of the working class, money is of preeminent importance. Those who have it, or are believed to have it, are variously termed *los ricos* ("the rich"), *los grandes* ("the big guys"), *los capitalistas* ("the capitalists"), and *los gordos* ("the fat guys"); those who do not are called *los pobres* ("the poor"). For most people in Monteros there is truth in the proverb *Tanto tienes, tanto vales* ("You have so much, you're worth so much"). Either you have money or you do not. In either case, it is believed, the economic situation into which one was born basically determines his entire pattern of life, including whom he will marry, with whom he will associate, and in what manner he will think and conduct his affairs.

Degree of occupational independence is another important criterion, which has yielded a tripartite scheme of social rank, existing alongside the purely financial one. Hence, laborers sometimes distinguish among three groups: the *ricos* or "rich," including those who do not have to work for a living or those who have somehow acquired a lucrative profession; the *medianos*, or "those of the middle range," who are made up mostly of shopkeepers, merchants, and others who have to work for a living but are their own bosses; and, finally, the *obreros*, or "workers," who live on either temporary or fixed wages and have no independent source of income.

The existence of cross-cutting modes of classification, combined with competing value systems, means that even though everyone considers rank important, nobody has a secure sense of social identity. If I am from an old, landed family, for example, and yet am forced by declining economic fortunes to open a store for a living, I can command a certain amount of respect from some townspeople to whom family background is critical, but I will be treated with condescension by others for whom the fact that I work is most important. If I am a large, wealthy landowner and have therefore never felt the need to educate myself to a profession, many townspeople will defer to me, but others—speaking behind my back because of my powerful economic position—will criticize my relative ignorance and lack of formal training. If this is the situation for those from the upper strata of society, it may be imagined how much more difficult it is for many commoners who, despite education and considerable financial success, are forced into a position of having to defer to those from superior family backgrounds. Under these ambiguous circumstances, people seize upon titles, modes of address, and naming to express their sense of rank and to manipulate their place in the system—a system that everyone seems to find inimical and yet inevitable.

Titles

Titles in Monteros set people apart by investing them with an aura of distance and respect. This is especially true of the most commonly employed title, *Don* (for women, *Doña*), which is supposed to have a restricted application, but which in reality is applied rather broadly. Pitt-Rivers' discussion of how this title is employed in Alcalá (1971, pp. 72–74) accurately outlines the situation in Andalusia generally: "People assert that the courtesy title of *Don* is the privilege of those who hold a university degree, who have a 'career'. In practice the use is heavily influenced by other criteria, such as age, wealth, appearance and occupation" (ibid. p. 72). In Monteros, when a person has a university degree, it is said that he "has his *Don*"; the title is spoken of and conceived as if it were some sort of material possession. Schoolteachers, lawyers, and medical specialists of all types are the prinicipal, fully legitimate possessors of their *Don*, so to speak. In actual usage, however, the term *Don* is much more broadly applied. Everyone from government bureaucrats to wealthy landowners, who may or may not have higher education, carries the title.

If an outsider asks why such a theoretically unqualified person is addressed by the title *Don*, he is likely to be greeted by one of two reactions. The first is to search for some legitimizing factor in the person's past. Of wealthy landowners it may be said, "He is a lawyer though he doesn't practice." *"No ejerce"*—"He doesn't practice"—is the justification many people use to explain why they address a person as *Don*. The second reaction, equally common, is simply to admit that social reality forces people to act deferentially towards those who might prove influential or of assistance sometime in the future. "We of Monteros are like that," states a farm administrator. "We call anyone *Don* who thinks he's the least bit important." There is a look of disgust on his face as he makes this admission, for ingratiation of any kind is repugnant to pride-conscious Andalusians. On the other hand, pragmatism is a necessary survival mechanism, and to rationalize debasing themselves temporarily, men will quote the popular saying: *Dame pan y dime tonto* ("Give me bread and call me a fool"). Some people, in overenthusiastic adherence to this philosophy, become known for their consistent and exaggerated deferential behavior. These people, in an unusual deviation from standard Spanish, are called *caciques* for their fawning attitude and comportment, which is termed *caciquismo*. [1]

Those who carry the title *Don* never use it, either in reference or address, among themselves. However, they do append the title to one another's names whenever speaking of one another to a social inferior. This practice effectively guards the distance between speaker and listener, for it accentuates the obvious fact that these two people have entirely different relationships with the person about whom they are conversing. When speaking with social superiors, a non-titled person will always refer to upper-class people by the titles *Don* and *Doña*. This, from the perspective of the elite, is to accord due respect to one's betters. From the lower-class point of view, however, it is a pragmatic response to social reality, which can be justified on the grounds that the social superior exerts some actual or potential power over the speaker.

One more title, *Señorito* (feminine, *Señorita*), deserves special discussion. As a term of address it is virtually obsolete. In my experience, only old people who have labored most of their lives as servants still call anyone *señorito*. (Our seventy-year-old laundress regularly addressed me by this term.) Until about 1960, the title was a commonly employed, affectionate, and respectful way to address one's social superiors, particularly one's patrons. Nowadays, it has acquired a markedly derogatory connotation of economic parasitism.

"The authentic word *señorito*," as one of my working-class informants put it, denotes a young unmarried man of whatever social station. [2] The term is never used in that sense, as the informant correctly noted; but that is its "official" meaning, and a meaning that

---

[1] The term *cacique* derives from ancient Mexico, and throughout the Spanish-speaking world has come to mean a political boss; *caciquismo*, then, is political bossism. I cannot explain why the meaning of the term is so different in Monteros from the rest of the Hispanic world, though it must be cautioned that this usage is restricted to the less educated segments of town society. On *caciquismo* as a political phenomenon in Spain, see Brenan (1964, pp. 7–8, 18, 94, 122), Herr (1974, pp. 115–16), and the classic essay on the topic by Joaquín Costa (1967 [1902]).

[2] This may explain in part why in Pitt-Rivers' Andalusian community the term *señorito* was applied primarily to young men of the upper classes (Pitt-Rivers 1971, p. 74). In Monteros no such age distinction exists in contemporary times, insofar as the use of the title is concerned. George Foster (1964, pp. 115–16) discusses how diminutives operate as an affectionate mode of address in rural Mexico.

bears at least some correspondence to its actual usage as well. Long ago the word *señorito* probably conjured the image of a carefree young bachelor, still unburdened by economic responsibilities; with time, it came to apply to any male adult, married or not, who was wealthy enough to live from capital, rents, and labor exploitation.

A few elderly members of the landed elite in Monteros—men who have never had to be burdened with the administration of their estates, much less with regular employment—still conceive of themselves as *señoritos*, fully worthy of the respect and deference that the term at one time conveyed. Most upper-class people, however, strive to maintain a modern image of themselves as responsible, working members of the community, even if their labor consists of nothing more than regular visits to the fields to consult with their farm administrators. They resent any implication of parasitism and correspondingly denigrate that handful among them whom they believe still to be living in the supposedly obsolete, exploitative fashion of their ancestors.

For working-class people, more lies behind the appellation *señorito* than the freedom from labor. It is clear, for example, that a *señorito* has to be wealthy. As we shall see in the following chapter, Gypsies are often thought to be exploitative in trying to live without working. But nobody would confuse a poor Gypsy with a *señorito*. Nor are most schoolteachers and clerks, who live on a limited monthly salary, considered to be *señoritos* unless they happen to be from wealthy landed families or act as if they were. The *señorito* is distinguished by comportment as well as by private income. If a man demonstrates by consistently haughty behavior that he considers himself intrinsically superior to manual laborers, then he will be referred to as a *señorito*. If, on the other hand, he maintains a proper distance from, though basic respect toward, these laborers, he will not be held in this derogatory light.

The title *Don* and the term *señorito* have thus come to symbolize not only particular statuses or positions in the social hierarchy, but also certain personal qualities. They are thereby easily manipulated in social intercourse to create different impressions, according to the relationship between speaker and audience. To flatter and demonstrate respect to a social superior one should address him as *Don;* to call him *señorito*, except under highly special circumstances, would be insulting. The people of Monteros are highly sensitive to the implications of using a title in one context or another. To demonstrate respect, for example, some men called me Don Estanislao in public, but omitted the title to achieve intimate familiarity when we were alone. Even the frequency with which a title is repeated in conversation is significant. To address a person as Don Fulano too often may be seen by one's equals as unnecessarily obsequious; for the purpose of staying on a superior's good side it is sufficient to utter the title respectfully only once during a verbal exchange.

Two lower-class men occasionally address one another jokingly as *Don*, at the same time adopting a pseudo-elegant tone of voice. Such joking is carried out, of course, with the full realization that only social equals can make common mockery of the social hierarchy. But if using titles jokingly implicitly defines status boundaries, we may also speculate that it operates on a symbolic level to destroy those boundaries as well. To address a person of equal status by a title—even if this is accomplished humorously—in a way implies that the speaker deserves such special treatment himself. Such usage transforms the title into something like the symbolic mirror described by Fernandez (1976, p. 15). It becomes a device by which people can see themselves reflected in another, thereby linking themselves with the actual other—their social equal—as well as with their symbolic others—the real Dons in town. In this manner, to address a person of equal low status by *Don* at once draws boundaries because it is a joke that only true equals can share, and eliminates boundaries because it is an assertion of symbolic unity with and similiarity to those of superior status. If only in humor, dominance and control over the real or imagined oppressors must be expressed.

Just as the title *Don* is resented by the lower classes and turned to their own psychological advantage through humor, so the appellation *señorito* is treated humorously by the elite. One highly educated man, a lawyer, refers to a male nurse (*practicante*) jokingly as a *señorito consorte*, a "*señorito* by association," because the nurse keeps constant company with those whom the lawyer considers to be the most propertied and yet least productive and industrious people in town. By using this term in the presence of other educated and well-to-do men, he dissociates himself from status equals whom he considers parasitic and unrepresentative of his values and lifestyle. The term is also used by the upper-class elite in irony, as when my wife and I were invited several times to join wealthy, educated members of the community for a drink in the Corredera, "where the *señoritos* sit." This phrase, lest we be misled as to the intent, was always followed by a small chuckle. The term *señorito*, when used by the elite in mockery, enables them to objectify themselves, thereby freeing themselves from an odious stereotype. This, too, is an important means of asserting dominance and achieving control, for nobody in Monteros, regardless of status, likes to be victimized by other people's oversimplified social categorizations.

However, when lower-class men refer—usually with an expression of thinly disguised disgust on their faces—to "the *señoritos*," they create a bond of equality among themselves by placing themselves in common opposition to the detested elite.

Pronouns

Any discussion relating Spanish speech forms to social rank would be incomplete without consideration of the use of *usted*, "you" in the formal mode of address, and *tu*, "you" in the informal mode. George Foster has already pointed out that these terms perform at least two psychological functions for the speaker: "a) To reassure the speaker where he stands *vis-à-vis* the person, being, or creature addressed. b) To let the addressee know how the speaker regards the relationship between the two" (Foster 1964, p. 111). In Monteros, as elsewhere in the Spanish-speaking world, the word *tu* indicates intimacy, trust, and equality, while the word *usted* symbolizes at least some measure of social distance, formality, guardedness, and inequality. The terms are constantly manipulated as a means of signifying relative rank.

Monteros adults, regardless of relative social status, generally reciprocate by calling one another either *usted* or *tu*. It is this implicit rule that enables pronouns to operate as markers of social rank. Hence, people tend to use *tu* almost immediately after being introduced to someone for the first time, *if* they have reason to believe that the person is a social equal. The most significant test of this rule is the occasional elimination of relative age as a criterion in pronoun use. All adults of the social elite—regardless of relative age—address one another by *tu*, even if there is a generation between them. Their common social rank in Monteros weighs more heavily in their perception of relative social distance or closeness than does their age difference. As for my wife and myself, members of the town elite called us by *tu* as soon as we were introduced, thereby indicating their acceptance of us—with our obvious economic and educational advantages—as social equals, and inviting us implicitly to treat them likewise. Workers, however, addressed us as *usted*, and only after a long time passed and they knew us well would they slip into using the *tu* form. Some, to the very end of our field stay, refused to address us by the familiar form in public, and preferred to reserve this for more private, intimate occasions when they could not be accused of overstepping the bounds of respectfulness.

Usted is almost always employed between two people of different status. The title *Don*, for example, is automatically accompanied by the formal mode of address: if you address a person as *Don*, you invariably also use *usted* in addressing a lower-status person—a reciprocity that even characterizes relationships between masters and servants who have been associated in the same house for years. Upper-class informants state that they continue to address their servants and other workers by *usted* as a sign of respect, to assure these people that they are neither treated nor perceived condescendingly. Lower-class people, on the other hand, insist that *usted* is a survival mechanism of the *señoritos*, who try at all costs to avoid the type of intimacy between themselves and laborers that would derive from the reciprocal use of *tu*.

Though nonreciprocal modes of address between adults are extremely uncommon, I witnessed two instances of their use. One was a casual encounter between a large landowner from an old, prominent Monteros family and a construction worker from a very poor, economically insecure background. The other was an ongoing relationship between a widow of late middle age, also from a prominent family, and her younger servant woman. In both cases, the elite person addressed the other by *tu* while receiving *usted* in return. Several factors might explain the asymmetry of address. In the first case, I would speculate that the vast difference in status between the men coupled with the facts that they have little to do with one another on a daily basis and that the landowner is a good deal older than the construction worker all operate to make the asymmetry nonthreatening. In the second instance, the servant had been reared from childhood in her mistress's house, and to call her *tu* was simply a natural retention of the form used when she was much younger. If the servant were suddenly to change employers, it is certain that those in the new household would address her as *usted*.

I suspect that asymmetrical address was common until a generation ago, when workers started migrating from Monteros in substantial numbers. Massive emigration to Catalonia and other parts of the industrial north initiated a chain of circumstances, including a labor shortage and the consequent increase in wages, that has led to a vast improvement in the standard of living for working people. Some of the most traditional and time-honored symbols of elite status, like elaborate tombstones, elegant dress, and attendance at the Town Hall dances during festivals, are being taken over by those who have been upwardly mobile economically. The threat that this economic mobility will in time be expressed socially must operate as a strong motivation for the elite to guard their distance carefully.

It is not only among people of different status that the *usted* form is employed. Under special circumstances, it is considered wise for those who ordinarily address one another by *tu* to adopt the formal mode temporarily. During the olive harvest, for example, each work team is assigned a leader, who is charged with maintaining the order and productivity of the group. The leader is invariably of the same social category as his workers, but the fact that he is placed in a position of authority, which requires that he be respected, means that he is supposed to adopt the appropriate symbols of his status. Wise and effective team leaders, it is said, address their workers by *usted*. More than once it was pointed out to me how a team's low productivity could be explained on the basis of the leader's over-familiarity with his workers, including his reciprocal use of *tu*.

In a highly status-conscious society, there is no more sensitive expression of social intimacy or distance than mode of address. The use of *tu* and *usted*, in this sort of atmosphere, becomes not only a symbol of class affiliation, but also a means by which people assimilate and project status images about themselves and others. It is a critical speech form indicating and shaping one's sense of being.

Nicknaming

There are two aspects of naming in Monteros that bear heavily on the question of social identity and social hierarchy: nicknames and diminutive names. In an earlier work (Brandes 1975c), I hypothesized that, for southern Europe generally,

> The nicknaming phenomenon flourishes where settlements are small, egalitarian, and traditional enough to provide for moral unity and effective informal sanctioning mechanisms; they reach their greatest fruition where such settlements are large enough to support some internal differentiation through formation of strong voluntary friendship bonds. Nicknames in Spain are born of the pueblos, of medium-sized villages. Hamlets and cities may partially share in the nicknaming tradition, but they lack the essential environmental conditions which permit that tradition to thrive (Brandes 1975c, p. 147).

Monteros, with its profound sense of hierarchy and its ethnic diversity, is both more populous and structurally more complex than I believed would be ideal for the highest development of nicknaming. To the extent that nicknaming is neither as ubiquitous nor as structurally significant in Monteros as in the small, egalitarian communities of Castile, my hypotheses have been borne out. Nonetheless, nicknaming in Monteros does exist, and has been molded to conform with the basic concerns of rank and reputation in this society.

Nicknames in Monteros are termed *nombrajos*, that is, "big names" or "gross names." (The usual Spanish terms are *motes* and *apodos*.) As with nicknames everywhere (see, for example, Antoun 1968; Barrett 1978; Bernard 1968–69; E. N. Cohen 1977; Dorian 1970; Foster 1964; Kenny 1966; Pérez-Díaz 1969; and Pitt-Rivers 1971), they are based on witticisms about personality or physical characteristics. Hence, in our town, a man known for his extraordinary strength is known as Sansón ("Samson"), a usurious moneylender is referred to as Al Capone, and a man who is thought to look like Richard Widmark is called Richa, which is approximately how the English name is pronounced with a Spanish accent. Here, as elsewhere, nicknames are restricted largely to men. Thus, if a woman is known by a nickname, it is usually through a form of teknonymy; she is "the wife of Sansón" or "the wife of Piojo Verde," and does not have a nickname of her own. In addition, nicknames are inherited patrilineally. They are passed down from a father to his children and then to his grandchildren. As a woman grows up, she gradually loses her father's nickname and acquires that of her husband, so that, taking account of considerable flexibility in the system, nicknames in Monteros are traditionally transmitted approximately in the same manner as are English surnames.

Monteros nicknames rarely refer to a single individual. In the vast majority of cases, the nickname belongs to an entire family, like the Viñas (the "Grapevines"), the Barriches (a nonsense term), the Pela'os (the "Winners"), and so on. Significantly, however, each nickname has come to symbolize a particular moral or personal quality. Hence, the Chumbos ("Prickly-pear Fruits") are said by many to be untrustworthy; the Bonitos ("Pretty Ones") are hard workers; the Gandumbas (a nonsense term) are stupid. I would estimate that, partially because of migration into Monteros by professionals and bureaucrats, fewer than half the inhabitants of the town bear nicknames. But where a nickname exists, it operates to impart to a family a collective reputation that is transmitted from one generation to the next.

This raises another aspect of the status system in Monteros: ranking according to personal qualities. Overlaying the distinctions of social category and existing concurrently with them but not in any way modifying them are estimations of personal decency. There are several components of decency: *honradez*, or "honor," which in women refers to sexual fidelity and modest conduct, and in men to honesty and the willingness (as distinct from the ability) to defend themselves and their families against outside attack; and *nobleza*, or "goodness," which refers particularly to the disinterestedness of motivations and intentions. Reputation also is bound to the concept of *vergüenza*, or "shame," the best discussion of which can be found in Pitt-Rivers' *People of the Sierra* (1971, pp. 112–21). To Pitt-Rivers, *vergüenza*

> means shame, the possibility of being made to blush. It is a moral quality like manliness, and it is persistent, though like manliness or innocence, which it more closely resembles, it may be lost. Once lost it is not, generally speaking, recoverable, though a feeling remains that it is only lost by those whose shame was not true shame but a deceptive appearance of it. It is the essence of personality and for this reason is regarded as something permanent (ibid. p. 112).

In Monteros, *nobleza, honradez,* and *vergüenza* are usually associated with whole families rather than with individuals. The presence or absence of these qualities is part of a different hierarchy from the one discussed earlier; it is a hierarchy based on the moral qualities available to everyone in all times and places, rather than on material advantages and possessions or family background. Townspeople make moral judgments about one another based largely upon family reputation but also on individual acts—acts that of course ultimately operate to create that collective reputation. It is in this respect as much as any other that nicknames are employed in Monteros. They come to symbolize not only a family group but also its moral complexion. The combination of family name—that is, reputation—and its social status operates above all to define eligible or desirable marriage partners, so that the potential influence of the nickname is enormous.

Thus far we have been discussing nicknames as terms of reference. But they are also significant as terms of address, when they operate as functional equivalents of the pronoun *tu*. Just as a worker never employs the second-person singular pronoun in addressing his superiors, so he refrains from using the superior's nickname to his face. Likewise, the superior never addresses his social inferiors by nickname. Workers tell the legend of two local men, now both dead: a barber known by the nickname Maestro Lucas, and a *señorito* called Piojo Verde ("Green Louse").

> Every day, at a given hour, the *señorito* would pass the barber-shop and call out, "Good day, Maestro Lucas." To this the barber would reply, "Good day, Don Tomás," using the respectful, titled version of the *señorito's* name. Finally one day the barber tired of being treated condescendingly and answered the *señorito* by saying, "Good day, Piojo Verde!" After that, the two men never spoke to each other.

This legend clearly provides a safe, verbal means for workers in Monteros to rebel vicariously against their social superiors. At the same time, it shows dynamic symmetry in speech between people of unequal status, a symmetry that workers attribute to the elite's status anxieties. The argument the workers provide to support this point of view is the same one they offer as an explanation for the use of *usted* between people from different classes: to use a nickname symbolizes more familiarity than actually exists, or than members of the elite would ever want to exist, between those of different social categories. Nickname use, then, is restricted to, and operates to define, social equals.

There exists another effective block to nickname use: ignorance. Many members of the elite have so little contact with the world of the workers that they are unfamiliar with working-class nicknames. The same may be said for the workers' knowledge of elite nicknames, which is even more restricted. In fact, many workers are unaware that the titled members of their community have nicknames at all. "They don't have nicknames," I was repeatedly told, "because they have their *Don*" ("*ellos tienen su Don*"). Thus, the very knowledge of a nickname as well as its employment as a mode of address becomes an important demarcator of social status.

Names, however, can be used to break down class barriers. In this context, I wish briefly to discuss diminutives, which must be distinguished from nicknames. Nicknames, in the strict sense, are what Nancy Dorian (1970) has termed "substitute names." They derive neither from given names nor surnames, but rather have an entirely separate linguistic point of origin. Diminutive names, in contrast, are either shortened or affectionately familiar forms of the first or last name. In English, we could say that Red or Curly is a typical male nickname, while Jim or Bob or Smitty is a diminutive.

Among the Monteros elite a small number of men are viewed by the working classes as *corriente*, or "ordinary," and *campechano*, or "unpresumptuous." These men are known to mingle and joke with the workers, to share drinks with them frequently, and generally to demonstrate themselves to have egalitarian sentiments. Workers address these men with the respectful *Don*, but they refer to them among themselves by diminutive names. Two cases in particular come to mind: Don Antonio, who is known in working-class circles as Antoñete; and Don Alfredo, spoken of as Alfredito. In both instances, the diminutive is employed without the title *Don*. I have discussed this matter with both men, who claim that their social peers neither address nor refer to them by diminutive. They are aware that working-class people call them by the diminutive, and attribute this use to the affection in which they are held.

But more than affection is revealed by this naming pattern. To refer to a member of the elite by a diminutive, rather than by title, is to demonstrate to one's audience a close social bond with the person so named. It is as if one worker were saying to the others present, "I have such an intimate relationship with Don Antonio that I can call him Antoñete." The use of the diminutive, then, becomes the symbol of an intimate tie to the elite. Its employment in ordinary speech operates symbolically to elevate the rank of the speaker to that of the person to whom he is referring. Interestingly, however, the use of the given name without the title—as Antonio or Alfredo—is as inconceivable in reference as in address. The diminutive acts in such instances as an honorific, albeit an affectionate one.

There is one final use of naming in Monteros that stands somewhere between nicknames and diminutives. It occurs when a given name, of either a living or a dead male relative, is applied to a family as a whole. Thus, there are the Basilisos, descendants of a man named Basilio. There are also the Chelos, descendants of a man named Consuelo.[3] (*Chelo* is the diminutive form of *Consuelo*.) This seems to be a purely working-class phenomenon. It is a special case where names and diminutives are used in precisely the way that I have already described for family nicknames. (To my knowledge, no special term exists to describe this unique form of naming.)

Naming of all types in Monteros is thus a critical means by which social identity may be derived and expressed. Used as terms of

---

[3]Throughout the Spanish-speaking world, the name *Consuelo* is almost universally applied to women alone. Monteros is an exception, because many men (and a few women as well) are named after El Señor del Consuelo ("Lord of the Consolation"), the principal devotional image in the town. (*Señor del Consuelo* and *Cristo del Consuelo* are alternative ways of referring to the same image. The former mode is the more colloquial and frequent of the two, while the latter is the image's official title.)

reference, names allow men to express their relationship to the person under discussion. Used as terms of address, they are a sensitive barometer of the status affiliations of the persons involved. Nicknames and diminutives received from others permit men to assimilate the way others perceive them; nicknames and diminutives given to others project the givers' self-image with regard to the status hierarchy. Women are influenced considerably less than men by the nicknaming phenomenon, if only because their own nicknames—in the few cases they have them—derive from their closest male relatives. Nicknaming in particular is a male-dominated domain, seized upon and utilized unconsciously for the expression of status.

Gypsy Jokes and the Andalusian Self-Image

Gypsies seem to have been born into the
world for the sole purpose of being thieves:
they are born of thieving parents, they are
brought up with thieves, they study in order to
be thieves, and they end up as past masters
in the art of thieving. Thieving and the taste
for thieving are inseparable from their existence, and they never abandon them until
they reach the grave.

Miguel de Cervantes, "La Gitanilla" (1613)

No discussion of stratification in Andalusia would be complete
without taking account of Gypsies, who loom large in the Spanish
mind generally but even larger in the mentality of southern Spain,
where most of the Spanish Gypsies have lived and traveled. To
Europeans, Gypsies have always seemed mysterious in nature and
origin. We know of course that their probable origin lies in north India, whence they spread westward, first into Asia Minor and North
Africa during the late Middle Ages and then into Europe throughout
the early modern period. There is evidence that they reached
Switzerland by 1414, Rome by 1422, Paris by 1427, and England by
1514 (Clebert 1967; McDowell 1970). In 1425, they were already
residing in Barcelona. It is presumed that Iberian Gypsies entered
the peninsula from both France and North Africa, but exactly in
what sequence or proportions they came via the northern and
southern routes is still open to question.

As is true of Gypsies in other countries, Spanish Gypsies are in
reality a caste living among, but apart from, the main national
ethnic majority. Phenotypically, they manifest a wide range of ap-

pearances, from the dark skin and hair of their Indian ancestors to occasional blond hair and blue eyes. Certainly their physical appearance overlaps with that of the olive-complexioned Andalusians. They are more distinguishable by their culture, including their strikingly flamboyant dress, their at least perfunctory knowledge of a separate language, known in Spain as Caló, and their extreme endogamy and loyalty to their own. They are also famous for specializing in certain occupations, like horse trading, entertainment, and artisanship.

There is little doubt that in recent years Gypsies through the adoption of formal education and a sedentary lifestyle have become increasingly integrated into the mainstream of society. They remain ethnically separate, however.[1] It is difficult to state definitively whether Gypsies isolate themselves or have their isolation imposed upon them by outsiders. In Monteros, at least, one can identify both processes at work simultaneously: Gypsies strongly discourage intermarriage and intimate contact with those among whom they live, and yet even from early childhood they suffer from severe discrimination and derision. Here, as throughout the country, they are a pariah group. Understandably, they have developed defense mechanisms to protect themselves against the verbal and other abuse heaped upon them daily by the non-Gypsy majority.

It is difficult to estimate the size of the Gypsy community in Monteros because it changes dramatically by season. It is my impression that Gypsies themselves underestimate their numerical strength, while I am certain that the non-Gypsies—known in contradistinction to the Gypsies as Castellanos, or Castilians—vastly exaggerate it. At maximum, during the winter olive harvest, there could be no more than four hundred Gypsies in town. In summer, when many of them leave for construction work and agricultural labor in the north, their population is probably about half that figure. If we compromise and say that there are about three hundred Gypsies in Monteros, which is probably close to the true yearly average, they would comprise no more than 3 percent of the total population. Yet their presence is much more important, especially to working-class Castellanos, than that low figure would suggest.

In this chapter, we shall be interested not in the Gypsies themselves, but rather in jokes told by Castellano men about Gyp-

---

[1]This is not to say that all Gypsies are or have been itinerant. In Spain, as well as in eastern Europe, there have always been pockets of sedentary Gypsies, the most famous such colony in Iberia being located on the outskirts of Granada in the Sacro Monte. This group receives full description by Quintana and Floyd (1972, 1976). See San Roman (1975, 1976) for additional studies of Spanish Gypsies.

sies. (This is just another route through which we can come to understand how Monteros men perceive themselves, for these jokes, like all the other projective forms we are investigating, tell more about their narrators than about their purported subject.) For a full comprehension of Gypsy jokes, however, we shall also have to turn to other joke motifs, especially to those regarding fools and foolish behavior. All of this humor imparts a good deal of insight into the Castellano consciousness of status and of a man's position within the status hierarchy.

My treatment of jokes here, as in subsequent chapters, focuses on texts rather than on performance. I believe that in the case of this genre—at least as manifested in Monteros—texts, when combined with basic knowledge about narrators and audience, provide a rich opportunity for content analysis and in and of themselves can yield a good deal of information. During fieldwork, I recorded jokes as closely as possible to the original at the time they were spontaneously narrated. The vast majority of jokes in my collection emerged when men were relaxing together over some drinks in the bars. In this atmosphere I could usually count on men repeating jokes for me until I had written them down. During particularly animated joke-telling sessions, however, this method proved frustrating and intrusive, so that I would simply jot down key phrases to remind me of the stories, and later, at the narrators' leisure, record them on tape. The joke texts in this chapter as throughout are translations of verbatim or near-verbatim texts.

Before turning to the jokes themselves, however, we shall have to speak specifically of the social position of Gypsies within Monteros, and particularly of the stereotypes by which they are branded.

The Gypsy in Monteros Society

If an outside observer like myself asks the people of Monteros to list the various *clases sociales* ("social classes") or *categorías sociales* ("social categories") represented in town, the classifications discussed in the preceding chapter almost invariably emerge. Though some informants emphasize one component or determinant of class at the expense of possible alternatives and some respond in greater detail than others, the answers all have one thing in common: the unconscious exclusion of Gypsies from any part in the scheme. This omission might be explained, at first, by the fact that the appellation *gitano* is an ethnic category, while the term *social class* is not. On the other hand, whenever I tried to clarify the social divisions that were presented to me, I would always ask, "And what about the Gypsies?" to which informants would respond, "Them? Nobody cares for them or wants anything to do with them! They're a bunch of good-for-nothings!" It is as if they were perceived as existing altogether outside the boundaries of society, just as untouchables are in India.

In Monteros, unlike some other parts of Andalusia (Pitt-Rivers 1971, p. 186), Gypsies are certainly thought of as *cristianos,* the term generally used to refer to "human being." But at the same time they are believed to have a special manner of thinking and acting that sets them apart from the rest of society. In fact, many people in Monteros resent sharing their town with Gypsies, who live dispersed throughout all the poor neighborhoods of Monteros; it would be preferable, these people think, if Gypsies were herded into their own special neighborhood or, better yet, were assigned to separate villages or towns.

It is easy to identify some of the more common stereotypes that Castellanos hold of Gypsies. Gypsies are said to be inordinately dirty and malodorous. One Castellano even told me that "it is questionable whether we have excluded Gypsies from our society or they have excluded themselves by being so smelly." They are also said to be inferior to Castellanos intellectually, though superior to them in genital endowment and sex drive; Gypsy men are believed to have enormous penises, and one Gypsy even bears the nickname Pijando ("Big Prick"), which is used in both reference and address and which is supposed to describe his primary physical attribute.[2] Finally, Gypsies are also said to be lazy and incompetent on the job. They are thought to be unwilling to work for a living, but when they are forced to do so, their performance falls far short of Castellano standards.

Racist attitudes toward Gypsies perform at least one critical function in Monteros society: they unite Castellanos who are otherwise opposed to one another because of either economic competition or class affiliation. Time after time, I witnessed the dissipation of potentially explosive situations between Castellanos as argumentative conversations were transformed into vague, generalized denunciations against Gypsies, upon whom the blame for the grievance between the parties, whatever it might be, could be pinned. It is the stereotyped image of Gypsies, rather than in-

---

[2]For a comparable case, in which great sexual endowment and drive are attributed to blacks, see Abrahams and Dundes (1969). Seidenberg (1952) discusses the sexual image of enemies in general.

dividual Gypsies themselves, which is called upon by Castellanos engaged in a disagreement. The mere mention of *"gitanos"* in a conversation is enough to steer all attention away from the essential, divisive issue at hand. Gypsies, like all despised peoples, are a scapegoat.

Actually, when defining the caste division in Monteros it would be more accurate to pose the opposition "Gypsy versus non-Gypsy," rather than "Gypsy versus Castellano." *Castellano*, meaning "Castilian," can variously refer to a resident or native of the vast central regions of Spain known as Old and New Castile, which few of the inhabitants of Monteros happen to be; to a person whose first and native language is Spanish, which would include the Gypsies; or to a citizen of Spain, which would also include the Gypsies. The term *Castellano* in popular usage, however, is much broader than any of these categories would suggest. As far as I can tell, it simply refers to a non-Gypsy of European descent, so that my family and I, for example, were called *Castellanos*, but only in conversations that posed this group in opposition to Gypsies. The term *Castellano*, then, is usually employed in a specific context. The same can be said of the pejorative Gypsy term *payo* (literally, "clown" or "churl"), which has essentially the same meaning, with derogatory overtones, as the term *Castellano*. In either case, there exists an important semantic unification of all non-Gypsies under the same term, which at least reflects—and perhaps influences as well—the actual, albeit rather shallow and ephemeral, unity that they achieve through common opposition to this minority group.

I stress the common opposition of the Castellanos or *payo* to Gypsies because I have observed numerous instances in which this commonality has expressed itself. Nonetheless, it is necessary to point out that members of the Monteros elite pride themselves on being less derogatory in their remarks about Gypsies than are the rest of the populace. It is not that members of the elite subscribe to a different opinion of this minority, for they do not. It is rather that, from the upper-class perspective, Gypsies are so far removed in status that they are not worth even the time of idle conversation. One upper-class *payo* put the matter bluntly: "There is no Gypsy problem here in Spain. We simply don't pay any attention to them. I've never once spoken with a Gypsy or had anything to do with one. So, you see, there *is* no Gypsy problem." Educated, wealthy elite members believe that it is only their social inferiors who are forced to associate with Gypsies, and so it is they who form and voice the strongest opinions about them.

Though I have heard occasional derogatory references to Gypsies from the mouths of the elite, my impression is that the upper-class estimate of the situation is in general correct. On the one hand, nobody likes Gypsies, and every non-Gypsy holds more or less the same stereotype of this despised minority. On the other hand, the constant denigration of and preoccupation with this group is a working-class phenomenon. Of course, this stands to reason. Working-class Castellanos, just a notch above Gypsies in the socio-economic hierarchy, are more highly motivated to differentiate themselves from this group and to raise their own status at the expense of the others than are members of the elite. This is no doubt why the vast majority of Gypsy jokes that we shall analyze come from working-class informants. It will become evident, however, that even though the overt intention of the jokes is to make fun of Gypsies, many of them serve simultaneously to laud Gypsies. Jokes, more than any other type of expressive culture in Monteros, reveal an underlying ambivalence in lower-class Castellano attitudes toward Gypsies. Before exploring this theme, however, I wish to analyze the jokes that simply tend to reflect the Gypsy stereotype.

Gypsy Jokes and the Gypsy Stereotype

One of the most common views about humor and ethnicity is, as Walter Zenner has pointed out, that "it perpetuates negative stereotypes and that it constitutes a form of aggression against the out-group. . . . This view of ethnic humor fits the 'superiority theories' of humor which hold that laughter is directed at those who are considered inferior and is, in itself, a form of triumph and superiority" (Zenner 1970, p. 93). Zenner's own analysis of Druze jokes in Israel confirms this important function of humor, a function that has been either postulated or substantiated by numerous other scholars as well (e.g., Barron 1950; Berlyne 1968; Burma 1946). There is no doubt that a "limited good" type of mentality (Foster 1967), in which people assume that there exists a finite amount of prestige or esteem in the world, underlies much ethnic joking: if one can deflate one's opponents, albeit only through ridicule and stereotyping, one may correspondingly enhance one's own social status and self-image. It is with this unconscious goal that many jokes about Gypsies are told in Monteros.

The Gypsy's alleged naïveté is frequently held up for ridicule. It is to convey this stereotype that the following is told:

One day in the middle of winter, when it was very, very cold, a Gypsy was walking through the streets wearing a short-sleeved shirt. A passerby stopped him and asked, "Aren't you cold?"

("*¿No tiene frío?*"), to which the Gypsy replied, "Why should I want the cold if I don't even have any clothing?" ("*¿Pa' qué quiero yo frío si no tengo ropa?*")

To interpret this joke, it is necessary at the outset to explain that it depends on the Gypsy's misunderstanding of the verb *tener*. In Spanish, as most readers probably realize, if one is cold, it is said that one "has cold" (*tiene frío*). In this joke, the Gypsy stupidly misconstrues the question to be an inquiry about whether he is in possession of cold, as if the air temperature were some tangible item that could be bought and sold. Thus, it is not simply Gypsy ignorance of language that the joke is designed to impart, but also the commercial mentality of Gypsies, who will supposedly convert any passing comment into a bargaining exchange. When we consider that the joke also incorporates the infamous tendency of Gypsies to dress poorly or inappropriately, then this brief joke—however odious it may seem to democratic sensibilities—is a truly impressive condensation of various derogatory stereotypes.

The commercial mentality attributed to Gypsies is never presented as a hard-working effort to get ahead. It is, rather, shown as a manipulative, scheming attempt to gain financially at the expense of someone else without exerting the labor or investing the capital that would legitimate the profit. Castellanos in Monteros employ the verb *gitanear*—literally "to Gypsy"—which is not far removed from our often unintended English-language ethnic slur "to gyp." *Gitanear* implies a mixture of underhanded persuasion and petty cheating. A storekeeper who tries to animate a customer to buy what he or she really neither wants nor needs is said to be *gitaneando*, or "Gypsying." So is a merchant who consistently rounds off a customer's change to the nearest low figure. To *gitanear*, then, is knowingly to take advantage of another person's goodwill, trust, or naïveté. Castellanos describe some of their own behavior in these terms, but the etymology of the word clearly indicates its origin in ethnic stereotyping.

Gypsies themselves, of course, are thought to do more than simply *gitanear*. They are, from the Castellano point of view, outright thieves and cheaters, even, as the following joke illustrates, in relationships with their own people.

There were two Gypsies who wanted a drink. One asked the other, "How much do you have?" The other said, "Only two *reales* [equivalent to less than half a cent]. And you?" "I have only six *reales*," he answered. "Well, then, why don't we combine our funds to buy one glass of wine and split it in half?" suggested the first Gypsy. So they bought the drink. When the bartender brought it to the counter, the Gypsy who had made the suggestion about buying it immediately picked it up and finished it off in one gulp. "But I though we were splitting it," said his companion. "We are," responded the first, "I drink it, and you say, 'Ahhhhhh!' "

As the narrator pronounces "Ahhhhhh!" he exhales deeply, as if he has just enjoyed a great treat. The underhanded tactics employed by the Gypsy in this joke are mild in comparison with the usual Gypsy reputation for theft and outright lying. The joke does, however, characterize Gypsies as trying to get something for nothing, which is ultimately the basis for all the stereotypes about their untrustworthiness.

Several jokes explicitly concern themselves with Gypsy indolence. One states that:

There was once a large crowd gathered for a public demonstration at a meeting where Franco was speaking. The crowd chanted over and over, "Bread and work! Bread and work!" A Gypsy in the crowd, upon hearing this, became frantic, and shouted out to those around him, "Wait a minute! You guys all have the wrong idea. We don't want work! We should shout, 'Bread and wine! Bread and wine!' "

This joke implies that, to the Gypsy way of thinking, merely the opportunity to work for a living is insufficient; as long as requests are being made of the government, they might as well include all the necessities for subsistence, provided as a free handout rather than in return for labor. The same basic message is incorporated in the following joke:

One very cold winter a Gypsy family was suffering tremendous discomfort because they had no way of keeping warm. So the Gypsy man said to himself, "Come next summer, I'm going to find myself some work, so that I can earn enough money to buy us a blanket for next winter." When summer came, he thought back to his idea of finding employment, considered it for a while, and then dismissed it. "It's so hot," he said to himself, "why should I want a blanket?"

In this joke, the Gypsy is seen as doing anything to rationalize staying away from work. There is also more than a touch of simplemindedness about the protagonist, thereby reinforcing this stereotype as much as that of the lazy Gypsy.

The curious thing about the two major stereotypes we have already considered—the Gypsy as lazy and the Gypsy as stupid or unsophisticated—is that they portray characteristics about which the lower-class Castellanos feel ambivalent. On the one hand, there is no doubt that when Castellanos tell these jokes they mean to denigrate the Gypsies and thereby unconsciously aim to raise their own status and self-esteem. On the other hand, in the above jokes, as much as in others we have yet to consider, Castellanos identify with the Gypsies; the stories are a safe, indirect outlet for the dissipation of Castellano anxieties about personal traits that they find it difficult to admit to themselves.

To demonstrate this proposition, let us examine in turn each of the major Gypsy stereotypes that appear in the jokes. With regard to the image of Gypsies as stupid and naïve, we must recognize that the Gypsy jokes are just one of several types in Andalusia that exploit the theme of intellectual and cultural inferiority. There are numerous jokes, for example, concerning *catetos*, roughly translated as "country bumpkins," whose ignorance operates to their distinct disadvantage.[3] A few representative stories follow:

> There was a *cateto* who went to Madrid to learn something about the world. He met up with a gentleman who placed his outstretched hand against a wall and asked the *cateto* to punch it hard. The *cateto* said, "Oh, no, I wouldn't want to do that. I'd hurt you." But the gentleman insisted that the *cateto* punch him and punch him hard. So the *cateto* wound up and gave a strong blow; but as he did, the man took his hand away from the wall, so that the *cateto* smashed his own hand. When the *cateto* returned home, his father asked him, "Well, what did you learn in Madrid?" Answered the *cateto*, "I'll show you." So he placed his hand against his eye, and asked his father to punch it. But as the father punched, the *cateto* removed his hand and got a black eye.

---

[3]*Cateto* jokes bear close resemblance to the "Fool" stories in folk literature throughout the world, which are categorized under Thompson's motifs J1700–J2749 (Thompson 1957, pp. 137–230); I cannot locate any exact analogues to the jokes I reproduce here. Moron stories in the United States, which share characteristics of the Andalusian *cateto* humor, are discussed by Davidson (1943), Mt. Pleasant (1955), and Wolfenstein (1954).

There were two *catetos* who decided to take an airplane trip. So they went to an airport, got into a plane, and tried to start it, but it refused to start. They tried a second plane, and the same thing happened. Said one to the other, "You'll see what bad luck we're going to have today. The first thing bad that happened is that the planes didn't start." Then they got into a third plane, and it started. While they were flying they decided to parachute. So they jumped with their parachutes on, but neither parachute opened. As they were falling, one said to the other, "I told you this was an unlucky day. First the planes didn't start; then the parachutes didn't open. The next thing is that there won't be a bus waiting for us when we land on the ground!"

The clever man (*el listo*) said to the *cateto*, "I'll describe some animals for you, and for each one that you can't name you give me a nickel (*duro*)." The *cateto* agreed to this plan, and in playing the game the wise man managed to earn seven nickels in a row from the *cateto*. Afterwards the *cateto* said, "I'll describe an animal for you, and if you can't guess which one it is, you give me twenty nickels." The wise man agreed to this. So the *cateto* asked, "What animal has wings, flies, swims in the water, and then comes out to eat grass from the meadow." The wise man thought awhile and then gave up, saying, "I don't know." Answered the *cateto*, "Here, take a nickel. I don't know either!"

To be sure, each one of these jokes and numerous others with a similar motif may be analyzed from a variety of perspectives. The final joke, which incorporates riddles within its frame, is especially interesting for its implicit confirmation of the class basis of riddle-telling in Monteros, which I describe in chapter 7; riddles, in the joke as in life, are a way for people who perceive themselves as intellectually inferior to raise themselves above their allegedly low cultural level. What above all interests us here, though, is the existence of a variety of narratives that exploit the theme of the fool and particularly of intellectual and cultural awkwardness. Jokes that utilize Gypsies as the main fool type convey a message about this specific caste. But the *cateto* jokes make a general statement about the intellectual and cultural inferiority of certain groups in Spanish society as a whole.

We must remember that Monteros is in no sense a peasant community. It is a typical Andalusian agro-town, populated by a sizable number of people with a high degree of education, sophistication, and awareness of the latest literary and cultural developments throughout western Europe. Juxtaposed to this group are the illiterate or semiliterate masses, who rub shoulders with the elite daily in a relatively small, compact settlement, being constantly reminded of their own intellectual disadvantage. Telling jokes about simpletons, then, becomes an outlet for unconscious self-parody. There is a terrible anxiety generated among lower-class men in particular by the conflict between their enormous, overbearing pride on the one hand and the recognition of their lack of worldliness and sophistication on the other. Jokes are in this situation a psychologically safe, indirect means for workers to admit to themselves their educational deficiencies.

There is thus reason to believe that Gypsy jokes are designed not only to ridicule Gypsies but also to provide an outlet for the inferiority feelings of the Castellano narrators themselves. The jokes are popular and effective (i.e., received with outbursts of laughter) because they elevate the Castellano self-image in two ways: first, by reinforcing the negative stereotype of a despised ethnic minority, and, second, by dissipating lower-class male status anxieties. The jokes are therefore delicate and subtle, for they enable the narrators and audience at once to denigrate and identify with the Gypsy protagonists.

A similar process operates with regard to the second major stereotype embodied in the jokes: the Gypsy as lazy or unwilling to work. Here we must digress a moment to elaborate from the previous chapter on the attitudes towards time and labor that are encountered among the Castellanos of Monteros. Until the early 1950s it was a disgrace among the elite to have to work. If a man was forced to engage in labor, he and his family were excluded from *sociedad*. One man from this group, Don Joaquín, considers himself the first *señorito* (he uses this word with pride) in Monteros to go to work. "It really upset my family," he says. His first job was as director of an olive oil factory. This was in 1951; his parents were no longer alive, but his widowed aunt, who had assumed family leadership, protested vigorously that taking a job would destroy not only Don Joaquín's reputation but that of all his kin as well. He simply told her that if she wished him to refrain from working, she would have to provide him with a sizable private income. She refused and within a few years came to accept Don Joaquín's decision because he was shown to be only the first of many elite men who were forced to go into business, seek a position in the government bureaucracy, or find other means of income to supplement their earnings from olives.

Nowadays, there are no more than fifteen or twenty members

of the elite—most of them, in fact, residing only part of the year in Monteros—who can afford to live exclusively on the earnings from their property. Not surprisingly, cultural values, which usually lag behind social and economic developments in situations of rapid change, have altered to suit the new circumstances. Most of Monteros' educated upper class today see the pursuit of a career or the direction of a business enterprise as a necessary and rewarding aspect of life. To be sure, it is still considered essential to hire servants and laborers to carry out whatever manual chores may be required. And elite women in particular are mortified even to be seen carrying a package through the streets. But the parasitic life of yesteryear is for the most part scorned, and the few who still lead this type of existence are criticized and ridiculed mercilessly behind their backs.

From the perspective of the working-class majority, however, the values and attitudes that the elite has discarded remain very much in effect. For most workers, labor of any kind is an intrinsically unpleasant enterprise in which no sane person would willingly engage.[4] One has only to ask male informants from this stratum of society how they would lead their lives if given the opportunity. The response of one man, a butcher, is a telling and typical fantasy. He would awaken at noon. Then he would laze around drinking coffee and vermouth until perhaps 3:00 P.M., when he would eat dinner. He would then take a nap until 8:00 P.M., when he would play cards or just relax. After poker, he'd look for four or five *nenas* ("broads"), who would be reserved just for him, and then return home at three or four in the morning. This is only one man's fantasy. But it is representative in its absolute disregard for the value of work. Again typically, it also emphasizes the pursuit of a time schedule conspicuously unsuitable for any economic enterprise. There are still a few men of the elite who pursue a schedule totally in conflict with that of the working men of the world; to pursue such a schedule was, in fact, a virtually uniform symbol of the *señorito* lifestyle until recent developments made that aspect of upper-class life impossible. It is not surprising, then, that working-class men still regard such a schedule—disdainful of responsibilities as it is—as the ideal.

When considering attitudes toward work, we must remember, too, that from the perspective of the working class, very few of the people they classify as *señoritos* even today engage in actual labor.

---

[4]The discrepancy between the values of different social classes that I describe in these passages has been dubbed "lagging emulation," a process that Friedl (1964) has analyzed fully and effectively for rural Greece.

Bank employees, government bureaucrats, schoolteachers, engineers—none of these people, nor those with similar occupations, can be said to work. When speaking of *trabajo*, or "work," a man is likely to extend both hands with tightly clenched fists, indicating manual labor. Jobs that rely primarily on the brain, frequently indicated by simply pointing to the head, are not classified as real work. Mostly, I think, this attitude derives from being unable to conceive of what such labor might consist. But also undoubtedly it is the lengthy vacations and undeniably conspicuous presence of white-collar men and professionals in the most elegant Monteros bars and cafes at every hour of the day that adds to the impression that they do not engage in *trabajo* in the usual sense of the term.

With this background, we can now return to the issue of the lazy Gypsies. For it is significant that Castellano workers should openly envy what they consider to be an indolent *señorito* lifestyle while denigrating the alleged tendency of Gypsies to avoid labor. After all, the Gypsies might just as well be admired for their adherence to Castellano cultural ideals. But there is, of course, an obvious difference between the *señoritos* and the Gypsies: one group is rich, the other poor. Castellanos deeply resent Gypsy determination to remain free from the constraints of a laborious time schedule. As we have seen, the resentment cannot stem from a belief that labor, in and of itself, is worthwhile. It derives rather from the fact that Gypsies seem simply not to *care* that they are poor and are therefore unwilling to bend to the requirements of the materialistic Castellano society around them. Gypsies remain outside the Castellano social system because they do not measure their own worth by the same standards as do Castellanos. Under such circumstances, Castellano workers, who find themselves at the low end of their own hierarchy, can only envy what they suppose is a Gypsy immunity from feelings of status inferiority. Gypsies, in other words, live better than Castellanos, despite their relative poverty. Castellanos may be relatively poor, but they are forced to work in order to maintain even a low social position.

It is only by understanding the complex feelings with which Gypsies are regarded that we can finally see why Castellanos laugh heartily at jokes that confirm the stereotype of the lazy Gypsy. The jokes provide a means by which Castellano men can assure themselves of the validity of their own lifestyle. Castellanos of the working class envy Gypsies their freedom from regular labor. Bound by the requirements of their own hierarchy, they are unable to emulate Gypsy freedom. They therefore deride it in an attempt to justify their own basically inconsistent mode of life: the vigorous pursuit of heavy labor in the face of the perpetually low, degrading status such work accords them.

When the Gypsy man in the joke calls out for "Bread and wine!" instead of "Bread and work!" it is the Castellano narrator who secretly wishes he could do the same. Unable, for his own and his family's honor and well-being, to abandon the Castellano standards that bind him to manual labor, he turns to the ridicule of those who can. The joke of the lazy Gypsy is, simply put, a Castellano defense mechanism, and a rationalization of a paradoxical lifestyle.

Gypsies and the Civil Guard

Perhaps the most numerous and, on the surface, most puzzling of the Gypsy jokes are those that portray a confrontation between Gypsies and the Civil Guard, an organization that needs a brief introduction. The Civil Guard, whom Michael Kenny (1966, p. 47) aptly refers to as "the aristocrats of the many police bodies in Spain," was constituted in 1844, and has been in continuous existence ever since. Members, who are drawn largely from the Spanish working class, are organized by military rank. Except for the highest echelon among them, they live in barracks in rural towns and villages together with their families, who, like themselves, are invariably non-natives of the places where they are stationed. Famous for their fierce loyalty to the ruling government (except during the Civil War of 1936, when they favored the Franco rebels), as well as for their extreme austerity and incorruptibility, the Civil Guard has come to be known as *la pareja*, "the pair," because guardsmen are required to travel and patrol in twos; when in uniform, they literally never go unaccompanied. Richard Herr provides an excellent summary of the Civil Guard's traditional function and image. After this force was founded, he says, its

> first task was to prevent political subversion. It also fought banditry, making rural Spain safe for travel and commerce. Later, when peasant revolts occurred, the Civil Guard put them down. Gradually it became a typical institution of modern Spain, well disciplined, humorless, cruel, and loyal to its superiors. The Civil Guard came to personify the law, the state, and the ruling classes throughout the small towns and countryside of Spain (Herr 1974, p. 91).

The Civil Guard barracks in Monteros today house eleven men and their families, somewhat fewer than during the two decades following the Civil War, when the repression initiated by the Franco regime was at its height. The relationship between the officers and the townspeople is a good deal less severe and restricted than it used to be, and the mutual distrust with which these groups have traditionally regarded each other has in large measure disappeared in Monteros and in rural Spain generally. Nonetheless, the popular image of the Civil Guard as a repressive body with a single-minded interest in maintaining order and control still prevails.

This image is still maintained for at least two salient reasons. First, though individual officers of the Civil Guard may fraternize with the local populace more than previously would have been permitted, it is recognized that the force as a unified body retains the discipline, organization, and loyalty necessary to transform itself instantaneously into an arm of political repression. In conflicts between the people and the state, there is no question of the side the Civil Guard would support; one has only to live through a political crisis in Spain, like that occasioned by Franco's death in November 1975, to know that the popular fear of the Civil Guard is only tentatively suspended, to be fully revived with every unpredictable circumstance.

Second, the traditional image of the Civil Guard is still accurate with regard to their relationship with Gypsies. I myself have no direct evidence of Gypsy mistreatment at the hands of the Civil Guard. What I do know, however, is that most Gypsies have an intense hatred and fear of the Civil Guard and cite instance after instance of totally arbitrary, often sadistic, actions performed against them by these rural police. True, there exist a handful of well-publicized cases in which Gypsies have joined the Civil Guard and risen in the ranks. But these Gypsies are regarded by their own as traitors, a good deal worse than Uncle Toms.

I have never heard a Gypsy himself joke about the Civil Guard; perhaps the fear is too immediate and intense to permit it. But Castellano men tell numerous humorous stories that pit these traditional enemies against one another and usually portray the Gypsies as victorious. Some of the jokes seem to be no more than simple expressions of Gypsy hostility toward the Civil Guard:

> Once there was a Gypsy who passed by a *cuartel* (Civil Guard barracks). The guard on duty asked him, "Why don't you salute? Don't you know that this is a *cuartel* and you're supposed to salute every time you walk by?" [The Guardia was just trying to rile the Gypsy; this is not an actual requirement.] "How was I supposed to know that it's a *cuartel*?" asked the Gypsy. "Well, there's a sign up there that says so," answered

the Guardia, pointing to the sign suspended above the main entrance to the building. "But I don't read," the Gypsy protested. "When I want fruit, I know there's a fruit stand because I see peaches or bananas hanging in front. When I want meat, I know there's a butcher because I see hams hanging in front. Why don't you hang up a Guardia, so that we illiterates can tell it's a *cuartel*? Then we'd salute!"

"What are we supposed to do?" asked the Guardia sarcastically. "Leave a guy hanging from a flagpole forever?" "Well, if you can't leave one there permanently," answered the Gypsy, "at least you could cut him down and change him every month for another!"

At first appearance this joke, like some of those that follow, seems to be a mere confirmation of the stereotype of the stupid Gypsy, as, indeed, on a superficial level it is. Yet Gypsies, in the Castellano mind, are at least cunning, if not intelligent. They are compared to the wolf (rather than the fox, as in our culture), for their allegedly high development of mechanisms of self-defense. These mechanisms include feigned innocence, which is what is portrayed in this joke.

But there are other hanging stories that illustrate Gypsy rebellion against the authority of the Civil Guard. In the following example, as in the one above, the Gypsy is accorded the final clever retort.

A pair of Guardia approached a Gypsy, and to agitate and disturb him they said, "Look, we want you to say something bad about us." The Gypsy seemed perplexed and modestly responded, "But, sirs, you haven't done anything to me to merit such a thing." "But we want you to say something bad about us anyway," responded the Guardia. "We demand that you do so." "Well, then," said the Gypsy, "may you die neither on earth nor in heaven." "May we die neither on earth nor in heaven? What's *that* supposed to mean?" asked the Guardia. Answered the Gypsy, "May you die in the air—hanged! (*en el aire—¡horcado!*)"

With this, the joke ends, and the narrator, a laborer, bursts into loud laughter. Though one supposes that the Guardia were trying to provoke the Gypsy into insubordination so that they would have an excuse to mistreat him, it is the Gypsy who is given the last word. And it is a hostile wish that this word reveals.

As mentioned above, a number of the Gypsy jokes contain overt sexual references. Some, of which the following is the best illustration, portray Gypsy deflation of the sexual power and prowess of the Civil Guard.

> There was a Gypsy who went to the fair in [the nearby town of] Baza to sell donkeys. One of the donkeys had an erection, and to play a trick (*gastar una broma*) on the Gypsy,[5] a Guardia approached him and demanded that for the sake of public decency he get rid of the erection. "If you don't," the Guardia threatened, "I'm going to have to fine you heavily." The Gypsy protested, "But I don't know what to do with him. I don't have any control over these matters!" "I don't care how you do it," said the Guardia, "but if you don't get rid of that erection right away, you're going to be fined."
>
> Then the Guardia walked away, and the Gypsy took hold of the donkey's ear and bit it hard. The pain caused the donkey to lose the erection. After a while, the Guardia returned, and was amazed to discover the erection gone. "How'd you do it?" he asked the Gypsy. "Oh, I don't have to tell you, do I?" asked the Gypsy. "It was really nothing." "Yes," insisted the Guardia, "I want to know how you did it. It's an amazing feat." "Well, if you really want to know," answered the Gypsy, "I told him that if he didn't put it down, the Guardia would suck it!"

This joke is, of course, more than an expression of Gypsy cleverness and insubordination, though these traits are undoubtedly an important part of the message as well. To understand the story fully, we must know that Gypsies, like donkeys, are said to have inordinately large penises. Given the close association between donkey and Gypsy in this joke, it would be difficult to deny that the animal's sexual organ represents the Gypsy's, and that its erect state symbolizes the threatening sexual power and absence of control attributed to Gypsy men. The uncontrolled power is portrayed as so great, in fact, that only the infliction of pain can remove it.

By contrast, the Guardia is portrayed as sexually passive and unappealing. The Gypsy's suggestion that the Guardia suck the donkey's penis places the Guardia in the supposed feminine role, that of being a mere bodily receptacle, which, as discussed in the following chapter, is totally contrary to Castellano ideas about appropriate masculine sexuality. It is also notable that the mere suggestion of sexual contact with the Guardia is said to be sufficient to

[5]For a full discussion of *bromas* in Monteros, see chapter 7.

reduce the donkey's erection; political power, in other words, is seen as existing in inverse proportion to sexual power. In the joke, the Gypsy not only undercuts the Guardia's mildly sadistic attempt to scare him but also challenges the Guardia's sexual potency as well. For if a donkey rejects him, where can he possibly turn?

Time and again, it is the sexual power of Gypsies that in combination with their cleverness enables them to win in their apparently ceaseless struggle against the Guardia.

> There was a Gypsy who was walking through the fields, and he stole a duck. Along came a pair of Guardia, and to hide the duck from them, the Gypsy stuck it down the front of his pants. On their ride to the *cuartel*, the two Guardia stopped with the Gypsy at a tavern. [Why they apprehended him remains unstated.] The tavernkeeper put out drinks and olives. When the duck smelled the olives, he stuck his head out of the Gypsy's pants and stole one of them. With that, one Guardia turned to the other and said, "Did you see that? I've seen them [i.e., penises] fat. But one that eats olives? Never!"[6]

Thus, the Gypsy not only gets away with theft but also is credited with a sexual organ that performs remarkable feats. And while Gypsies, in the jokes, are shown to be sexually assertive and powerful, they are also successful in foiling the Guardia's attempts to place them in the receptive, "feminine" sexual posture.

> There were two Gypsies who had just come from robbing the fields. One carried a sack of olives on his back, and the other a sack of melons. They met a Guardia on the road [inexplicably, the *pareja* here is incomplete], and he asked them what they were doing with the fruit. They answered matter-of-factly that they had stolen it. "OK," announced the Guardia, "I'll teach you guys not to steal. I'm going to stick the fruit up your ass." So the Guardia got hold of the Gypsy with the olives first, and began sticking olives in his anus. But as he was doing it, the Gypsy began to laugh. "What's so funny?" asked the Guardia. Replied the Gypsy, "The olives go up my ass easily. But just wait until you get to the guy with the melons!"[7]

---

[6] Alan Dundes of the University of California at Berkeley has told me that he has heard an American version of the same joke, in which a duck, emerging from a man's pants, is seen eating popcorn in a movie theater. I have been unable to locate this version in the literature.

[7] This is obviously a version of Tale Type 1689, "Thank God they weren't peaches" (Aarne-Thompson 1961).

This joke is just another manifestation of the typical Monteros male fear of attack from behind, which I discuss fully in chapter 5. Like the other Gypsy jokes, this one also accords a member of the oppressed minority the final laugh.

Now that we have examined some of the more representative Gypsy-Guardia jokes, it should be evident why they presented a tremendous puzzle: here is a despised minority being portrayed as successful in their struggle against a powerful, respected, and feared Castellano police force. Should not the working-class Castellanos who narrate these jokes align themselves with their fellow Castellanos, the Guardia? We turn now to the multifaceted reasons why they fail to incorporate such an alignment into their humor, and why they seem to take pleasure in the apparent defeat of the Guardia at the hands of the hated pariah group among them.

There is, first, the simple observation that Guardia and Gypsies symbolize opposite principles in Spanish life: the Guardia represents order, the Gypsies disorder; the Guardia represents law, the Gypsies absence of law, for they steal; the Guardia represents the state, the Gypsies freedom and autonomy. In fact, the Gypsies—or, more accurately, Gypsies as perceived by lower-class Castellanos—seem to enjoy all the privileges of the educated, wealthy town elite, who are also said to rob through exploitation and legal manipulation and to live unconstrained by the confining rules to which the common man is subjected. Working-class Castellanos yearn for this type of freedom, and to the extent that Gypsies represent it, they become an unconscious focus of identification. Humor permits empathy with the Gypsies, and the vicarious release that their rebellion against authority brings. Only through what Wolfenstein (1954, pp. 159–91) calls the joking facade may the real Castellano feelings about Gypsies emerge.

I must disavow credit for this partial explanation of the jokes, for the idea was originally presented to me by a wealthy Monteros lawyer and landowner. When I asked him why working-class jokes seem to elevate the position of the Gypsies when confronted by Guardia, he immediately reminded me of the Andalusian anarchists of the previous century and of the fact that this movement was popular largely [because common people in southern Spain value personal freedom and independence above all else.]Gypsies, in the popular mind, represent freedom. They live as they please, travel where they want, and are unbound by the mores of Castilian society around them. Thus, according to this lawyer, Castellano jokes reveal identification with and envy of Gypsies despite their everyday treatment of them as an inferior race apart.

And, of course, if we examine the historical record, there is no more likely or appropriate object for Andalusian rebellion than the Civil Guard, which for decades was the main organ of elite repression and exploitation. Gerald Brenan sums it up by saying that "the hatred between them and the villagers made many parts of Spain ungovernable" (1964, p. 57). Vicens Vives, too, declares that "Civil Guards maintained order not only against bandits and criminals, smugglers and highwaymen, but against peasants whom years of misery had stirred into rebellion, and against workers kept down by iniquitous labor conditions" (1970, p. 133).

Thus, if the Gypsies, with their reputation for freedom, are an understandable focus of identification for working-class Castellanos, then the Civil Guard, the most visible organ of repression and outside interference, is an understandable object of ridicule in the jokes. Gypsy insubordination against the Civil Guard is thus equivalent to rebellion against the elite with whom the Guardia has been historically associated. It is also probable that the Civil Guard is the focus of reaction against all the forces of control—including those both internal and external to the individual—and that the jokes provide a safe, cathartic means of expressing release from these forces.

Only by moving from the level of society to the level of the individual can we explain why many of the Gypsy-Guardia jokes incorporate sexual themes. The jokes, we must recall, are told by working-class men. In the following chapter, I try to demonstrate that in Monteros men perceive will and power as emanating from the male genitals. The sexual superiority of the Gypsies as portrayed in the jokes must be explained on the basis of this evidence. The larger size of male Gypsy organs, their sexual potency, and the unwillingness of Gypsies to submit to anal penetration are all essential ingredients of the rebellious, insubordinate spirit that Gypsies exhibit in Castellano jokes. The male narrators associate the two themes of sexual superiority and social defiance, for, in the male mind, the two are inextricably linked and dependent upon one another.

It is perfectly reasonable, we can now realize, that Gypsies should be elevated to a victorious position in their struggle against the Guardia. Like the working-class Castellanos who narrate these jokes, the Gypsies suffer from low status and constant infringements on their freedom and autonomy. But unlike the Castellanos, they rebel against the oppressor, and are endowed with unusual sexual attributes that enable them to do so. The rebellion against authority is expressed in sexual terms; this is a theme we encounter over and over in Monteros male folklore. Gypsy jokes are a grand Castellano fantasy, enabling working-class men to rise above the low status and attendant constraints under which they suffer.

In this respect, it is significant that the people of Monteros have adopted the term *Castellano* to differentiate themselves from Gypsies. Andalusians, paradoxically, are accused by the actual Castilians to the north of being carefree, sexually assertive, and lazy. Andalusians know what Castilians think of them and to a considerable extent have incorporated these views themselves. We may presume, therefore, that Andalusian perceptions of the Gypsy are no more than a projection of a negative self-image onto a despised pariah group. By calling themselves *Castellanos*—"Castilians"— Andalusians can identify with a regional group of higher national status and political power. Through the same means, they divorce themselves from the undesirable, stereotyped traits of which they are accused by other regional groups. The term *Castellano*, then, is a mechanism of defense and projection that solidifies the Andalusians' sense of superiority against Gypsies and thereby elevates their self-esteem.[8]

[8]The ideas in this paragraph developed out of the perceptive comments of Dr. Anita L. Alvarado of the University of New Mexico. The comments were offered publicly at the Symposium on Social Stratification and Class Conflict in Western Europe: Anthropological Perspectives, held at the Annual Meeting of the American Anthropological Association, Houston, 29 November–3 December 1977. Some of the analysis in this chapter was first presented at that symposium.

Masculine Metaphors in Folk Speech

When the Son of man shall come in his glory
... he shall set the sheep on his right hand,
but the goats on the left.

Then shall the King say unto them on his
right hand, Come, ye blessed of my father, in-
herit the kingdom prepared for you from the
foundation of the world ...

Then shall he say unto them on the left
hand, Depart from me, ye cursed, into ever-
lasting fire, prepared for the devil and his
angels....

   Matthew 25:31–41

Unquestionably in Monteros, as throughout Andalusia, men can maintain a positive image of themselves only to the extent that they preserve their families' honor and reputation. Pitt-Rivers has offered a neat formulation of the manner in which the honor of the family and that of the individual are closely intertwined: "There is a near-paradox in the fact that while honour is a collective attribute shared by the nuclear family it is also personal and dependent upon the will of the individual; individual honour derives from individual conduct but produces consequences for others who share collective honour with this individual" (Pitt-Rivers 1977, p. 78). This means, among other things, that a woman's sexual purity must be main- tained lest her entire family's image be tainted. It is the husband's prime responsibility to control the conduct of his wife and daughters. If the females should go astray, their behavior reflects as much on him as on them.

It is for this reason that men in Andalusia have tried—often successfully—to seclude women from public view and to limit the range of their activities. Men, in the end, feel severely threatened and powerless when confronted by women. They consider women potentially dangerous, as we shall see in this chapter. It is the fear of women and the self-proclaimed male struggle against them that in large measure impel men to dominate and suppress them.

These male attitudes, I believe, cannot easily be dismissed as a mere rationalization for the political and economic exploitation of women. The attitudes must be understood on their own terms as a strong motivating force in determining relationships between the sexes. Certainly the vast majority of men, and particularly working-class men, articulate a basically defensive posture when describing their attitudes toward women. It is this defensive posture, in a variety of metaphoric manifestations, that we shall now explore.

The Moral Dichotomy Between the Sexes

Before explicitly analyzing why men feel victimized by and vulnerable to women, we should first understand an essential moral dichotomy between the sexes. In Monteros, as elsewhere in Spain (Cátedra Tomás 1976, p. 35), men believe themselves to be inherently more virtuous than women. They justify this opinion primarily on religious grounds. "Women are of the Devil," a worker once explained to me as three of his friends listened and nodded in agreement. "God created the world in seven days. Let's say that the first day He made the earth and plants, the second day the sun, the third day . . . well, I don't quite remember it all. But the fifth day He made man. And from the ribs of man He made woman on the sixth day. That's why women have one more rib than men. If you have a chance to see a human skeleton, you'll find this out for yourself."

The narrator then went on to explain that the original man and woman were called Adam and Eve and that they lived together in Paradise. God told them that they could reside there as long as they did not eat an apple. Then one day the Devil appeared to Eve in the form of a serpent, and he tempted her to eat an apple off a tree. Eve, in turn, tempted Adam to eat the apple. "And that is why woman is of the Devil," said my informant, continuing his rendition of the Fall. "She was that way from the very beginning, and she has been trying to tempt and dominate man ever since." As for man, he "is of God because he did not sin and he remained pure. He only sinned after he was tempted by woman to sin. He was and still is closer to God than is woman."

Referring to this Biblical myth, men frequently state that women "dress like serpents" (*se visten de serpientes*) in order to create harm and dissension among men. Female iniquity is particularly evident in sexual matters, about which it is asserted contemptuously and assuredly that all women are seductresses, possessed of insatiable, lustful appetites.⟩ When women wield their powers, men cannot resist temptation and are forced to relinquish control over their passions. This is why men believe that: *Pueden más dos tetas que cien carretas* ("Two breasts can do more than a hundred carts"). Women who are determined to get their way will always win in the end; thus there is no alternative, men claim, but to capitulate to them from the start.[1]

But it is not solely in sexual matters that women rule. Women are also blamed for perpetuating the Monteros class system and for being much more exclusivist than men. It is said that women of the elite refuse to associate with commoners, and that they urge their husbands, who are thought to be more egalitarian by nature, to act likewise. Female exclusivity also manifests itself in discrimination against "outsiders" (*forasteros*), people who are not Monteros-born and -bred. Wives who have married into Monteros from elsewhere complain that they are forever rejected by women from long-established Monteros families. Lengthy residence in Monteros, complain these outsider women and their husbands, does nothing to alter native female attitudes. Men who marry in, however, are said to be integrated rapidly into town society. No wonder, then, that the people of Monteros proclaim: *La mujer es de pelo largo pero intentamento corto* ("Women have long hair but few good intentions"). Or, alternatively: *La mujer es de pelo largo y sentimiento corto* ("Women have long hair and little feeling"). Whether describing a woman's goals or emotions, Monteros proverbs rarely portray her in a favorable light. Man is good, woman evil.

Similarly, some men of Monteros unconsciously express a binary opposition consisting of two distinct metaphoric chains: God is associated with men and sheep, while the Devil is linked to women and goats.[2] Sheep, like men and God, are good; goats, like women

---

[1]There are similar proverbs in Old Castile, where there exists a more egalitarian relationship between the sexes than in Andalusia; however, these proverbs are employed to describe the great power of a woman's love (Brandes 1975b, p. 177) rather than the scheming nature of females in general.

[2]I have refrained in this volume from analyzing binary oppositions per se, though it should be clear from the discussion of Giants and Big-Heads in chapter 2, as well as from what follows in the present chapter, that they are an important structural feature in Monteros. Henry Schwarz has carried out a binary structural analysis for a town in Extremadura (Schwarz 1976, pp. 115–40).

and the Devil, are evil. People who watch over animals say that God was the original shepherd and the Devil the original goatherd.[3] God and the Devil one day decided to have a race to see who would get to the river with his animals first, so they could drink. To win, God sent a curse (*echó la maldición*) on the goats and the Devil, forcing them high up into the hills in the opposite direction from the water supply. Ever since then, goats have been destined to graze in the hilliest, poorest terrain, just as women are forced to accept a formally subordinate niche within the human domain.

Shepherds claim that at night when it is perfectly dark, if you run your hands along a goat's back it will emit sparks—the fire of the Devil. They also state by way of proof that if a goat eats the tips off an olive branch, the branch will remain forever stunted; but if a sheep nibbles at the tips, the branch will regenerate. These phenomena occur despite the fact that olive trees are a natural and appropriate food supply for goats, which subsist on trees, shrubs, and bushes, while sheep prefer to eat grasses and other herbage from the ground.

Shepherds further assert that goats, as punishment for their association with the Devil, were banished from Christ's manger at the time of his birth, while sheep were permitted to flock there in great numbers. Again in order to demonstrate their claim, they point out that Christmas creches always contain sheep but never goats. Indeed, Spanish artistic representations of the Nativity—from medieval retablos all the way to contemporary greeting cards—invariably exclude goats from the flock of animals in attendance. The Spanish image of the goat, by contrast, is nowhere more accurately portrayed than in Goya's painting *Escena de Brujas* (usually translated as *The Witches' Sabbath*), dominated by a gigantic horned goat representing the Devil, who is surrounded at the base of the painting by countless female witches.[4]

---

[3]In Christian symbolism, of course, sheep are of extraordinary significance, sometimes being associated with Christ himself. One scholar asserts that "sheep are accorded a larger share of attention in the Bible than any other animal and their names—ewe, lamb, ram, sheep, and flock—are found seven hundred and forty-two times, in seven hundred and three verses, which exceed one forty-fourth of the whole number of verses (Wiley 1957, p. 370). An important segment of the Roman Catholic Mass is entitled "Lamb of God." Interesting discussions of animal symbolism in Christianity can be found in Ferguson (1954), Rowland (1973), and Wiley (1957).

[4]The painting dates from 1798 and is housed in Madrid's Lázaro Galdiano Museum. The painting is not to be confused with Goya's later canvas with the same title, which hangs in the Museo del Prado and receives interesting interpretation by Julio Caro Baroja (1964).

In Monteros, the association between humans and animals is more subtle than is reported, for example, among the Sarakatsani shepherds of northern Greece, among whom "Women and goats are conceptually opposed to men and sheep" (Campbell 1964, p. 31), and whose sexual division of labor is in effect determined by this conceptual opposition (ibid., pp. 31–5). Nonetheless, in Monteros the symbolic associations between people and animals emerge in unexpected ways. When men speak of sexually promiscuous women, for example, they are likely to say: *La cabra que es de monte siempre tira al monte* ("The goat from the woodlands always heads toward the woodlands"). That is, once a woman begins to sleep with a series of different men, she will forever continue doing so. Although it would be possible to generalize from this proverb in other ways, I have never heard it applied to any other context. Similarly, when several men depart from a gathering in order to conduct private business, the ones who are left behind state, by way of explanation: *Deja la oveja mear* ("Let the sheep piss"). In other words, men should be left to conduct their affairs undisturbed. Women, in my experience, are never referred to metaphorically as

Men with sheep.

sheep. Spanish literature, I might add, embodies the same associations between animals and the sexes as is found in Monteros.[5]

An important expression of the metaphoric chains linking animals and humans is the evil eye, a destructive, invisible, and often involuntary emanation causing illness or death.[6] Because of their inherent wickedness and close association with the Devil, certain females, and females alone, are accused by the people of Monteros of being possessed by the evil eye (*mal de ojo*). And certainly it is more than coincidental that animal victims of the evil eye in Monteros, as throughout Mediterranean Europe (Blum and Blum 1965, p. 131; Campbell 1964, p. 338), are often sheep and rarely goats. In one particularly interesting case, a woman nicknamed Culona ("Big Ass") is believed definitely to have the evil eye, which she regularly though unconsciously uses to destroy sheep. "Only last year," a shepherd confided, "she was staring at a perfectly healthy, well-fed sheep. 'What a beautiful sheep!' she remarked. The next day the animal died."

We may surmise, in anticipation of the forthcoming analysis, that the female destruction of sheep through the evil eye is a symbolic projection of woman's destruction of man. Furthermore, in the case of Culona's evil influence, we have a clue to one important source of man's downfall: the *culo*, referring variously to the buttocks or the anus. It is significant that a woman who has been dubbed with the nickname Culona should also be perceived as destroying sheep.[7] For, as we shall presently see, men believe themselves to be threatened as much by their attraction to women—an attraction that centers primarily on the female buttocks—as by their potential anal penetration by other men.

Serpents and Human Sexuality

In an attempt to uncover some of the important ways in which women seem threatening and dangerous to men, I wish to explore further the symbolic connection between women and serpents. We have

[5]In Lope de Vega's *Fuente Ovejuna*, for example, Laurencia addresses the men of her town as *ovejas* or "sheep" (1969, p. 120). Bernarda, in Lorca's *La Casa de Bernarda Alba*, refers critically to the women who have come to pay their respects at her husband's funeral as "*una manada de cabras*," "a herd of goats" (García Lorca 1960, p. 1361).

[6]Bibliography on the evil eye is vast. See Elworthy (1958), Gifford (1958), Meerloo (1971), Maloney (1976), and the references contained therein.

[7]For extensive discussions of nicknaming in Spain, see Barrett (1978), Brandes (1975c), and Pitt-Rivers (1971, pp. 160–69).

already noted that in Monteros men say that women "dress as serpents"; since, in standard Spanish, the word *serpiente* is often used as a synonym for the Devil (Real Academia Española 1956, p. 1194), there is a clear implication that women become transformed conceptually into the Devil through their symbolic metamorphosis into serpents. In this respect, it is noteworthy too that the word *serpiente* is feminine in gender (*una serpiente*),[8] which is consistent with a strong artistic tradition in southern Europe of portraying the serpent in the Garden of Eden with a woman's face (Rowland 1973, p. 144). Overall, the Monteros symbolic system suggests an identification of serpents as female. Here, at least, it is decidedly wrong to apply the usual psychoanalytic link between this creature and the phallus, a connection that Ernest Jones once termed "one of the most constant and invariable symbols" (1949, p. 101).[9]

Besides the serpent in the Fall of Man, serpents have two other important sources of reference in Monteros. The first is a well-known working-class rendition of the Holy Family's journey to Bethlehem. The pregnant Virgin, it is said, was seated on a mule that was plodding along the road. A serpent suddenly appeared in front of the mule, scaring the beast so greatly that it tossed the Virgin onto the ground, nearly causing the death of her unborn child. In those days the serpent still had its legs. But as a punishment for endangering the Virgin and child, God deprived it of its legs and forced it to crawl along the ground forever after. God also punished the mule—referred to in the legend as a *mula*, the female of the species—by making her permanently barren, the price for scaring easily and hurling the Virgin to the ground.

The significance of this story becomes understandable only if we recognize that the two culprits, the serpent and the mule, both represent females. They endanger the lives of another female, the Virgin, and her male child. We have here one of the clearest possible expres-

[8]Despite the usual assumption that the gender of Spanish (and other Latin-derived) nouns is arbitrary, many Spanish speakers have told me that serpents must be female because the term *serpiente* is feminine. Death (*la muerte*) is also considered to be feminine for the same reason. The issue is complex and obviously cannot be resolved here. I merely report that there is supporting evidence from informants for my interpretation.

[9]This is not to suggest that all psychoanalytic thought conforms to Jones's formula. Roheim early recognized that the snake's infamous tendency to devour, i.e., incorporate, makes it analogous to a "dangerous vagina" (Roheim 1924, p. 408). More recently, Slater has offered a sensitive and subtle analysis of the bisexual symbolic qualities of the serpent (Slater 1971, pp. 75–122). Here the serpent is portrayed as particularly feminine in nature, for it is the ingestive, incorporative function of the beast that receives primary emphasis.

sions of the intense, indissoluble bond between mother and son, which is characteristic of Monteros, just as it has been of the entire northern Mediterranean world at least since ancient Greece (Slater 1968, pp. 3–74). The son's fate is bound to that of his mother, an idealized, pure version of womanhood. To the pure Virgin, we can contrast the dangerous serpent and the disruptive *mula*, who represent negative manifestations of the feminine character and embody the potential destruction of family well-being. Indeed, according to Monteros men, it is women in their role as Devil who pose the greatest threat to family unity in Monteros, just as it is women in their role as mothers who solidify the family bond. The legend of the journey to Bethlehem is a superb reflection of male ambivalence toward women.

The second significant reference to serpents is a folk medical belief concerning infants that is now confined to the poorer and older residents of Monteros but that, until the early 1960s, was quite widespread among all but the educated elite. It is said that at night a serpent may crawl surreptitiously into the bedroom where an infant and its nursing mother are sleeping. When the child awakens from hunger and begins to cry, the serpent suckles the mother's breast and inserts its tail into the infant's mouth. In this manner, the serpent draws nourishment from the mother's body at the expense of the infant. This deception continues for a period of several weeks until the child finally withers and dies. The mother remains unsuspicious throughout this period because the tail acts as a soporific to the infant while the sucking motion of the serpent's mouth exactly replicates the child's. It must be noted that the efficacy of this belief depends in large measure upon the assumption that breast milk is a "limited good," in George Foster's sense of the term (1967). If it were not, the child could simply compensate for lost nighttime nourishment by nursing more during the day. What happens, however, is that the serpent consumes so much milk at night that it completely exhausts the mother's restricted supply, leaving nothing for the infant.

This belief, as I said, is fast disappearing. It no doubt arose as a culturally shared and codified projection of anxieties concerning infant mortality and the availability of an adequate supply of mother's milk in the days when as many as half of all infants died and wet-nurses or, later, bottled formulas, were available only to the wealthy elite. However obsolete, the belief still represents a powerful symbolic portrayal of masculine attitudes toward women.

Let us note, at the outset, the structural parallel between this folk medical belief and the legend of the Virgin's journey. In both, the serpent plays an aggressive, destructive role directed toward the death of an infant. In both cases, too, the infant is masculine. The gender is clear in the instance of the baby Jesus, while in the medical belief the comprehensive masculine term *niño* is always used when referring to the victimized nursing child. Furthermore, the medical belief, like the legend, incorporates contrasting portrayals of females, the serpent representing the evil dimension of womanhood, the mother representing the positive one. In both folkloristic references, the disruptive aspect of women threatens to destroy or does destroy their creative, productive side (giving birth, providing milk). In both, too, the strength and well-being of the mother-son bond are also endangered. Overall, the two folklore references may best be viewed as expressions of the ambivalent attitude toward women that prevails in Monteros.

There is one critical element appearing in the medical belief alone, however, which we cannot afford to overlook: the *leche*, or milk. The milk is at once denied to the nursing child and incorporated within the serpent, to the beast's immediate benefit. To recognize the full significance of the serpent's thievery, we must realize that in Monteros as throughout Spain, *leche* means "semen" as well as "milk"; it is, in fact, the most universally and commonly employed word to refer to male sexual fluid. Moreover, the linguistic association between milk and semen is not merely incidental, but rather is codified in and popularized by jokes that turn on puns for the term *leche*.[10] It is not surprising that semen and milk should be so closely linked when we consider that both substances, besides being white fluids, are connected with the creation or sustenance of life. (In English, *cream*, rather than *milk*, is given the dual denotation.) Just as a man in infancy depends on milk to survive, so too he relinquishes *his* milk in adulthood in order to produce children. And just as the people of Monteros consider a mother's milk to exist in limited supply, so too do they perceive semen as a finite substance, permanently depleted with each ejaculation.[11] Since people consider semen to be an essential ingredient for main-

---

[10]One joke, for example, tells of a Spanish emigrant working on a German farm. Among all the laborers, he was the only Spaniard. One day they held a contest to see who could get the most milk out of the cows, but they assigned to the Spaniard the only bull on the farm. When the laborers presented their results, they each had milked eighteen to twenty liters, except the Spaniard, who brought in only half a liter. Said the foreman, "Aren't you ashamed to show up with only this small quantity of *leche* [milk]?" "But, sir," the Spaniard replied, "you gave me a bull to milk and I had to jerk him off to get even this much *leche* [semen]!"

[11]In parts of Nigeria, too, a man's lifetime supply of semen is considered to be finite (Foster 1967, p. 309).

taining a man's vigor, energy, and youth, its dwindling supply can only lead to his more rapid demise.

We can finally understand how the medical belief of the suckling serpent relates to the sphere of adult sexuality in Monteros. Just as the serpent deprives the child of milk, woman deprives man of his semen. Just as the serpent benefits from the nourishment of milk, it may be supposed that woman benefits from incorporating semen into her body. In both cases, man is victimized by woman. The serpent's role, in other words, replicates that of the wife, and reflects the male fear that women pose a serious threat to masculine well-being.

Body Substances and Bodily Strength

For many men of Monteros, women are inherently evil, and on this account alone can challenge their very existence. But it is also women's sexuality that men fear, primarily because it threatens in various ways to rob them of their masculinity and convert them symbolically into females. The men of Monteros have a sexual identity that must constantly be guarded and defended against potential assault. This assault may take one of three principal forms, each of which we shall discuss in turn: the wife's attempt to drive her husband to a premature death; the wife's adultery, which feminizes her husband; and the man's enforced adoption of a feminine, passive role.

To explain the first point, let me begin by summarizing how a traditional Monteros man views sexual relationships. When women are in their early teens, they begin to use make-up and dress provocatively so that they will attract and be able to capture men (the usual verbs here are *atrapar*, "to trap," and *cazar*, "to hunt"). While the prospective husband is courting, a woman acts submissive, shy, and compliant, but this is just part of her overall plan of attack. Once the man is bound by an official, indissoluble wedding ceremony, the woman begins to demonstrate her true ambition, which is nothing less than to dominate completely, to rule her husband and children, and above all to sap her husband's strength by forcing him to engage in heavy sexual activity and physical labor until he gradually expires. Her ultimate goal, it is believed, is twofold: to live from her husband's social security or insurance premiums without having to share the income with him; and to satisfy her voracious, indiscriminate sexual appetite without the restrictions imposed on her by marriage.

Men consider women to be constitutionally much the stronger

sex. In the short run, to be sure, men—especially young men—are demonstrably stronger than women. They can run longer and faster, lift and pull heavier objects, and do more strenuous labor. But men lack the long-range bodily resistance and durability of women, and therefore die at a much younger age. Especially in matters of sex, women are said to have superior strength and drive to that of men.

The main reason given for this female corporal superiority is that women have "clean" blood. The menstrual flow, men believe, freshens the blood supply every month by divesting it of impurities. Like most Mediterranean people (e.g., Blum and Blum 1965, pp. 33–34, 40, 138, 170; Blum and Blum 1970, pp. 20, 46; Campbell 1964, p. 31), as well as some from other parts of the world (Douglas 1966, pp. 121, 147, 151, 176; Schieffelin 1976, p. 67), the people of Monteros consider menstrual blood to be polluted for the specific reason that it carries away the filth that inevitably accumulates over the course of a woman's cycle.[12] As one informant put it, a woman is like a bottle of water that receives periodic washing and refilling. Her blood supply remains fresh and renewed. Man, on the other hand, is like a bottle of water that becomes stagnant. The impurities of his body continuously build up with no means of release. He therefore naturally becomes weaker over time than does woman.

To compensate, however, men have one great source of strength that women lack: semen. Semen, as we have already noted, is said to be life-giving and beneficial. Given the inability of male blood to regenerate and cleanse itself, semen is without doubt man's single most important bodily substance, the one upon which his very existence, as well as his continued enjoyment of sexual pleasure, depends. In fact, one could almost say that just as a man's genitals are the locus of his strength and will—a notion we shall examine in the following section—so, too, his semen, which is located within the genital region, *is* his strength and will.

Considering this point of view, it is understandable that men are greatly preoccupied by the allegedly debilitating aspects of sex, which deprives them of valuable semen after each ejaculation. In Monteros, I have observed no concern among men that coitus or sexual contact of any kind with women is immoral or contrary to religious standards. Nor do men seem to fear that their sexual relationships will cause them to be punished in the afterlife. In other

---

[12]For a thorough discussion of the topic of menstruation from a cultural standpoint, see Delaney, Lupton, and Toth (1976); their scholarly citations on the subject are wide-ranging.

words, men are totally unconcerned that women will lead them into sin. What does worry them, however, is that their wives will, through sexual activity, deprive them of their strength and youth and drive them to an early grave.

I became aware of this male preoccupation soon after my arrival in Monteros when I visited a tavern where there hangs a prominently displayed glazed tile upon which is written the following rhymed proverb: *Agua de pozo y mujer desnuda/Llevan al hombre a la sepultura* ("Well water and a naked woman/Lead men to the grave"). I asked the three or four men who were gathered at the counter to explain the saying to me. The first part of the proverb, concerning well water, they dismissed as self-evident; anyone knows that well water is bad for you, they said. As for the reference to the naked woman, one of them opened his eyes wide, furrowed his brows in a knowing sort of glance, and began moving his outstretched arm and tightly closed fist back and forth to and from his chest in the typical Spanish gesture depicting coitus. By way of further explanation to the perhaps untutored foreigner, the man simply said, *"Debilita"*—"It weakens."

Though the tavern tile was manufactured elsewhere than Monteros and in fact does not bear a traditional town saying, the proverb accurately reflects the Monteros male point of view. Townsmen grow up hearing their own proverbial wisdom to the same effect: *Si quieres llegar a viejo/Guarda la leche en el pellejo* ("If you want to reach old age,/Keep your semen within your skin"). Since semen, the life-giving element, exists in limited supply, men should be careful to preserve it as much as possible. This means, for male youth and unmarried men of all ages, that self-control should be exerted against masturbation. After marriage, when intercourse becomes the main avenue of sexual release, abstention is the best way for a man to conserve his vigor, especially as he grows older.[13]

Men take note of cases that demonstrate their perception of women's ultimate goals. In one instance, a fifty-nine-year-old widower eloped with a forty-year-old widow, who, it was said, had been trying to seduce him for months. Within days after the elopement, word was out that the man had left her with the complaint that she had a voracious sexual appetite. Every time he would turn over to sleep she would try to arouse him into another encounter. It was more than he could take, and all the men I knew seemed to sym-

---

[13]Most Monteros men, in fact, do not abstain from sexual activity, despite their undeniable fear of its long-term consequences. As discussed in chapter 10, men seem to enjoy sex virtually free of guilt feelings.

pathize with the man's lot. It was assumed that the woman was after his money, and was trying to do him in.

Men claim that widows immediately gain weight and acquire a lustrous glow after their husbands die; this demonstrates their happy state. They also are likely to become sexually promiscuous. Pitt-Rivers' data from elsewhere in Andalusia confirm my own observations:

> It is a matter of popular consensus that women uncontrolled by men will throw caution to the winds and indulge in the most abandoned love affairs; no matter how improbable on account of her age, the widow, it is thought, is likely to take on the predatory male attitude towards sexual promiscuity. I have often been astounded by the amatory conquests credited to septuagenarian peasant ladies (1977, p. 82).

Widows with whom I have discussed the matter explain that it is only after their husbands have died that other men can begin to notice them openly without fear of reprisal. I know at least one widow who is deeply hurt by the constant implications that she and others like her wanted their husbands to die. Yet there are some who admit they are better off alone, and quote the popular Monteros saying: *Te casaste, te cagaste* ("You married, you shit on yourself.") In fact, in one conversation between a group of married women concerning the topic of widowhood, not one could think a widow whom she regarded as worse off economically or in any other way than when she was married. In part, this may be explained by the fact that married men invariably spend a good part of the limited family income in treating their friends to drinks in the bars. In part, too, women are resentful of the vast amounts of time that husbands spend away from home. If men feel trapped by marriage, women consider themselves even more so, and wives sometimes transmit their sentiments through means both subtle and overt to their husbands. It is hardly surprising, then, that on occasion men should perceive their wives' frustration and anger and should explain these feelings on the basis of a sexual ideology provided men by their culture.

Horns, Super-Goats, and the Preservation of Masculinity

For men, women are dangerous not only because they try to sap their husbands' strength but also because their intense sexuality creates the constant threat that they will enter into an adulterous union. Men operate in daily affairs on the assumption that their wives want to deceive them, and in fact will deceive them if given the least opportunity. José Cutileiro's description of male attitudes in southern Portugal holds equally true for Monteros:

> A man enters marriage hoping that he will not become a cuckold. The bride's virginity and the wife's fidelity are the basic moral assumptions on which the family is built. The ideal state for a woman is a state of purity, but purity is only part of her nature: her *vicio* (vice), the predisposition responsible for the potential social dangers attached to her active sexual life, is also part of it (Cutileiro 1971, p. 99).

A wife's infidelity threatens the moral reputation of her entire family. But it affects no one so profoundly as her cuckolded husband, who is charged with the responsibility of harnessing her rampant sexuality and confining it within the secret walls of their bedroom.

In Monteros, as throughout Spain, the predominant symbol of the cuckold is the *cabrón*, or super-goat, and its *cuernos*, or horns. The term *cabrón*, in fact, has become so purely synonymous with cuckold that it is no longer usefully applied to the actual male animal, who is referred to instead as a *macho cabrillo* ("little male goat") or simply, where conversational context permits, *macho* ("male"). And the goat's horns have become so representative of the cuckold that the word *cornudo*, "horned one," is employed interchangeably with *cabrón*.

Interestingly, in the technical use of the term, the *cabrón* is not simply a cuckold but rather a cuckold who is aware that his wife is engaged in extramarital affairs and who continues to live with her despite this knowledge. According to the Monteros male view of the world, any woman is capable of sexual deceit; in fact, men commonly state that "All women are whores" (*Todas las mujeras son putas*), and then, if this remark is greeted with surprise, emphatically repeat the word "All" (*Todas*). What is shameful for a man is not so much that his wife should suddenly adopt her natural role. The true humiliation comes first from having been unable to control her, and second from tacitly tolerating her behavior by continuing to reside with her. In fact, this type of conscious cuckoldry, for all I can determine, is extremely rare. Informants of mine could name only two known cases in 1975–76.

Nonetheless, no man in Monteros is anxious for his wife to have an affair even if he never learns of it. The specter of a wife's infidelity haunts men daily, for they know full well that: *El cabrón es el último que se entera* ("The cuckold is the last one to find out"). For this reason, I believe, men seem completely unashamed to admit that *so far as they know* their wives have been faithful, but that they can never be one hundred percent certain. By stating this repeatedly (in some cases, several times a week) men advertise their total ignorance of their wives' behavior should the latter actually have betrayed them. In this manner they demonstrate at least a technical disqualification from the category *cabrón*, and they announce to their friends that they are ready to hear the worst.

In matters like this, however, technicalities are hardly satisfactory. Men worry that people might be pointing to them behind their backs, pitying them for their wives' infidelity and yet embarrassed to confide the truth to them. For this reason, the people of Monteros are hesitant to state that a child, especially a newborn, looks like the mother, for this is an indirect way of raising the question of paternal identity. In Monteros, no matter what their actual appearance, the vast majority of newborn infants are said to resemble their legal fathers. Such a statement is at the very least a correct and polite opinion to express to an infant's parents and kinsmen, despite what might be said privately.

Throughout the course of a year in the field, I was told countless times that because of my coloring it would not be unusual if my wife gave birth to a blond baby. What most of the dark-haired men of Monteros fear, however, is that this fate should happen to them. Everyone cites the curious case of a married couple from a nearby town who emigrated several years ago to work in northern Europe. The woman became pregnant and returned some time before her husband to give birth among family and friends. Her progeny, however, turned out to be a pair of black (*negro*) twins. It is said that when her husband returned to town, he took one look at them and left that very day. She later was also forced to leave in disgrace. The story, which may or may not be true, clearly projects male anxieties about the actual paternity of their children. (It has nothing whatever to do with race relations.)

But we have yet to ask the critical question of why men should feel so threatened by the prospect of female infidelity, especially considering that such infidelity is actually rare. To answer, we must reconsider the meaning of the metaphors by which the cuckold is described. Julian Pitt-Rivers, who first introduced this matter into the anthropological literature nearly a generation ago, is still the only Hispanicist to have given it serious thought. One passage from his now-classic *People of the Sierra* is crucial:

> The word *cabrón* (a he-goat), the symbol of male sexuality in many contexts, refers not to him whose manifestation of that quality is the cause of the trouble but to him whose implied lack of manliness has allowed the other to replace him. To make a man a cuckold is in the current Spanish idiom, "to put horns on him." I suggest that the horns are figuratively placed upon the head of the wronged husband in signification of his failure to defend a value vital to the social order. He has fallen under the domination of its enemy and must wear his symbol. He is ritually defiled (Pitt-Rivers 1971, p. 116).

Here, as in another passage (ibid., p. 116), Pitt-Rivers implies that the horns themselves symbolize the masculinity and virility of the cuckolder—indeed that they are the emblem of the cuckolder—which he places symbolically on the head of the cuckold.

Though Pitt-Rivers' interpretation of Andalusian symbolism is appealing and has been uncritically accepted, it needs to be challenged. In Monteros, as in Pitt-Rivers' community, people commonly use the expression "to put horns on him" to mean "to make a man a cuckold." But it is not the male rival who puts on the horns, as Pitt-Rivers implies; it is the wife! Thus, one man will say of another, *"Pobrecillo, que no sabe que su mujer le está metiendo los cuernos"* ("Poor guy, for he doesn't know that his wife is placing the horns on him"). Men also jokingly wonder aloud of their wives, *"No sé si me habría meti'o los cuernos"* ("I don't know if she ever put horns on me"). In these as in countless other expressions it is clear that it is the cuckold's wife, not his rival, who bears primary responsibility for the horns on his head.[14]

It is only by clarifying this seemingly minor, yet critical, point that we can explain why men fear being cuckolded: to be cuckolded is to be transformed symbolically into a woman. The horns, originally associated with or belonging to the woman, are placed

---

[14]Occasionally the people of Monteros speak as if it is the illicit couple who together put the horns on the cuckold, but this speech form is not nearly as common as the one in which the wife alone puts horns on the husband. *Never* is the husband's rival spoken of as the sole source of the horns. Very rarely it is also said that a man has put horns on his wife by engaging in an extramarital affair. This usage, I suspect, is a recent introduction into Spanish sexual ideology, but because of its rarity, I have not investigated this notion thoroughly enough to speak of it with authority.

upon the head of a man, thereby feminizing him. The cuckold not only wears horns but also simultaneously becomes symbolically converted into a *cabrón*, or super-goat. And the goat, as we have seen, is closely associated with womankind. Here it is perhaps significant that female goats, unlike female sheep, have horns. It is, in fact, safe to extrapolate and say that goathorns in Monteros, and probably throughout Andalusia, represent the harmful, devilish dimensions of the feminine character. The cuckold, who suffers the consequences of his wife's uncontrolled sexuality, becomes forever branded with this female symbol.[15]

But it is necessary to state also that goathorns are sometimes said to grow from within the cuckold as well as being placed upon him from without. The men of Monteros are careful never to rub their foreheads lest people begin to wonder whether horns are beginning to disturb them. "I wouldn't touch myself on the forehead too often," advised one close friend. "I don't even like to *think* of touching myself there," stated another, "much less actually do it." I remember, in particular, one uncle's campaign to try to get his nephew to leave his girlfriend because she was reputed to have slept with a string of other men. After private conversations proved to have no effect, the uncle and some of his friends resorted to public ridicule. In the marketplace, the bars, and wherever else crowds were gathered, they would call out to the young man, "*¡Cabrón!* After you marry her, let me have a turn with her, will you? She's a real piece! The horns are already sprouting from you! (*¡Ya te están saliendo los cuernos!*)"

The thought of goathorns is especially horrible to the men of Monteros when they are said to emerge from within the body, for this indicates that the man not only wears a symbol of femininity but also to some extent actually becomes a woman. No wonder, then, that men are so fearful of their wives: by an act of infidelity, an act toward which women are in any case said to be naturally inclined, a wife can deprive her husband of his precious masculinity and even go so far as to convert him symbolically into a member of her own sex. This potentiality, of course, invests her with an awesome power.

---

[15]Of course in this analysis I refer specifically to goathorns. As anthropologist Honorio Velasco pointed out to me while discussing the matter with him in Madrid, the symbolism of horns in general is much more complex than I have indicated here. Hence, the horns of the bull connote male aggressivity, and horn-bearers across the board seem to represent a challenge to stability and the approved social order.

Male Genitalia and Masculine Behavior

In order best to understand the third threat to masculine identity—the enforced adoption of a symbolically feminine, passive role in the sexual act—we need to examine further some masculine notions of how the male body relates to the male being. We will begin with an incident that occurred while I was collecting a genealogy from a young, highly educated member of the landowning elite, a native of Monteros and currently town judge. During the course of the interview, I found out to my surprise that one of my informant's brothers was married to an Englishwoman. "To a Spaniard it's not important who he marries," said the judge jokingly, "not even if she's from England!" With that, a Monteros bureaucrat who was listening in quickly interjected, "Didn't you know? Spain conquered America not by the sword, but by the prick (*polla*)." Eager to better the bureaucrat, the judge then recalled that one of his professors at the University of Madrid used to say, "America was conquered by Spaniards who were carrying the cross in one hand and the prick in the other."

These ideas, to be sure, were stated in typical Monteros jest. Nonetheless, they reveal an important component of the masculine self-image throughout Andalusia: the locus of power and will, of emotions and strength, lies within the male genitals. Men speak as if they are impelled to act according to opinions and desires that originate in their testicles or penis. In this particular speech pattern, the most common colloquial expressions for penis—*chorra, polla, pijo*—and those for testicles—*cojones, huevos* (literally, "eggs")—are employed interchangeably. Thus, if a man impulsively decides to miss a day's work and is asked to justify himself, he may likely say, *"Porque me sale de los cojones"* (literally, "Because it comes to me from the balls"). Similarly, if a man's wife should ask why he did not come home earlier the previous evening, he will answer, *"Porque no me salió de la chorra"* ("Because it didn't come out of my prick"). In all such cases, the speaker proclaims total freedom from obligations and responsibility on the grounds that conformity to the rules is contrary to his will, which emanates in some fashion from his genitalia. To rationalize one's action by reference to the penis or testicles is, above all, to assert one's complete individuality. It is an extreme, yet very common, expression of the obstinate refusal to comply with ordinary behavioral expectations. And just as this particular manifestation of the human will is somehow related to the male genitalia, so too is it perceived as being especially characteristic of men. For nonconformity of any kind requires the fearlessness and sense of abandon that only men are thought to possess and that, with the single exception cited below, they alone are permitted to express.

This is why a man who is considered especially assertive, aggressive, and fearless in Monteros is called a *cojonudo*, a "big-balled man." His extreme masculine behavior is projected linguistically onto his genitals, as if normal-sized testicles were not large enough to accommodate the full force of his personal strength and will. There is also the rare woman who is called a *cojonuda*, a "big-balled woman," because she is courageous and determined, especially in business affairs, and shows herself willing to work alongside her spouse for the greater financial benefit of the household. Of such female entrepreneurs it is said that "they have balls inside," and that "God made a mistake, for they should have been born as men." A *cojonuda* is equipped with a highly desirable personality trait ordinarily reserved to men, and therefore she is similarly associated metaphorically with masculine physical attributes.

Sometimes, however, even the strongest of human beings is overwhelmed by life circumstances beyond his control. To act *por huevos* or *por cojones* ("by the balls") is to do something out of force or necessity. Thus, if one has to pay an outstanding bill lest his property be attached, the payment is made *por cojones*. Similarly, to flatter a potential employer, a detested member of the elite, is to act *por huevos*, for if one were wealthy and independent one would certainly not stoop to such demeaning behavior. A woman may also speak of being forced into an action by circumstances beyond her control, but she will employ the euphemism *por papas* ("by potatoes") or *por pantalones* ("by the trousers") instead of openly saying "by the balls."

Let us now turn to the question of the degree to which the people of Monteros actually believe that the penis and testicles are repositories of masculine personality traits—of force and will and determination—in the manner, say, that we in the United States locate these characteristics in the brain. For the people of Monteros, does masculinity actually reside within the male genitalia, or is it only spoken of *as if* it resided there?

On the one hand, men justify some of their speech patterns by making an explicit analogy between their emotions and bodily processes. When a man becomes angry and is at the height of fury, just before lashing out with a punch, he shouts at his opponent, "*¡Me sudan los huevos de tí!*" ("My balls sweat from you!") By way of explanation, men claim that this is said only when a person is so furious that his emotions rather than physical labor or the heat of

the day are enough to make his testicles sweat. Similarly, when a
man is fearful with what seems to be good reason (in one such case, a
man was trapped inside a truck that was perched over a cliff), he
can say that he has *cojones en la garganta*—"balls in the throat," the
equivalent of our "heart in the mouth."[16] Men claim that even
though this is the standard way of expressing legitimate fear, a man
might just as well say that his testicles are anywhere in his body
other than the place they belong. The critical metaphoric message is
that the testicles are displaced from ordinary position, as is said actually to happen through the shriveling of penis and testicles when a
man is afraid.

Of course, the above examples demonstrate a conceptual link
between emotions and their effect on the male genitalia, not that
the genitalia are themselves repositories for the emotions. Regarding
the latter issue, a fortuitous circumstance allows us to assert that the
people of Monteros almost certainly speak *as if* masculine attributes
reside in the genitalia, rather than believing that they actually do. It
is well known that the former mayor of Monteros, a man who held
that post for nearly thirty years, lost one of his testicles in combat
and for this reason was believed unable to have children. The man
ruled with the tight political control required of mayors by the
Franco regime in the years immediately following the Civil War
(1936–39), and was decorated by that regime for his valiant service
in the Blue Division, the volunteer unit that Franco deployed to
Germany during the Second World War to assist Hitler. This man is
detested by some, revered by others. But all say that "even though
he is missing a testicle, he has acted in this town as if he had seven or
eight of them." Reference to the genitals in matters of masculinity is
clearly metaphoric.

So is the following popular joke, by the way, which arose in
Monteros in the early 1970s when the town acquired (through ap-
pointment by the provincial governor) its first *alcaldesa* or woman
mayor. "In Monteros, we're going ass backwards. First we had a
mayor with two balls, next we had a mayor with one ball, and now
we have a mayor with *no* balls!" It is difficult, given the overween-
ing importance of the personality attributes associated with the male
genitals, for men to understand how a town can hope to function
and survive under such circumstances.

---

[16]In Monteros, as throughout the Western world (Firth 1973, p. 231), the heart is
also considered an important repository of emotions, though this organ has not found
its way into popular speech nearly to the degree that the genitalia have.

The Threat of Anal Penetration

We can now return to the main discussion of how women threaten men. If masculine behavior, for the people of Monteros, has its conceptual locus in the male genital region, then feminine behavior is concentrated linguistically on the anus. Men show themselves to be constantly aware that the anus can be used in homosexual encounters, in which cases the passive partner is perceived as playing the feminine role and indeed of being converted symbolically into a woman. It is this sexual transformation that men fear. As a defense, male speech forms reveal a constant attempt to force masculine rivals into the feminine role, in a quest to avoid adopting this role themselves.

Perhaps the most common expression along these lines is *tomarlo por culo* (literally, "to take it by the ass"), which has more or less the same meaning as the colloquial "shove it up your ass" in American English. The important difference, however, comes with usage rather than meaning. In Monteros I have never actually heard one man insult another by telling him to "take it by the ass." This would be an uncommonly grave attack in which the rival would in effect be transformed symbolically into a woman. Instead, men who are angry at one another commonly state behind each other's back that they are going to *mandarlo tomar por culo*—"order him [the rival] to take it by the ass." When women are present, the euphemism *saco* ("sack" or "bag") is substituted for the word *culo* ("ass"), a clear example of symbolism by analogy to biological function.

Men generally think of strategic weakness in daily affairs, be they economic or political, in terms of potential anal penetration. To *bajar los pantalones* ("lower your trousers"), for example, implies being forced into readiness for phallic attack by a male rival. On one occasion, two wealthy landowners were discussing the recent labor shortage in the olive harvest, made all the more serious by their inability to mechanize the collection (see chapter 8). In disgust, one of them blurted out, "We're fed up with having to *bajar los pantalones a los obreros*" ("lower our trousers for the workers").

But again, as with the male attitude toward horns, we have to ask whether speech patterns regarding the anus are merely metaphoric or whether they reflect an actual fear of playing the passive role in a homosexual encounter. Here, medical beliefs and practices can lead us to the answer. Throughout Spain, suppositories are one of the most widespread forms in which drugs are administered, and they are regularly prescribed for both children and adults. In Monteros, men and women differ radically in their views of suppositories: women accept this form of treatment readily and without complaint, while most men categorically refuse ever to permit a suppository to be inserted into their anus. The male fear—sometimes expressed jokingly, sometimes seriously—is that through consistent use of suppositories, a man can become accustomed to having objects placed there; he may then begin to derive pleasure from it and will become transformed into a homosexual and, worse, one who is relegated to the female, passive role. "There's a plague of suppository prescriptions here in Spain," complained one bank employee. "Can't they find some other way of curing disease?" I know of several cases in which men suffered fever and sore throat for weeks before their wives could persuade them to follow the doctor's advice and use suppositories. "They think it's only for homosexuals," explained one woman, whose husband stubbornly refuses this form of medication, and whose seventy-year-old father has done likewise throughout his entire life.

Interestingly, men in Monteros, as throughout the Mediterranean (Dundes and Falassi 1975, p. 189; Dundes, Leach, and Ozkok 1970), are unafraid to joke about playing the phallic, "male" part in homosexual intercourse. This role, at least, is consistent with masculine notions of genital assertion and aggression. It is, rather, the dread of assuming a feminine posture—of being the victim of sexual attack, instead of the perpetrator—that preoccupies the men of our town. This theme, as well as the others we have examined, emerges clearly in male jokes and joking, through which men can dispel, however momentarily, the anxieties these feelings arouse.

Jokes and the Male Identity

Una vez te casarás y mil te arrepentirás.

You'll marry once and regret it a thousand
times.

    Monteros proverb

6

    In the introduction to Gershon Legman's massive two-volume
compendium of sexual humor (Legman 1971, 1975), the author
states that a main function of joke-telling is "to absorb and control,
even to slough off, by means of jocular presentation and laughter,
the great anxiety that both teller and listener feel in connection with
certain culturally determined themes" (Legman 1971, pp. 13-14).
Through the growing literature on jokes and humor we have come
to recognize that what is funny in one cultural context may prove
dull or trite, or even repugnant, in another, Humor, in fact, may be
said to be the most sensitive barometer of the concerns and preoccupations that are shared by a group of people. Without an
understanding of humor, of what makes people laugh, we can never
hope to penetrate to the core of a people's mentality in order fully to
understand what motivates them to act as they do.

    In Monteros, nowhere do the meaning and functions of male
humor become more evident than in the jokes men tell one another
and the pranks they play on one another. Jokes and joking are so important, in fact, that they can be said to provide the main fabric by

which men are bound to each other on a daily basis. It is no exaggeration to say that a good part of each man's day in Monteros engages him, either as actor or recipient, in joke-telling or prankstership.

Arthur Koestler has rightly remarked that "the more sophisticated forms of humour evoke mixed, and sometimes contradictory, feelings; but whatever the mixture, it must contain one ingredient whose presence is indispensable: an impulse, however faint, of aggression or apprehension" (Koestler 1964, p. 52). In Monteros there are aggressive and defensive components to both joke-telling and prank-playing. But it is nonetheless clear that the element of defensiveness (what Koestler calls "apprehension") predominates in male jokes, while the aggressive impulse receives release primarily through pranks. In jokes, Andalusian men reveal and share their most deeply buried anxieties with one another, and thereby achieve a feeling of intimacy and camaraderie that they would find difficult to express through more overt means. Through pranks, on the other hand, men find a safe, jocular release for the hostile, competitive attitudes with which they also regard one another. Men are as ambivalent in their feelings toward one another as they are toward women, and nowhere is this ambivalence better expressed than in their humor.

To demonstrate, let us turn first to narrated jokes and postpone the discussion of pranks until the next chapter. In Monteros jokes are told in a variety of social settings, but for the most part they emerge in sexually homogeneous situations. Thus men, the prime joke-tellers in town, tend to narrate their humorous stories in the exclusive company of other men, with whom they in fact spend most of their time. Men and women from all social classes agree that sex-exclusive groups are more animated and relaxed than are groups composed of both sexes. (The main exception, as we shall see in chapter 8, is during the olive harvest, when normal social relations are disrupted by the nature of the activity at hand.) Since many men spend most of their waking hours in the sole company of other men, it is hardly surprising that their jokes should reveal an underlying concern with homosexuality.

Regardless of whether we wish definitively to attribute an explicitly homosexual dimension to male joke-telling in Monteros, there is no doubt that the most popular jokes reveal the same anxieties and concern about masculinity discussed in the preceding chapter. Four prominent themes, paralleling those found in metaphoric speech, emerge in the jokes: the quality and size of the male genitals; the power of women to emasculate; the voracious sexual appetite of women; and the male fear of being cuckolded. Let us discuss them in turn.

Jokes about Genitalia

Extreme physical modesty prevails within the Monteros home, and fathers make an effort never to reveal their genitalia to their sons. Nonetheless, it is clear from the jokes that men suffer from the feeling that their phallus is of inadequate size, whether it be in relation to the father's genitals or to some other supposedly more universal standard. In the following joke, we must understand the explicit metaphoric comparison between poor men, whose economic limitations reduce their ability to conquer women, and small dogs, who are jokingly considered incapable of mounting a female. (A popular *copla*, or short poem, for example, states that *El amor del hombre pobre es como el del perro enano; que en querer y no poder se le pasa todo el año*—"A poor man's love life is like that of a dwarf dog; he spends the whole year wanting and not being able to do it.") A working-class man, in fact, told me this joke:

> There was a big female dog who was in heat, and two small male dogs came near her to try and mount her. One tried, then the other, then the first again, then the other, but they had no success. Then along came a big male dog, who barked at the little dogs to get them away from her and fucked the big female. The two little dogs had been looking on, and one said to the other, "See what a good lay you get with a big prick!" (*"¡Te das cuenta con un buen pijo qué bien se folla!"*)

An Oedipal theme is at least suggested in this narrative: the small sons are frightened away by their genitally superior father, who is all too willing to demonstrate his sexual superiority.

Filial awe at the size of the father's organ is explicit in the following joke:

> There was a son of seven or eight who saw his father's penis accidentally for the first time. He asked his father what it was, and the father said it was his "conscience" (*conciencia*). The boy had been out of school for a few days, and when he returned, the teacher scolded him for being absent. "Were you ill?" she asked. "No," answered the boy. "Then what's the

reason?" she inquired angrily. "Doesn't your father have a conscience?" "Does my father have a conscience!" blurted out the
boy. "He has a conscience *this* big!"

As he gives the punchline, the narrator stretches his right arm in
front of him and crosses it about halfway to the shoulder with the
left hand, in the characteristic gesture indicating massive genital
length.

In Monteros jokes, men show that they are concerned not only
with how they measure up to their fathers, but also with the related
matter of impotence.

> There were a lieutenant and a soldier in the army, and the
> lieutenant was urinating. The soldier looked over and noticed
> that the lieutenant was wetting his shoes. "Pardon, sir," he
> said, "but I think you're getting your shoes wet." "I am?" asked
> the lieutenant with glee. "That's the best news I've heard in a
> long time, because for the past two years I've been wetting my
> balls."

My informant explained that the lieutenant's penis had been so flac-
cid that the stream of urine had been hitting his testicles. That the
stream should arch out so as to hit his shoes was an indication that
the penis was at last beginning to reacquire its potency.

In the following joke, also concerning impotence, the male narrator and his audience at least have the opportunity to fantasize
about the genital defeat of the awesome father.

> There was a little boy who passed by a bakery with his father,
> and there was a donkey outside, waiting to be loaded up with
> breads to be distributed throughout the town. Well, the donkey
> had an erection, and the son didn't know what it was. So he
> asked his father: "Papá, what's that the donkey has?" "Oh,
> that's only an illness," answered the father. The next day the
> boy passed the same bakery with his mother, and the donkey
> again had an erection. "Look, Mamá," said the boy, "that
> donkey has an illness." Replied the mother, "What a pity your
> father doesn't have such an illness."

Of the jokes we have thus far related, this is perhaps the most complex, because male listeners can identify with any one of three
figures: the boy, the father, or the donkey. To identify with the
father is at once to recognize and mock one's own sexual inade-

quacy. In this instance we would do well to recall Legman's analysis of jokes as a protective or defensive psychological mechanism. By means of humor,

> the seriousness, and even the physical *reality*, of the situation can be denied and made light of, by telling it—or by accepting some serious original anecdote describing it—simply as a joke; as something allowing the accumulated tension of living this situation, or telling about it, or listening to it, to relieve itself in the harmless but necessary explosion of laughter (Legman 1971, pp. 17-18).

Of course, it is not necessary that a man actually be impotent to enjoy this joke; the mere fear of sexual inadequacy should be enough to make the joke effective.

On the other hand, men listening to this joke may just as easily identify with the young boy, who is, after all, the story's protagonist. In this instance, to learn that the father is impotent and that indeed the mother denigrates his sexual abilities must provide comforting reassurance about one's own abilities in comparison with one's father. Perhaps more than anything, this joke tells the story of discovery and affirmation: men, in the guise of the young boy, first question their own sexual potential, wondering what it is and whether it really exists. Then they find reassurance and affirmation of their sexual potency in the powerful figure of the donkey. Finally, they overcome the previously awesome figure of the father by winning the confidence of the mother, whose intimate words to her son place the two of them in opposition to the absent adult male, whose erection—if it could be achieved—would only be like an "illness." This joke, as much as any, represents an Oedipal wish fulfillment.[1]

For the most part, the Oedipal themes that are so evident in Monteros jokes remain disguised, whether by the substitution of animals for humans or by some other symbolic device. In several jokes, however, filial hostility toward and victory over the father are more explicit than in the stories we have already examined. The dialogue in the following joke is accompanied by mimicry of a lilting Mexican accent.

> Two Mexicans were walking together. "Here comes my father," said one Mexican, pointing to four men coming from the opposite direction. "Which one's your father?" asked his compan-

---

[1]Animals are used to express similar Oedipal themes in American jokelore (see, for example, Abrahams and Dundes 1969).

ion. With that, the first guy took out his pistol and shot one of the oncoming men. "The one who's doubling over," the man answered.

There is a symbolic facade here, in that the joke allows Spaniards to couch their feelings toward the father in the guise of a stereotype of Mexicans. Hostility toward one's father is presented as only as extreme manifestation of a more general racial characteristic. The implication is that Mexicans are so violent that they would casually kill their own fathers, not that the fathers are the specific object of hostility. Defeat of the paternal rival is thereby given indirect expression and in this manner made more palatable to the men of Monteros.

In other jokes, the rivalry with the father for possession of the mother is fully explicit.

There was a man who went for his army physical, and [to be released from military obligation] said he was the son of a widow. "What do you mean son of a widow? Your father is alive." "He was alive until today," answered the young man.

The implication is that the protagonist killed his father in order to be relieved from military service. But, as the narrative indicates, another consequence of his action—and the only consequence the joke-teller actually states—is that he is now alone with his mother. Significantly, the informant who told me this joke had lost his mother at the age of five and was reared thereafter by an older sister and their father. It is not surprising that this man should express his Oedipal wishes with greater directness than most men in Monteros. The Oedipal theme in Monteros jokes is important, as it is elsewhere, as a symptom of psychosexual development and the incomplete resolution of intrafamilial conflicts. But it is also necessary to view these jokes as only one more expression, among those to which we have already been introduced, of rebellion against authority and control, qualities that are in this case represented by the father. The father, more powerful than the son, is appropriately endowed with genitalia of superior size and strength. To overcome his domination, it is necessary to deprive him of his sexual potency or remove him from the scene through murder. Both of these goals, inconceivable in actual life, may be achieved vicariously and symbolically through joke-telling. Here we have a perfect example of how humor, like play, "soars beyond ordinary boundaries and creates a world in which extraordinary things are possible, where the unthinkable is thought and the forbidden is performed as commonplace" (Salamone 1976, p. 147).

Woman as Emasculator

Monteros jokes not only help men to express their feelings of powerlessness and genital inferiority, but also reflect the typical male beliefs concerning female aggression, sexual insatiability, and marital infidelity. Men, who fear that their wives crave to destroy them, need emotional release from the tensions that the threat from women generates. Jokes provide both an affirmation of conflict between the sexes and a means by which men can minimize, however incompletely and ephemerally, the importance of this conflict.

Men, as indicated in the previous chapter, fear that their wives would prefer to be widowed, a prospect that is, to say the least, disturbing. Their anxieties may be temporarily dispelled and converted into laughter through the portrayal of feminine hostility in jokes:

> There was a mason who went to his house every day after work. One day he arrived home and said to his wife, "Something terrible has happened to me. Another worker and I were under a scaffold and a brick fell on him and killed him. Awful, just awful!" Responded the wife, "And what's wrong with *you*? It's just that you're never in the right place at the right time!"

My informant, laughing heartily as he narrated this joke, explained that the wife in the story was regretful that her husband had been the one to escape death.

Men believe that widows, far from mourning their husbands, revel in their freedom. On All Saints' Day (1 November), the annual occasion for decorating graves and honoring the memory of deceased relatives, a male informant related to me a joke of two widows who went to the cemetery together to pray for their husbands' souls.

> The first widow knelt down, prayed, and started to cry, but the other simply pulled down her underpants and urinated on her husband's grave. "Do you realize what you did?" asked her companion. "You urinated on your dead husband's grave! Why in the world did you do that?" Responded the other, "Each woman cries through the place that she most feels it."

This joke manifests the common male belief that women heap scorn—here represented by urine—on the memory of their dead husbands. It is also a commentary on female sensuality, most explicitly on the widow's unfulfilled sexual desires.

In actual life, of course, men express the very attitudes about their wives that they attribute specifically to women. Thus, once men are married and have children, they begin to recognize the economic burden and sacrifice that raising a family entails and complain good-naturedly but seriously about the situation. Married men often yearn openly for the freedom from responsibility that they enjoyed when they were younger. They also speak nostalgically about the days when they could womanize without the fear of being criticized for endangering the family's reputation. If their wives died, they claim, they would be free to pursue whatever sexual or economic adventures they liked. The family, to be sure, provides men with a critical source of security; I know a number of men who are obsessed by the fear that their wives might die and leave them alone. But at the same time, men experience a sense of being hemmed in and constricted by the indissoluble bond to their wives, which they perceive to be as much a burden as a blessing. Most men undoubtedly believe that their wives would, at the very least, be indifferent to their death. But this view may best be explained as a projection of men's own ambivalent desire to be liberated from the marital yoke. Certainly, the criticisms of marriage that men themselves express—the absence of economic and sexual freedom—are the ones most frequently attributed to women, despite the fact that women almost never complain about their lot. By projecting their own feelings onto women, men can avoid a sense of guilt at wanting to be rid of the family bond—a bond that in many ways provides them a sense of personal warmth and security and that confers upon them full adult status.

Of the two sexes, women are the ones who live the more constricted lives. For the most part, they bear their powerlessness and lack of freedom without complaint. They have learned, however, to wield an important weapon against their husbands: the verbal attack against masculinity. Women know that men perceive their masculinity in almost purely genital terms, so that the best method of keeping men in line is to criticize their virility. On several occasions I heard old or late-middle-aged men tell their wives, in front of friends, that they expected to return home late or that they would be unable to be with the family for dinner. The women responded in such cases by saying to the friends, "What do I need *him* [the husband] at home for, if he's no longer able to do it anyway?" Everyone laughed, but the emasculating image could only be painful to the husbands, who were at a loss for retort.

Women attack their husbands' masculinity even when their cause for resentment is the spouses' assertion of masculine power. Women whose husbands exert no sexual control in their marriage find themselves almost constantly pregnant. In one such instance, the wife had given birth seven times, the last birth endangering her life. She was burning with fury at her husband for having impregnated her yet an eighth time, and let no opportunity go by without reminding him of it. Once, while peeling a cucumber she said to him, poking the vegetable under his face, "Here, you'd better take this if you're thinking of getting another woman, because you'll need it. You don't have one of your own." Attacks like this occur because they are the only permissible and effective means by which women can openly express antagonism toward their husbands.

For men, in turn, these biting remarks only confirm their opinion that women are seductresses who use their inordinately great sexual powers or desires toward male destruction. Jokes reflect the view that women are emasculating creatures. In some of the narratives, women arouse men only to turn around afterwards and scorn or reject them.

> A woman was walking along the streets of Madrid holding a dog in her arms so that it wouldn't get run over. She was beautiful, the woman, and a man walking alongside her said, "If only I were that dog, there in your arms!" Responded the woman, "I'm taking him to have him castrated. Want to come along?"

In this joke, the symbolic castration that women utilize against men in everyday affairs threatens to become reality. We should make note, too, of the explicit association between man and dog, which lends credence to the merely implicit symbolic connection between animals and humans that we have already analyzed in previous narratives.

Another, similar joke portrays a cruel female rejection coupled with public ridicule.

> There was a man who was very skinny, very skinny, who met a sexy woman (*buena hembra*) on the street. She invited him up to her house, and he said to himself, "Well, I have nothing to lose," and he followed her up there. When they entered the apartment, she told him to go into the bedroom and get un-

dressed. "Get undressed, get undressed," she said. When he was undressed he called out to her, "OK, I'm undressed." The woman gathered her children around her. Then she called the man out of the bedroom so he would stand in front of them all. When he appeared she said, "See, children. If you aren't good, you're going to wind up just like this guy!"[2]

The woman in this joke uses her femininity to lure the man. Instead of providing him the expected sexual gratification, however, she disparages him for his appearance. This joke, I suspect, concerns genital size as much as anything; for if the woman were only interested in ridiculing the man's general bodily appearance, the plot would not require that he get undressed. Humiliated, the man is made to suffer from the accusation of being skinny, that is, of genital inadequacy, which is similar to the threat of castration that we analyzed in the previous joke. In both narratives, a provocative woman is portrayed as depriving a man of his sexual potency. For many men of Monteros, of course, this deprivation is practically equivalent to robbing him of life.

Woman as Sexually Assertive

To belittle a man's sexual endowment or power is only one way of depriving him of life, however. Another, as we have seen in chapter 5, is to engage him in so much sexual activity that he quickly withers and ages, especially from the loss of semen. However much interest men may demonstrate in sex, it is always rationalized on the basis of female seduction. As one woman put it, "If a man sticks his foot out to trip a woman she is supposed to remain standing, but if a woman puts out her foot, a man can fall." Capitulating to sexual attraction is a male luxury, but the ultimate source of all sexual activity—at least from the male point of view—is feminine. This is why Monteros jokes portray women as being at least as desirous of sex as men, if not more.

The jokes show that, for women, coitus takes primacy over any other activity. A version of the following joke, just one of many concerning traveling and the marital separation it entails, also appears in Legman's collection of English-language sexual humor (1971, p. 236).

---

[2]This joke, I have been told, is also part of the American folk tradition, though I have been unable to locate it in published sources.

There was a man who'd been away from his home for a month working. When he arrived back home, he asked his wife, "Well, what are we going to do? *Echar un cohete* ("launch a skyrocket," that is, have intercourse), and then eat?" "Yes!" she answered enthusiastically, "there's no hurry to eat!"

The message here is clearly that the woman has longed for sexual activity during the period of separation as much as the man.

Other jokes also portray the man as initiating or suggesting sexual intercourse, and the woman agreeing all too eagerly.

There was a girl in the fields with a miniskirt. She was bent over, attending to the crops, when along came a young man. Her skirt was quite high, and the guy felt a desire to have her. So he approached her from behind, and, before she could say anything, parted her dress to one side and stuck it up her. The girl at once turned her head around and protested indignantly, saying, "What do you think you're doing?" and similar things. The man, still with his prick inside her, answered, "So do you want me to take it out?" The girl thought to herself for a moment and said, "No, as long as you have it in there, you might as well leave it."

The above two jokes, like others we have already analyzed, must be considered to contain a strong element of projective fantasy. Unlike some stories, these at least reflect the actual life situation of men initiating sexual contact. But what they do, in addition, is to attribute equally burning sexual desires to women. They say, in effect, that even though women may protest about having intercourse, females want and need this activity as much as males. Women's protests are merely a show, an act, a facade.

Women in real life, as in narrative fantasy, are thought to be *viciosa*, that is, "hooked" on sex. Normal men are incapable of satisfying their extraordinary desires.

There was a man who asked a woman if he could have intercourse with her and she responded, "Look, I'd like to but I'm sort of afraid. They say that yours is very long and thick." The man answered, "Don't worry. What I'll do is wrap a couple of handkerchiefs around it so that it won't go far inside you." So he took out some handkerchiefs, tied them together, and wrapped them around his erect penis, so that only a small por-

tion remained naked. Then he entered her. "Is it in?" the
woman asked. "Yes," answered the man. "Then unwrap it a
wind or two," she instructed. He did this, and the woman continued to ask him to unwrap the handkerchief until his entire
penis was inside her. But the woman wanted still more. So,
without her knowing it, he took an umbrella and put it inside
her. She asked again, as always, "Is it inside now?" He
answered, "What do you mean, is it inside? I even have an umbrella inside you!" "Then for God's sake open it up!" she cried
out.

The woman in this joke, as in others, plays an initially reticent role.
But very quickly she becomes converted into the sexual aggressor,
until her desires exceed the capabilities of even the most well-
endowed partner.

The same message is imparted by another humorous tale of a
woman who was dissatisfied with her husband's performance in bed
and took him to witness a bull in action. As the couple looked on, a
cow was mounted by a bull thirteen consecutive times. The woman
tells her husband that he should take the bull's activity as an example, to which the man feebly defends himself by claiming that the
cow had been mounted by thirteen different bulls, not just one.

All these jokes reveal a uniformly male point of view. The jokes
are so male-centered that neither my wife nor I can conceive of a
Monteros woman narrating one; certainly, in all the time we spent
in Monteros no woman ever told one to us. We do know a few
women who seem proud that members of their sex are the responsible party in selecting sexual partners and in attracting and capturing
the men they most desire. These women derive a secret sense of
power and satisfaction from thinking that they were the ones who
chose their husbands, while creating the illusion that the choice was
really the man's.

But this is quite different from sexual activity, in which women
are supposed to play the passive role. Coitus in Monteros is ideally
male-initiated. To judge from joking encounters between wives and
husbands, many men force their wives to engage in intercourse far
more frequently than the women would like. In the case of a few
women we know, sexual enthusiasm is muted because they are fearful of pregnancy. In several other instances women resist advances
because they derive little or no pleasure from sex. I have been told
by at least two men that some townswomen—even educated
women—are totally unaware that females are capable of reaching
climax. Yet men accuse women, not themselves, of being oversexed.

Interestingly, however, most men enjoy and strive for occasions on which their wives participate actively in coitus. Sexual release in and of itself is not a sufficient sign of masculinity; it must be accompanied by female arousal as well. Men speak openly about wanting to satisfy their wives' sexual needs, and they certainly brag about their years of bachelorhood, which, if one could believe the tales, were filled with successful attempts at arousing initially shy, but fundamentally quite passionate, young women. Men like to think of themselves as capable lovers, which is precisely what they appear not to be in most of the jokes.

The humorous stories provide men a double way out. On the one hand they justify frequent coitus on the grounds that women enjoy and crave the act as much as men. At the same time, however, they rationalize any inadequacies in sexual performance by reinforcing the view that women are insatiable in their demands and that they crave more than any normal male can reasonably be expected to give. Jokes thereby relieve men of any possible guilt that they might be exploiting women and reduce male anxieties about the quality of their sexual performance. In both instances, the sexual component of male identity is protected and reaffirmed.

All things considered, it is tempting to accept Legman's sweeping though as yet unsubstantiated judgment concerning the invention of sexual humor:

> One fact strikingly evident in any collection of modern sexual folklore, whether jokes, limericks, ballads, printed "novelties," or whatnot, is that this material has all been created by men, and that there is no place in it for women except as the butt. It is not just that so preponderant an amount of the material is grossly anti-woman in tendency and intent, but also that the situations presented almost completely lack any protagonist position in which a woman can identify herself—*as a woman*—with any human gratification or pride (Legman 1971, p. 217).

Certainly in Monteros it is men, of the two sexes, who predominate as narrators of and audience to sexual humor.[3] Jokes, like other

---

[3]My wife and I occasionally heard women narrate jokes, and I possess a small collection of these. I avoid the discussion of female humor at this point not because it is unworthy, but because the topic would lead me astray from the main point of this volume. For interesting analyses of female humor, consult Johnson (1973), Mitchell (1977), and Weigle (1978).

forms of humor that we have seen, reinforce men's conception of themselves as men. In a society where one's sexual identity is under constant scrutiny, jokes contribute significantly toward maintaining a positive male self-image.

Female Infidelity

Jokes in addition to justifying and rationalizing men's sexual behavior provide a safe and necessary means of expressing sexual fears and anxieties. Here, I refer specifically to masculine concerns about the fidelity of their wives, an issue discussed at length in the previous chapter. Men, who are constantly preoccupied by the thought that their wives will be unfaithful, are nonetheless delighted by numerous narratives about the unfaithful woman. These jokes concern cuckolded husbands who openly and shamelessly display the horns their wives have placed on them. In telling or listening to these jokes, the men of Monteros can only derive a sense of relief that it is the pitiful, naïve protagonists of narrative fantasy who suffer the consequences of female infidelity, and not themselves.

This theme is one of the most popular in the entire repertoire of masculine humor. Many of the jokes speak specifically to the ever-present insecurity that one's wife might be having a secret affair.

There was a man who had been away from home a number of days, and when he returned he had a great desire to have intercourse with his wife. When he told her this she said,"I'm sorry, dear, but I'm sick [menstruating]. Here, take this money, and go do it with someone else." So the man took the money, and as he was going downstairs he met a neighbor woman. He told her where he was going, and she said that she would do it for him. When they were finished, the man climbed the stairs again to his own apartment, and his wife was surprised to see him. "But you're home so soon! How come?" "Well, our neighbor said she would do it for me, so I was only over at her place." "And didn't she charge you?" asked the wife. "Yes, of course she did. She took all my money." "The bitch!" said the wife. "And when her husband needs it, I give it to him for free!"

The surprise ending, of course, reveals that the husband has been an unsuspecting victim of his wife's infidelity for a long time.

One of the most popular infidelity jokes concerns a man who catches his unfaithful wife in the act.

> There was a drunk who came home late one night with a friend. And he wanted to introduce the friend to the people of the house. So he said, "And here is my son . . . and that one over there is my wife . . . and the other one"—indicating a strange man whom he saw in his bedroom—"well, that should be me!"[4]

A husband in actual life who occasionally comes home late in a state of drunkenness must wonder whether his wife has used the opportunity to get back at him by taking a secret lover. In the Monteros scheme of things, spouses are no less capable of deceit than anyone else.

Since horns are such an integral part of the infidelity syndrome in Monteros, it is not surprising that a number of jokes should mock the *cabrón* or potential *cabrón*. According to one narrative,

> There was a little boy who was absentmindedly kicking a horn down the street, as children often use a stone. Along came a man who stopped the boy and told him not to kick the horn. "Why not?" asked the boy. "Is it yours?" "No, no, no," said the man. "Go ahead and kick it if you want!"

In narrating this story, the joke-teller assumes a panicked tone of voice to relay the man's final disclaimer of ownership. This mimicry is designed to convey the idea that the man was so shocked by the thought that he might be associated with horns that he quickly retracted his original interest in the boy's harmless activity.

Another joke about horns speaks to the issue of the secrecy of an unfaithful spouse. Here we must recall the well-known Monteros proverb that *El cabrón es el último que se entera*—"The cuckold is the last one to find out."

> There was a Gallego who lit up an Ideal cigarette. The cigarette was so bad that it made him explode, and he landed on the

---

[4]An American version of this joke, in which the cuckold also consents to his wife's infidelity, is reported by Legman (1975, p. 74). Francis Child's Ballad No. 274, "Our Goodman," parallels the theme in this joke, a theme that is apparently found in folklore throughout western Europe (Child 1898, pp. 88–95, 281, 303–4).

moon. When he arrived there, he came across a man with antennae, and asked him, "Why do you have those things on?" Answered the man from the moon, "To find out what is happening on Earth." Responded the Earthman, "Boy, in my country, he who wears those things never finds out about anything!"

Gallegos, from the northwestern corner of Iberia, are poor and ignorant, according to general Hispanic stereotypes. This explains why a Gallego should smoke such a low-quality cigarette that it would propel him to the moon, and why, too, he should naïvely interpret antennae as horns. No matter, the story's main message concerns not Gallegos but cuckolds; here narrator and audience are reminded that a wife is fully capable of secret infidelity. This joke, more than any other, raises the haunting possibility that a man might at this very moment be a cuckold without knowing it.

The true *cabrón*, of course, is the one who knows about his wife's infidelity and consents to it implicitly by maintaining his relationship with her. Several jokes are designed to mock this pitiful figure. As one narrator put it:

They don't celebrate the fiesta of San Marcos here, but they do in Alcalá and Colmenar, and on this day the women take over and give the orders. The men take care of the children, and the women can say anything they want about the men. Well, anyway, they were in procession with San Marcos, and a man shot a skyrocket into the air, shouting, "This one for the *más cabrón* (most cuckolded man) in town!" With that, his wife quickly pushed him to one side, saying, "Get out of the way, Juan, before you get hit with the *caña* [tail of the skyrocket]!"

The humor of this story, of course, emerges from the incongruity of the wife's behavior. She has been careless enough of her husband's reputation to make of him a cuckold, but she exhibits a maternal, protective concern that he might get hit with the skyrocket. Here we have a perfect parallel with a frequent masculine belief that it is the most overtly nurturing, caring wife who is most likely to be the one who puts horns on her husband. She is, like the woman in this humorous tale, bound up in a ceaseless effort to hide her real feelings and activities.

Finally, Monteros jokes mock the clownish figure of the *cabrón* who is so devoid of pride that he does nothing to hide his status from society at large:

There was a man who was a *cabrón*, but the horns didn't sprout on him (*no le salían los cuernos*). So he went to the doctor to find out why. The doctor explained carefully to the man, "To say a person has horns doesn't really mean that they are supposed to grow on him. It's just something that's said, not something real." "Oh," responded the man, "I'm glad to hear it, because I was afraid that it was from lack of calcium in my body."

The cuckold's naïveté in believing that he should actually sprout horns is matched only by his simple-minded confession of his problem to the doctor. In Monteros, the constant objective in interpersonal relations is to maintain a favorable facade. The unfortunate aspects of one's life, which might give others cause for pleasure or ridicule, should remain obscured from public view.

It is curious that the men of Monteros, so preoccupied with the prospect of themselves becoming cuckolds, should find jokes about cuckolds to be humorous. Perhaps it would be more reasonable for men to shun such jokes in order to avoid the horrible specter of being publicly shamed by wearing the horns themselves. But avoidance would ignore the fact, pointed out by Freud a half-century ago, that

> humour has in it a *liberating* element. . . . Obviously, what is fine about it is the triumph of narcissism, the ego's victorious assertion of its own invulnerability. It refuses to be hurt by the arrows of reality or to be compelled to suffer. It insists that it is impervious to wounds dealt by the outside world, in fact, that these are merely occasions for affording it pleasure (Freud 1963b [originally 1928], p. 265).

This is not to say that the men of Monteros would seek horns, like the man in the joke who visited the doctor. Rather, by telling and listening to jokes about cuckolds, men derive two sources of pleasure: a cathartic release from an ever-present concern about the wife's possible deceit; and the public appearance of bravado, through participation in the joke-telling group, which asserts that one is not, in fact, a cuckold and therefore has nothing to fear from this topic of conversation. A real cuckold could never suffer the humiliation of joining in a joke-telling session where horns and marital infidelity were the main subjects under consideration. To participate actively in such a session, then, is to exhibit one's freedom from concern and the certainty of masculine control over a couple's sexual life. Jokes about cuckolds at once liberate men from their anxiety about being cuckolded and permit them to demonstrate their immunity from such anxiety. This double psychological function explains the enormous popularity of such humor.

It also explains why these and similar jokes can be told over and over among the same group of men and still be received enthusiastically with hearty laughter. Laughter, as Arthur Koestler reminds us, is a discharge mechanism which provides for the release of nervous energy (Koestler 1964, pp. 51–63). When tension builds up, as with the suggestion of uncomfortable topics related in jokes, it is harmlessly and pleasurably dissipated through "the puffing away of emotion discarded by thought" (ibid. p. 52). Even "the peculiar breathing in laughter, with its repeated, explosive exhalations, seems designed to 'puff away' surplus tension in a kind of respiratory gymnastics; and the vigorous gestures and slapping of thighs obviously serve the same function" (ibid. p. 59). In fact, this is why laughter is the best diagnostic criterion for the effectiveness and cultural sensitivity of jokes. Jokes, like those related here, are culture-bound, and only seem funny because they evoke certain anxiety-producing situations and emotions that are shared by a particular group.[5] These situations and emotions are as important for the success of a joke as is the story line itself. As long as a joke gives the narrator and audience the opportunity to release, however temporarily, the emotional anxiety that all of them share, it can and usually is stated repeatedly with humorous effect.

---

[5]This is not to say that everybody within a culture is equally capable of understanding jokes told by members of that culture. As Harvey Sacks (1974) has pointed out, jokes are to some extent "understanding tests," in which both narrators and audience try to demonstrate their cognitive and linguistic capabilities.

7

... the answer to an enigmatic question is not found by reflection or logical reasoning. It comes quite literally as a sudden *solution*—a loosening of the tie by which the questioner holds you bound. The corollary of this is that by giving the correct answer you strike him powerless.

Johan Huizinga, *Homo Ludens* (1955)

In Monteros, people operate under the assumption—so thoroughly discussed in Spanish literature and social commentary —that appearances are deceiving and that one must therefore always be vigilant against unexpected attack. Defeat, everyone knows, can be born of the most seemingly innocent circumstances. This is why people say, "May God free us from calm waters; from the rest, I'll free myself" (*De las aguas mansas nos libre Dios; que de las otras me libraré yo*). Calm water in this proverb represents in- dividuals who appear to be good and well-meaning, who never fight, argue, or contradict others. It is, in fact, these people, and not the open, demonstrative, combative types, who have to be guarded against. Consistently calm and agreeable people, it is thought, are the most likely to hide their real motives and to strive toward their own personal advancement by stealthily undermining the position and well-being of their competitors. Because these people are so deceptively kind and innocuous, it is difficult to combat them. The best protection, especially for Monteros men, is to be the aggressor rather than the victim, to fool others rather than to wait patiently and to be tricked oneself. In this chapter, we turn to manipulative techniques through which men attempt to maintain mastery over their social environment, and thereby demonstrate the assertiveness fully expected of them. Two kinds of activities are especially pertinent to this topic: pranks and riddling.

The *Broma*

The people of Monteros distinguish between two types of prank, the *broma* and the *cachondeo*. If you ask an informant to differentiate between these categories, he apparently has no difficulty with sorting them. The *broma*, you will be told, is a light-hearted jest performed by a well-meaning antagonist. *Bromas* are usually, though not exclusively, spontaneous; they occur at a moment's notice and arise out of real-life situations, including both conversational discourse and other forms of interaction. Insofar as the *broma* is both unplanned and integrated within ongoing social situations, it conforms nicely to Fry's definition of a "situation joke," in which "none of the humor participants have knowledge of their impending involvement in a joke" (Fry 1968, p. 56). With *bromas*, as with situation jokes in general, there seems to be a definite role differentiation between the antagonist and the victim. But the antagonist carries out his action in an entirely good-natured spirit, and the victim is aware instantly that he has been the butt of a humorous exchange. Antagonist, victim, and audience—if there is one—laugh, and all parties are left with a satisfied feeling when the incident is over. No harm was intended and none was rendered.

The *broma* exists in many forms, but the people of Monteros subsume all of them under the rubrics *broma de mano* and *broma de boca*. *Bromas de mano*, or "hand pranks," are those that involve physical action rather than speech. Commonly, a man sneaks up behind an unsuspecting friend and frightens him by grabbing his legs or pinching him in the thighs while making some unintelligible, animal-like shriek. Rare is the day in Monteros when this scene is not encountered at least several times. With similar frequency, a man approaches a friend who is nonchalantly having a drink in a bar, embraces him from behind, and lifts him off the floor for a quarter-minute or so, during which time the aggressor continues to hide his identity. Alternatively, the aggressor might place his hands over his victim's eyes and keep them there. All these *bromas de mano* share the guise of a friendly greeting, while actually they are as much an attack from the rear. The victim is usually at least temporarily displeased at being placed in a vulnerable position and tricked publicly.

Bromas de boca, or "mouth pranks" (i.e., "speech pranks"), arise out of verbal interchanges. Some of it is simple teasing. Young men, for example, often ask older men in their sixties and seventies, "How many times did you do it last night?" Or they will jokingly challenge their elders by saying, "I'll give you 100 *pesetas* if you have it hard!" Classified as *bromas de boca*, too, they are spontaneous, humorous bantering exchanges that occur in the course of conversation. In bars, after a man has had his fill, he will usually ask the bartender, "*¿Que se debe aquí?*" ("What is owed here?") meaning, of course, "How much do I owe you?" The bartender sometimes deliberately misinterprets the question, and responds by cataloguing the items in his business operation on which he himself still owes money: "the refrigerator, the counter, the wine . . ."

As the above examples indicate, many *bromas de boca* consist of familiar codified items of speech. Their humor derives as much from the element of surprise as from the fact that they touch upon sensitive aspects of the life circumstances in which the actors find themselves (whether this be indebtedness or impotence from old age). Occasionally, however, jokes are invented on the spot and skillfully woven into the conversation in such a way that they are classified in Monteros as *bromas* ("pranks") rather than *chistes* ("narrative jokes"). Two friends, for example, were in a bar one morning recounting the events of the previous evening to one another. "What a shame about that young girl suffocating last night," remarked one of them casually. Then, as if written into a script, the other responded with surprise, "Where'd it happen?" to which the first quickly retorted, "On a man's prick." A bona fide joke with a punchline had been told. But the main impact of this speech event was to trick the unsuspecting friend who had taken the news of suffocation seriously into participating in the verbal exchange. The humor lay in the pranksmanship as much as in the unexpected verbal incongruity of the punchline. It also lay, of course, in the fact that the unsuspecting friend—like the girl in the joke—symbolically suffocated from the more verbally aggressive and intrusive retort of his competitor. The friend, having been fooled, was left momentarily speechless, and hence conversationally impotent.

Bromas, as I have said, almost always have an identifiable antagonist and victim. Sometimes, however, antagonists are anonymous, and, as an expression of super pranksmanship, they play a trick on the community as a whole. For instance, in the spring of 1976 a rumor began to circulate in Monteros that the mayor had decided to impose a tax of ten *pesetas* on all flowerpots displayed on the town streets. Considering that the women of Monteros have enormous pride in their flowering plants and ostentatiously situate them in great numbers on the balconies and along the outside walls of their homes, this tax would clearly pose a serious financial threat to many families. The rumor circulated rapidly, so that within half a day many of the town streets had been stripped bare of flowers, their owners having retired them indoors. The following day the mayor issued an official statement denying that she had ever intended to tax outdoor flowerpots; all realized that they had been the butt of a practical joke, and the streets once again became resplendent with their dazzling display of colorful spring blooms.

Supposedly innocent, harmless pranks are so important in Monteros that there exist a host of institutionalized occasions on which pranksmanship is expected and, indeed, prescribed. On 24 June, the Day of San Juan, people until recently were permitted to play all sorts of water-related tricks on one another.[1] The most common was to dump buckets of water from balconies onto the heads of passersby in the streets below. Even today, anyone named Juan is fair game for such pranks, and in 1976 I witnessed two cases in which men with this name were threatened jokingly with being dunked in neighborhood fountains; they were carried to the fountains forcibly, though the act was not actually completed.

The Day of Los Santos Inocentes (the Holy Innocents) on 28 December is still an important occasion for *bromas*, but those of a special type. On this date, anyone who manages to borrow small quantities of money from friends or relatives is entitled to keep it. Thus, men (I have never witnessed women in this role) casually ask for spare change all day, hoping that their friends will unwittingly give it to them and find themselves tricked. If a potential victim hands over 100 or 200 *pesetas* (equivalent in 1976 to about $1.50 or $3.00 U.S.), the borrower calls out gleefully, *"¡Que los Santos Inocentes te lo paguen!"*—"May the Holy Innocents pay for it!" At this point the "lender" realizes that he has been tricked. Needless to say, most people maintain vigilance throughout the day, not so much to preserve money as to save face. It is embarrassing to be caught off-guard.

There is one final occasion when Monteros culture prescribes that *bromas* be carried out: the wedding night. Here, traditionally but not currently, it was the female relatives of the bride who were

---

[1]Traditions in the celebration of St. John's Day vary regionally within Spain. In the north, these rituals are generally associated with fire (see, for example, Lisón Tolosana 1971, pp. 303–14; G. M. Foster 1955; Gómez-Tabanera 1968b, p. 195), but they are also sometimes associated with water (Gómez-Tabanera 1968a, p. 71), as in Andalusia.

*The ubiquitous flowerpots, displayed
on balconies and rumored taxable.*

supposed to be perpetrators of the practical jokes. These women were almost always responsible for arranging the house where the bride and groom spent their wedding night.[2] The bed might be short-sheeted, thus preventing the couple from getting into it. Cowbells might be attached to the bottom of the mattress so that they jangled with vigorous bed motion. These, along with a host of similar pranks, seem to have been directed toward the same immediate goal: to create a temporary, humorous obstacle to consummation of the new marital union. The bride's female relatives, it would appear, were determined to take one last step to preserve her virginity, undermining her new husband's attempts to use her for his own selfish, pleasurable purposes. The women of her family would make a final symbolic attempt to rescue the bride from the subordination to her husband that would be her future lot.

The discussion of *bromas* should make clear that a wide variety of activities, subsumed under what we would term teasing, practical jokes, and banter, may be included within this category. *Bromas* without doubt contain an element of aggression, but they are basically harmless. When they take the form of practical jokes, they are similar to the numerous tricks that people in our culture play on April Fools' Day, or that children engage in while away at summer camp. A *broma* is, more than anything, a good-natured prank.

The *Cachondeo* and the *Broma Pesá*

Cachondeos, on the other hand, are, as my informants put it, "more serious." To *cachondear* is to fool a person through a conscious scheme that contains an element of malice.[3] The *cachondeo* is, in the words of one man, "more than a *broma*," for the ultimate intention is to harm or wound, usually through some thinly disguised form of ridicule. The interpretation of an action, particularly with regard to the motivation of the aggressor, ultimately determines whether it will be classified as *broma* or *cachondeo*. It is im-

---

[2]Most newlyweds in Monteros, if they can afford to take a honeymoon, wait until several days—or even several weeks—after the wedding ceremony to depart on their trip.

[3]Interestingly, the Spanish adjective *cachondo(a)* means "passionate" or "sexy," though I have never heard this word employed in Monteros. Gabriel Moedano, a Mexican folklorist, informs me that in his country the verb *cachondear* signifies "to seduce a woman," or "to arouse a woman sexually." The term *cachondeo* in Monteros, therefore, undoubtedly has some etymological connection to sexual matters though it has lost this connotation in contemporary usage.

possible, merely from examining the content of a prank, to decide whether it belongs to one category or the other.

Let me give an example from personal experience. Several months after my family and I settled in Monteros, a newly acquired friend asked me if I didn't want to collaborate with him to *gastar una broma a los gitanos*—"to spend a joke on the Gypsies"—as the usual phraseology puts it. His idea was to pretend that I was a wealthy millionaire with three or four oil wells in my possession and on the lookout for someone to sell me and care for two horses and two ponies—an animal for each member of my family. I was to play along with the Gypsies who would presumably bring a host of animals to my house for scrutiny, only to be completely frustrated in their attempts to make the sale. The scheme at the time seemed weird and distasteful, the product of an unfortunately idiosyncratic mentality, and I categorically refused to play along. (This was long before I recognized the prevalence and importance of pranks like this in Monteros culture.) Two days later, however, I was greeted by a long string of Gypsies at my door, coming one after the other to sell me horses. Embarrassed, I tried to squirm my way out of an uncomfortable situation by saying that there must have been some misunderstanding.

Later in the year, when I was trying to discover the distinction between a *broma* and a *cachondeo*, I asked informants to classify this incident. Universally, people stated that the Gypsies and I had both been victims of a *cachondeo* because we had been made to look foolish and because we had lost control over a situation that had been orchestrated without our knowledge or permission by a third party. When I asked the aggressor himself to classify the incident, however, he insisted that what he had done to me was simply a *broma*, but admitted reluctantly that he had inflicted a *cachondeo* on the Gypsies. His reluctance to make this final admission was perfectly understandable. Men are usually completely unwilling to admit, either to themselves or to others, that they mean to harm the victims of their pranksmanship. This is why, when initially proposing the scheme to me, my friend had characterized it as a *broma*. No man ever states overtly that he is planning a *cachondeo*, even though from the victim's perspective, as well as from the point of view of impartial witnesses, this is in effect what his prank turns out to be.

If a prank seems to have graver consequences than its perpetrator intended and if it really has victimized someone unjustly, then it may be referred to as a *broma pesá*, literally, "heavy prank," or one that has passed the bounds of mere joking or kidding. One evening at dusk I was quietly strolling across one of the principal Monteros plazas with a friend when suddenly a car came moving rapidly and dangerously toward us, pulling to a screeching halt nearly at our feet. When the driver, a neighbor of mine, saw that we were upset by the prank, he feebly attempted an explanation: "Just a *broma*." "A *broma*, yes," agreed my companion, "though somewhat *pesá*." The prank had passed the bounds of acceptability to the point where it might have done us serious harm. For the victim to call the incident a *broma pesá* was, in this context, a friendly way of relaying this message. Similarly, if the aggressor is forced to admit publicly that one of his pranks has resulted in unforeseen, deleterious consequences, he is much more likely to refer to it as a *broma pesá* than a *cachondeo*. In general, prank categories are manipulated to fit the prankster's and victim's separate images of the intended and actual outcome of a prank.

The term *broma pesá* may be, but is not necessarily, a euphemism for the term *cachondeo*. As already pointed out, *bromas*—and this includes *bromas pesás* as well as ordinary *bromas*—may involve physical actions as well as speech. In fact, some *bromas*, like pinching a person's legs or pretending to run a car into someone, involve no speech at all. *Cachondeos*, by contrast, are always basically verbal. In the words of one informant, to *cachondear* is "to tell someone that you know he's right when you really know he's wrong, or to tell someone he's wrong when you really know he's right." A typical instance was the time a town bureaucrat entered a bar slightly tipsy from having already drunk too much and walked up to me and some shepherd friends. The bureaucrat, in an attempt to impress me, boasted about how *culto* (educated and cultured) he was, in contrast to my drinking companions, who he said were "intelligent, but of course lack culture and have undeveloped minds." The others, playing the fool, kept reassuring the bureaucrat of his superior education and training, all the while laughing among themselves at the sight of this uncouth, impolite, inebriated man with a bloated self-image trying to pass himself off as someone he obviously was not. This is the *cachondeo par excellence*.

With the *broma*, the underlying aggression of an act is often disguised to the point where it is totally unconscious. The aggression of a *broma pesá* is overt, but is recognized only in retrospect, after the prank has already occurred and its actual effects can be measured. In the case of the *cachondeo*, however, there exists a conscious attempt—often organized among several individuals, as in the example above—to arouse a victim to the point of anger. The *cachondeo* thus becomes the test of a person's ability to maintain control over his emotions. It pits the determination of a group of men to provoke and anger another until he breaks, against the equally strong determination of the victim to maintain his composure or even, ideally, casually to dismiss his aggressors' actions through laughter and humor.

A common *cachondeo*, for example, is for two men at one end of a bar counter to begin to whisper secretly as if they were talking about a third at the other end of the bar. They press their mouths close to one another's ears, laugh occasionally and turn their eyes at strategic moments toward their victim so that he is sure to realize that he is the object of their conversation. If the intended victim ignores his aggressors long enough, they will tire of the game and stop. If the victim jokes with them, saying, "And what you're talking about isn't half of it! There's a lot more to what they're saying about me that even you don't know!" then the incident is liable to be converted into a lively joking session. The *cachondeo* becomes transformed into a series of *bromas*. In either instance, the intended victim shows himself the victor by exhibiting control. Should he become exasperated or angry, however, his aggressors will assure him that it was all just a *broma*. No matter how much they publicly dismiss the incident as insignificant, the aggressors will secretly regard their victim with contempt for his inability to maintain mastery over the situation and, by extension, over his life in general. The incident becomes a demonstration of overall willpower. Men who disintegrate under the threat of aggression are scorned, while those who withstand it courageously are admired.

Irritable victims, in time, find themselves without drinking partners. One of the favorite pastimes in bars—where most Monteros men spend a good number of hours each day—is to play any one of a large variety of games to determine who will pay for a round of drinks. The games differ in complexity and duration, but all are based on luck. Skill plays only the smallest role, if any, in determining the winner. Nonetheless, the loser is referred to as the *tonto* ("fool"). Not only does the *tonto* have to suffer this unflattering label, but he also is expected to tolerate the biting remarks of his drinking companions: "Man, if I were you, I'd really feel bad having to spend all that money"; "Well, looks like you're sixty *pesetas* poorer. Glad it's not me!"; "This wine sure tastes good, especially since I'm not the one who has to shell out the money for it. How does it taste to you [the victim]?" All of this, of course, is by way of *cachondeo*, though should the victim break out angrily he will be assured that it is all a mere joke, not to be taken seriously. His disintegration under pressure, however, serves to make him an unattractive drinking partner. Should he repeatedly blow up under these circumstances, he will be ostracized from the verbal and monetary exchanges that take place among men in bars. The ability to give and take abuse is therefore a prerequisite to the maintenance of normal social life in Monteros.

The Functions of Prank-playing

It is instructive, for the moment, to examine Monteros prank-playing in the light of Radcliffe-Brown's classic analysis of joking relationships:

> What is meant by the term "joking relationship" is a relation between two persons in which one is by custom permitted, and in some instances required, to make fun of the other, who in turn is required to take no offense. . . . The joking relationship is a peculiar combination of friendliness and antagonism. The behavior is such that in any other social context it would express and arouse hostility; but it is not meant seriously and must not be taken seriously. There is a pretense of hostility and a real friendliness (Radcliffe-Brown 1965, pp. 90–91).

The joking relationship, Radcliffe-Brown states, is one of "permitted disrespect" (ibid., p. 91). It arises, in particular, between individuals or groups (families, clans, etc.) who exist in a partly antagonistic, partly friendly relationship to one another. Joking incorporates the elements of "conjunction" and "disjunction" that characterize the relationship between these parties. The ability to tease and joke helps them cope with their ambivalent status.

Teasing, horseplay, and virtually all the varieties of pranksmanship that we have discussed fall under what Radcliffe-Brown would call "joking." Among the many issues that Radcliffe-Brown's seminal analysis raises, three seem most pertinent here: the social context of prank-playing or joking (which are, for purposes of this chapter, synonymous); the intentions of the actors in specific joking instances; and the social and psychological impact of joking on the participants. Let us discuss them in turn.

Radcliffe-Brown, like most of those who followed him with analyses of joking relationships in tribal societies (e.g., Christensen 1963; Colson 1962; Hammond 1964; and Rigby 1968), focused on the specific structural relationships between particular groups or individuals. The social context of prank-playing in Monteros is more diffuse in that it would be difficult to identify discrete parties—whether individuals or larger units—who have a special on-going bond of the type described by these authors. This much we can say, however: all men are ideally supposed to be able to joke, tease, and play pranks. They are seen as being much more prone to this type of activity, and in fact *are* more prone to it in general, than are women. There are some men who are known for being especially avid pranksters or for specializing in particular types of pranks: for example, greeting a buddy with a pinch in the ribs or tormenting the loser in a bar game. These people come to be known for their pranks, which seem to be appreciated with sincere affection as a source of humor or diversion. All men occasionally play pranks, and even those who do so only infrequently are required to accept them graciously. But there seem to be no specific partnerships, dyadic or otherwise, in Monteros prank-playing.

On the other hand, pranksmanship in Monteros is almost exclusively symmetrical in that the person who teases or plays a prank must expect similar treatment from his victim in the future. In Monteros, pranks tend to thrive among those who consider themselves equal, and they foster a sense of common membership in a particular social rank. Thus, in the words of Howell (1973, p. 7), acceptance of abuse becomes a "precondition of group membership." This does not mean that pranks never cross ethnic or social class boundaries, for they occasionally do. It simply means that if a man wishes to maintain a sense of distance from those he considers his inferiors, he will refrain from joking with or teasing them for he can only expect them to treat him similarly. Thus, in fact, people of the same status tend to be the ones who most frequently tease or play pranks on one another. In Monteros, there exists very little of what Zijderveld calls "joking-down" and "joking-up" (1968, p. 297), by which people of unequal status relieve tension with playful banter. Rather, one consequence of pranks in Monteros is to foster a sense of distinctiveness between those of different rank, who are unable to joke together.

There is only one exception to the overall social symmetry of pranksership in Monteros: the victimization of Gypsies. In chapter 4 we discussed the position of Gypsies in Andalusia. Here I simply wish to note that Castellanos seem to recognize few limits in the degree to which they inflict pranks on Gypsies without receiving equal treatment in return. To be sure, symmetrical joking between Gypsies and Castellanos occurs at the olive harvest where, as we shall see (chapter 8), there is a good deal of license and permitted disrespect between the sexes as well. But this is a special season during which normal relationships are temporarily suspended. In everyday town life, the joking between lower-class Castellanos and Gypsies is noticeably asymmetrical. I would attribute this asymmetry primarily to the infinitely sharp caste boundaries between Gypsies and Castellanos, particularly to the unthreatened superior status of the latter. Between the elite and the working class, who are becoming increasingly educated and prosperous, the dividing line is less discrete, but the traditional distance-maintaining mechanisms nevertheless remain in full force.

Let us now consider the specific intentions of Monteros pranksters. Certainly, as in all joking relationships, pranks in Monteros combine goodwill and antagonism, such that "there is a pretense of hostility and a real friendliness" (Radcliffe-Brown 1965, p. 90). In our town, as we have seen, it would perhaps be equally correct to say that pranks involve a pretense of friendliness and a real hostility. In the case of *cachondeos*, there is public recognition of the aggression behind an act. *Bromas* are perceived as being more purely friendly in tone, but even here it is clear that the friendliness is often obvious only to the perpetrator of a prank, not to the victim. And then, too, there exists the curious phenomenon of "retroactive joking," originally analyzed by Emerson (1969), in which a person denies the seriousness of a statement or action that has not been well received. In Monteros, a jokester may pass the bounds of acceptable teasing and then quickly withdraw in an attempt at appeasement by saying, "Don't take me seriously. It was only a *broma*." With this, he first relays the hostile message, then quickly denies it and covers it up. Both the flexibility of vocabulary referring to a prank and the utilization of recoil and denial techniques enable men to express their hostile message more frequently and more overtly than would otherwise be possible.

But why, we may legitimately ask, should men who are on basically friendly terms need an outlet for antagonism? There are several reasons, but perhaps most important is that Monteros men are constantly on their guard against deceit. Basically defensive in their posture, they at the same time have to assert themselves lest their opponents think them weak and vulnerable. Men must constantly demonstrate their potential for aggression, wherein lies the preservation of themselves and their families. To play a prank is to perform as a man should. The assertive action is a simple extension of masculine genital attributes. This is why pranks have to be reciprocated as well. They are received with goodwill because men understand, whether consciously or not, the inherent need for those of their sex to project and thrust through actions and words, as if these were metaphors for the male sexual role. To parry and not to give is to be weakened and feminized. One must always be ready to retort.

Then, of course, there are specific circumstances developing out of interpersonal relationships among men that impel them to express a veiled hostility toward one another. Perhaps most important in this regard are relations among business associates, competitors in the same line of work. A guild mentality prevails in Monteros in that people who share an occupation, even though they are economic competitors, are supposed to associate, assist one another, and maintain friendly relations. Storekeepers, butchers, and artisans bend over backwards to demonstrate their goodwill toward others in the same line of work. Nowhere is this custom better symbolized than in the expensive parties that people who enter a new business give for those already established in it. Naturally, the openly friendly relations among people in the same business are tinged with more than a bit of hostility. The undercurrent of aggression is released through pranks and joking.

Hostility also arises out of the potential loss of economic or social independence in a relationship. The economic system in Monteros is such that men are often required to labor under the order of those whom they themselves directed the month before. Within the working class itself, there is a constantly changing spectrum of economic alliances and patron-client relationships. In August, a small-scale sheep breeder may hire a shepherd. By December the shepherd, leading a work crew at the olive harvest, may sign on his former employer as one of the workers. In the winter, a mason may quit his job for more lucrative, if temporary, employment in the olive oil factory. By March, however, he needs the contacts of friends on construction crews to resume his normal work. Men, in other words, are forever dependent upon one another for work, and find themselves subordinate at every turn to those whom at other times of the year they were able to dominate. Economic pragmatism dictates that friendly relations be maintained with as many people as possible. The system, at odds with the high value placed on economic independence, breeds abiding resentments in those upon whom a man presently or in the future may need to rely. Harmless pranks are a safe manner of expressing these resentments.

Finally, the hostility inherent in close friendships needs a harmless means of release. Men in Monteros develop temporarily deep, though often fickle, loyalties to a few others with whom they spend great amounts of time daily. To my knowledge, Currier is the one scholar to have hit upon the time element critical in male friendships in southern Europe, and his description, derived from rural Greece, applies to Monteros as well: friends "are companions, yet however well they may know and trust one another, however closely their interests may coincide, and however long-standing their friendship, the basic feature of their relationship is the *time* they spend together" (Currier 1974, p. 148; italics in original). In Monteros, men demand an enormous amount of attention from friends in order to validate their relationships. If time is unavailable during the day, it must be granted in the evening. Aside from the demands of time, male friendships involve possessiveness and petty jealousies. Inevitably, as with the best-friend relationships of the teen-aged years in the United States, antagonisms and hostilities develop. Pranks, joking, and teasing pervade all of male culture in Monteros, but nowhere is this behavior more evident than between friends, whose ties depend upon these purportedly amicable, but simultaneously aggressive, mechanisms of release.

Riddles and Social Class

Riddling may be seen as a form of verbal chicanery in which the victim, or rather prospective victim, participates knowingly in his own demise. The listener wittingly exposes himself to possible—indeed probable—defeat. But at the same time he becomes an active participant in the verbal drama. He is, as Koestler says, "lifted out of his passive role and compelled to cooperate, to repeat to some extent the process of inventing . . . " (Koestler 1964, p. 86). To this important extent, the person who listens to a riddle differs from the unguarded and violated recipient of a prank. In riddling, the victim, merely by consenting to participate, shows himself to exert at least some degree of control over the situation.

Riddles have a more or less definite distribution within the Monteros population, a distribution that at first seems extraordinarily puzzling, dividing the populace by class as well as sex. Riddles show themselves to be a popular form of spontaneous verbal entertainment among men and women of the working class and women of the elite. There is a definite tendency for working-class men to tell riddles more than any other single group and for male members of the upper class virtually to refrain from riddling at all. There is a moderate amount of riddling among women of all social ranks, though, as I have said, it is more common among elite women.

I first received the clue to this distribution from a highly sophisticated, wealthy landowner, who omitted the sexual dimension but emphasized the fact that the uneducated segment of Monteros society knows and tells many more riddles than the educated segment. After thinking long and hard, in fact, he himself could come up with only a single riddle, and claimed that he had neither heard nor learned any while growing up. The reason, according to this informant, is that educated people have their "own knowledge"; they are free from reliance on the wisdom of the past or, for that matter, on pat, codified phrases of any type. Each educated person has his own ideas, which he elaborates in his own language. The uneducated masses, by contrast, have to rely on verbal play. This informant, consciously following Huizinga (1955, pp. 105–18), considered riddles to be *"una forma lúdica"* ("a play type") based on well-established, traditional items that do not require a creative mind.

This explanation perhaps reveals more about the informant and the attitudes of men of his class than about the distribution of riddling in Monteros. The phrasing of class divisions in terms of educational level, the exclusion of women from consideration, the interpretation of working-class people as basically uninventive—all of these show my informant to be a typical representative of his sex and socio-economic rank. Nonetheless, insofar as the men of Monteros are concerned, the informant's observations regarding the class distribution of riddling were borne out by my own field experience, and his analysis is at least partly correct.

One of the central features of riddles, as has been pointed out by various scholars already (Barrick 1974; Glazier and Glazier 1976, p. 199; Sutton-Smith 1976, p. 112), is the arbitrariness of the response. In Monteros, this is a component of virtually all riddles; however much the listener may guess, if he is not already familiar with the riddle, it is highly unlikely that he will respond correctly. The riddler, we may say, is accorded dictatorial authority to determine precisely what the answer should be. Nowhere is this better illustrated than in the following riddling sequence:

Riddler: *¿Donde tiene la mujer el pelo más rizado?*
            Where does woman have the most frizzy hair?

Riddlee: (tentatively):
            ¿En el coño?
            In the cunt?

Riddler: *No; en Filipinas. Bueno. ¿Puedes decir ahora donde lo tiene más rizado?*

No, in the Philippines. Good. Now can you say where she has it the most frizzy?

Riddlee: (definitively):
Claro, en Filipinas.

Of course, in the Philippines.

Riddler: *No. Donde antes me dijiste.*

No. Where you told me before.

Here, the riddler takes it upon himself to dictate a series of correct responses, in each instance declaring the riddlee wrong and determining in effect that the riddlee may never hope to guess correctly. There is good reason why Spanish riddles are called *acertijos*, from the verb *acertar*, "to guess." Guessing is all one can do; there is no hope for a rational solution to the verbal puzzle.

The above riddle also incorporates the folkloristic technique known as a "catch," in which the riddlee, convinced that he has been provided with the correct response, is caught off-guard and shown to be even less competent than he originally thought. The following riddle also employs this subtle type of verbal twist:

Riddler: *¿En qué se parecen una familia, un piloto, y un salvaje?*

How are a family, a pilot, and a savage alike?

Riddlee: *¿En qué?*

How?

                              pilot(e)a   (i.e., *en pelotas*)
Riddler: *En que el piloto pilota un avion y el salvaje va en pilota.*

In that the pilot flies a plane and a savage goes naked. [There is a clever use of language here, which is untranslatable into English.][4]

Riddlee: *¿Y la familia?*

And the family?

Riddler: *Muy bien, gracias.*

[They're] Very well, thanks.

---

[4]Folklorists will recognize this riddle as a "Spooneristic conundrum" (Brunvand 1968, p. 53).

In this sequence, the riddlee is made to believe that he has caught the riddler in an error, that is, not accounting for all elements in the puzzle. When he asks about the presumed flaw, however, he is given an appropriate, yet incongruous, response, showing that the riddler has kept the upper hand after all. Riddles are, in fact, a power struggle in which the riddler must and usually does maintain his superior position over the riddlee.

Now, if we recall the segments of Monteros that are most given to telling riddles—women and lower-class men—we can see immediately that these are the powerless elements of the society, the people who are either economically dependent or socially inferior. They are, in other words, unlike the Giants of chapter 2. It is natural that these people should choose a harmless way, like riddling, to assert control and domination, for to know the answer to a riddle is to have power. This analysis confirms Williams' contention that "riddling forms provide for situations of definition of social dominance and submission" and that riddling serves as a "rehearsal of dominance-submissive behavior forms" (Williams 1963, p. 104). To demonstrate this proposition, we only need cite the great sense of triumph and glee with which a Monteros riddlee occasionally responds by saying, "Oh, I already know that one, but you can go ahead and tell it anyway if you'd like." The riddlee, destined to be victimized, thereby deprives his questioner of the ability to dominate, and liberates himself, however momentarily, from the bondage of ignorance.[5]

Power that comes in the form of knowledge should make the riddle an especially attractive verbal device for women and members of the lower class, who without question share relative educational deprivation with respect to men of the elite. Women comprise the vast majority of illiterates in Monteros. Even women of the upper classes, knowledgeable as they are in literature and the arts, have until very recently rarely been given the opportunity for advanced formal education; the tutoring they received in piano playing and singing was considered more appropriate to their talents and expectable lifestyle. Among lower-class adults functional illiteracy is common. Until recently, again, child labor and restricted opportunities ensured that most working people would have to educate themselves if they were to be able to read and write at all.

---

[5]My analysis is consistent with Elli Maranda's contention about the distribution of riddles in Lau: "It is my impression that this art form is the 'underdog's channel' . . . utilized by those persons to whom other insitutionalized expression is denied: women, commoners, unmarried men, and children" (Maranda 1971, p. 58). Abrahams (1968, pp. 151–52) also perceives the role of riddles as an aggressive device.

Of course, members of the elite assert that until recently workers failed to manifest an interest in educating their children despite everpresent opportunities to become educated. Workers see the matter differently. Education, they claim, has been a tool for the maintenance of elite privileges and power. If workers tried to enroll their children in school, the children were denied entrance, or at the very least were discouraged from attending. Nowadays, workers point out, education is still not compulsory, which means that negligent parents are in effect permitted to condemn their children to a life of ignorance and dependency. Workers are fully cognizant of the power and personal independence that a good education accords, and are aware, too, of their own relative educational deprivation.

This situation perhaps accounts for the existence of riddles such as the ones below, which demonstrate familiarity with written language, a treasure in a semiliterate society.

1.   *En el medio del mar estoy*
     Sin ser de Dios ni del mundo
     Ni del infierno profundo,
     Y en todas partes estoy.

     I'm in the middle of the sea (*mar*)
     Without being of God or of the world
     Nor of the deep Hell,
     And I am in all parts (*partes*).

     Answer: the letter *a*.

2.   *Soy la redondez del mundo,*
     Sin mí no puede haber Dios,
     Papas y cardenales, sí,
     Pero pontífices, no.

     I am the roundness of the world,
     Without me, God couldn't be,
     Popes and cardinals, yes,
     But pontiffs, no [i.e., pontiffs could not be either].

     Answer: the letter *o*.

In each of the above riddles, the riddler offers no initial clue that the correct response is a letter. But in each case, too, comprehension of the answer requires a knowledge of Spanish spelling in order to determine in which of the riddle words the letter *a* or *o* appears. By telling these riddles, as much as by understanding them, a person is able to display a bit of linguistic mastery.

Uneducated people, for the most part, are not resigned to their lot. They resent the sophistication and greater literacy of the elite, especially because they recognize that this greater worldliness and knowledge confer material advantages and power. Riddling, I would suggest, provides a means for people to overcome briefly the powerlessness that comes from educational deficiency. It provides a temporary sense of domination and control over the world through just those techniques and skills in which people feel most wanting. If men riddle more than women—as is my definite impression—it is because the need to dominate and assert themselves is closely bound to their sense of masculinity. The discrepancy between ideal assertive behavior and actual subjugated position is, for them, greater than it is for women, who certainly feel the lack of control but who at the same time are not accorded much in any realm. To the contrary, as we shall see below, women are often victimized by male riddling, which becomes in a way a metaphor for male domination in other aspects of Monteros life.

Riddles as Sexual Aggression

In Monteros there exists an enormous variety of riddle types, but perhaps the single most common is what has come to be known as the pretended obscene riddle (Brunvand 1968, p. 52). Pretended obscene riddles are designed to evoke images of genitalia or sexual acts; the actual correct response, however, turns out to be a quite innocent object or action that suits the description in the riddle as well as does the obscene response. The riddle concerning frizzy hair in the Philippines, above, is only partly pretended obscene because one of the two correct answers is in reality a sexual image. With the true pretended obscene riddle, the correct answer is unambiguously innocent. This is important because it enables people to tell a riddle in mixed sexual company without appearing unseemly or indecent.

Both men and women know and tell pretended obscene riddles. There is a curious sexual distribution in the content of these riddles, however: men tend to tell riddles evoking male physical attributes, while women tell those concerning the female anatomy. In my collection, there are riddles from both men and women that raise the image of coitus.

From men, I have the following:

1. *De día colgado, de noche apretado.*

    By day hung, by night pressed tight.

    Answer: *La tranca de una puerta.*
    The cross-bar of a door.

2.   *Tan largo como un pragate* [i.e., *alpargate* or esparto-grass
      sandal] *y tiene pelos hasta el remate.*

      As long as a sandal, and it has hair up to the end.

      Answer: *El cepillo.*
            A brush.

3.   *Colorado le meto y colorado le saco.*

      I put it in red and I take it out red.

      Answer: *El pimiento.*
            The pepper.

4.   *Gordo lo tengo, más no quisiera,*
      Que entre las piernas no me cogiera.

      Fat I have it, more so I wouldn't want,
      For between my legs it wouldn't fit.

      Answer: *Un caballo.*
            A horse.

Now a few from women:

1.   *Bajé a la plaza,*
      Compré una moza,
      Le levanté la falda
      Y le ví la cosa.

      I went down to the market,
      I bought a young girl,
      I raised her skirt,
      And I saw her thing.

      Answer: *Una lechuga.*
            A head of lettuce [compared here to a young
            girl; the outer leaves are the skirt].

2.   *Entre dos paredes blancas*
      Hay una rosa amarilla,
      Y no la acierta
      Ni el rey de Sevilla.

      Between two white walls
      There's a yellow rose,
      And he will not guess it,
      Even the king of Seville.

      Answer: *Un huevo.*
            An egg.

3. *Ha venido un tío:*
    Me la ha metido,
    Me la ha sacado;
    Pídele a Dios
    Que me haga provecho.

    A chap came:
    He put it in me,
    He removed it from me;
    Ask God
    That he do well by me.

    Answer: *Un practicante pinchando.*
    A male nurse giving an injection.

What we are confronted with, it seems, is a situation in which men and women use riddles as a subtle means of displaying their own sexual organs. What psychological function can this serve? To explain the existence of pretended obscene riddles in Monteros, we should turn to Freud's analysis of "smut" (i.e., obscenity) in humor:

> We know what is meant by "smut": the intentional bringing into prominence of sexual facts and relations by speech. . . . It is a further relevant fact that smut is directed to a particular person, by whom one is sexually excited and who, on hearing it, is expected to become aware of the speaker's excitement and as a result to become sexually excited in turn. . . . Smut is thus originally directed towards women and may be equated with attempts at seduction (Freud 1960, p. 97).

Freud continues this analysis by pointing out the similarity between smut and exhibitionism: "By the utterance of the obscene words it compels the person who is assailed to imagine the part of the body or the procedure in question and shows her that the assailant is himself imagining it" (ibid., p. 98).

As we have already seen, under ordinary conditions in Monteros, there exists a strict avoidance of sexual topics between unrelated men and women; obscene words—excluding common swear words—are never uttered in mixed company. Pretended obscene riddles enable men, in essence, to expose their genitals verbally and to evoke images of the sexual act in the presence of women whom they covet but cannot otherwise take. In its mild form, it is a means of flirtation; when carried to excess, a form of verbal rape. For reasons we shall soon determine, pretended obscene riddles are commonly told at the olive harvest, the only occasion when women participate in riddling to the full degree that men do. Otherwise, women, especially elite women, merely use this folkloristic device as a means of expressing otherwise taboo desires and concepts while safely keeping this slight degree of licentiousness within the secret confines of their homes.

Pranks may be seen as a means for men to express aggression against members of their own sex, while pretended obscene riddles permit them to extend their sexual domination over women to those who are unrelated to them. Both pranks and riddles, however, operate to convey another message, which has been a primary theme in Spanish life and letters at least since the original issuance of *La Celestina* in the fifteenth century: appearances are deceiving; they do not represent reality. In pranks, a person is victimized essentially for being off his guard, for being too trusting of his physical and social milieu. In pretended obscene riddles, likewise, the riddlee is tricked into believing something to be correct that is incorrect; the accurate response is not at all what one imagines it to be. Pranks and riddles socialize people into a basically skeptical state of mind that, it is said, will serve them in more critical everyday affairs, particularly those dealing with the management of resources. No one, after all, wants to be like the bartender in the following popular joke:

> There was a man who went to a bar and asked for a brandy. When the bartender brought him the drink, the customer said, "Look, I've changed my mind, and if it's all the same with you and the price is the same, I think I'll have coffee instead." The bartender agreed, and brought the customer coffee. When the customer finished drinking it, he started to walk out without paying. Said the bartender, "Wait a minute. You haven't paid." "But I exchanged the brandy for the coffee," explained the customer. "But you didn't pay for the brandy either," protested the bartender. "Neither did I drink it!" retorted the customer. And with that he walked out of the bar.

The world in Monteros is conceived to be like this conversation; people taking advantage and slipping away unjustly through clever manipulation, verbal or otherwise. Pranks and riddles remind people to maintain their guard and prepare them for the numerous defeats, small and large, that life inevitably seems to bring.

Space and Speech at the Olive Harvest

Cogiendo la aceituna
se hacen las bodas;
la que no va de aceituna
no se enamora.
¡Qué tendrán, madre,
para cosas de amores
los olivares!

Picking olives
weddings are made;
she who doesn't go to the olive harvest
doesn't fall in love.
Oh mother, what the olive groves
can do for the things
of love!

> Traditional *sevillana* (flamenco song)

The Economic Importance of Olives

In Monteros, as throughout the entire province in which the town is situated, the economy depends almost exclusively on the collection and processing of olives. We have only to consider that of the approximately seven hundred thousand hectares of cultivated land in the province, five hundred thousand are devoted to olive groves (Instituto Nacional de Estadística 1972, p. 39). Among these groves, as Gerald Brenan has pointed out, "are to be found the largest and richest olive estates in the world" (Brenan 1964, p. 155). Nowhere else is there such an intense concentration and reliance on this crop. Even such people as bankers, bureaucrats, and shopkeepers are ultimately dependent on the vitality of the olive economy; not only do they service a populace that is overwhelmingly involved in rural agricultural pursuits, but in many cases they themselves also have some direct investment in olive production. Thus the character of economic and social life in Monteros is influenced enormously by the requirements of the extensive groves found in its vicinity.

The Spanish geographer Antonio Higueras Arnal has correctly noted that the technology of olive production is extremely simple, and that for most of the year the groves require very little attention (Higueras Arnal 1961, pp. 102–3). In the spring the trees are pruned and the land is fertilized and plowed. The pruning is a manual operation; the plowing and fertilization, accomplished simultaneously, are done by small tractors. Even for estates of one hundred hectares, these operations require the labor of only a handful of men. The same can be said of the insecticide spraying that takes place during the summer and of the plowing that occurs once again in the fall. Furthermore, olive trees, unlike the vast majority of fruit trees, virtually never need to be uprooted and replaced. If properly cared for, they will produce indefinitely, though of course yielding more in some years than in others.

Because of this relative paucity of agricultural activity, the casual observer can drive for dozens of miles through olive country without ever seeing a soul in the fields. To the untutored eye, it is an almost surrealistic experience to witness huge expanses of carefully plotted groves, imparting from the distance the impression of a vast, fluffy, polka-dotted quilt, but with nobody in sight nor any indication of who might be responsible for creating this supremely ordered landscape.

During only one brief but critical season does the scene change radically: from mid-December through mid-March, when the olives are black and ripe, the groves are filled with thousands of laborers working on the harvest. The harvest itself is called simply *la aceituna*—"the olive." And so important is this operation to the lives of the townspeople that the same word has come to be virtually synonymous with winter: "It gets very cold during the *aceituna*"; "we tend to go to bed early in the time of the *aceituna*." The olive harvest, requiring vast mobilization of the labor force, affects the life of the town profoundly.

Even today, when agriculture throughout Spain has become highly mechanized, the olive harvest requires huge teams of laborers. Large landowners, in whose hands most of the olive terrain is concentrated, have recently experimented with mechanical harvesters called *vibradoras* ("vibrators") because they embrace and shake the tree trunks, causing most (though not nearly all) of the olives to fall to the ground. One landowner who has been using such a machine over the course of a decade informs me that it reduces the number of laborers needed by more than half. But in Monteros, there are no more than five or six large landowners out of some forty or fifty who employ the vibrators. Not only are they very expensive, but also they are said to damage the roots of the trees unless they are run very lightly, in which case they perform inadequately.[1]

To date, then, there has been virtually no modernization of the most important agricultural task in Monteros. The olive harvest today remains in all essentials what it has been over the course of generations. Here is an anachronism in the annals of modern agriculture: highly concentrated land parcels, consisting of rich soil and yielding an immensely valuable crop, but without any sure means of replacing an age-old labor system.

It is only necessary to relate a few labor statistics to demonstrate how crucial olive agriculture in general, and the olive harvest in particular, is to the life of Monteros. In the 1975 census, out of a total population of 6,681 persons in the town proper (leaving aside the dispersed rural populace around it), 2,350 were listed as economically active. Of the latter group, 1,169, or almost precisely 50 percent, counted themselves as casual day laborers who work from one week to another at the jobs they can find without any employment security. An indeterminate though substantial number of others must also be placed in the same category. These are the townsmen who for reasons of status or self-image prefer to think of themselves as "farmers" (*labradores* or *agricultores*) rather than "day laborers" (*obreros eventuales*), even though they own only a few hectares of land and need to supplement this source of income with temporary wage labor.

All of these people—the officially as well as unofficially declared day laborers—participate in the olive harvest. Of equal importance, their wives and teenaged children in most cases also participate, despite the fact that these townspeople are almost without exception listed in the census as economically "inactive" (*inactivos*). In other words, the overwhelming majority of Monteros townspeople draw income directly from the collection of olives, and the harvest season is, in fact, the only time of year that these people can be certain of steady employment. The winter, then, is a time of hard work but substantial reward. It is the only period of real plenty in Monteros, a season when laborers and landowners alike benefit. In this sense, as in others, it is an extraordinary part of the year.

[1]In the olive harvest of 1976–77 a new, supposedly improved *vibradora*, imported from the United States, was introduced into Monteros by several innovative landowners. In one case, the work that in previous years took about seventy laborers to accomplish could be carried out with the vibrator and only twenty laborers. The vast majority of large landowners remain skeptical of the machine's economic value, however, and are especially fearful of the damage it might do to the trees. They say that they will wait a few years to observe its effects before using it on their own groves.

Space at the Harvest

We should term the olive harvest extraordinary not only for its economic importance but for its social and psychological significance as well. Like the pageant of Giants and Big-Heads, the harvest is an occasion when normal relations between the sexes and classes are both affirmed and symbolically reversed. Let us examine for a moment simply the spatial relations involved in the harvest to see how this can be so.

There is, to begin with, a reversal of the normal physical domains in which members of the various classes operate. Here we must introduce a distinction, common in Monteros as throughout the Hispanic world, between the *pueblo* and the *campo*.[2] The *pueblo* is the permanently populated residential center, replete with stores, schools, churches, and homes. The *campo*, on the other hand, refers to the vast tracts of agricultural land that, in Andalusia, also contain dispersed houses and farm buildings known as *cortijos*. The meaning of the term *cortijo* varies enormously from one part of Andalusia to another (see, for example, López Ontiveros 1974, pp. 490–544, and Rodríguez Becerra 1973, pp. 93–96), but in our region its strict contemporary usage refers to any house that is in the fields. Thus, a humble farmhouse with attached barn is as much a *cortijo* to the people of Monteros as is a sumptuous residential complex made up of a large elegant home and swimming pool, along with barns, sheds, and laborers' houses.

Throughout much of the year, from April through November, the *pueblo* teems with daytime activity. For such a small, rural town, there is a surprisingly heavy flow of traffic, enough, for example, to make it a constant source of anxiety for parents with small children. The stores and marketplace are filled with customers, as are the six banks and more than thirty bars. One always leaves one's

[2]David Gilmore, in a recent valuable article on "The social organization of space" (1977), explores what we might call horizontal spatial divisions within the Sevillian town of Fuenmayor. In distinguishing between the *pueblo* and the *campo*, I am also discussing a horizontal spatial division, though the major portion of my spatial analysis, as we shall presently observe, concerns vertical spatial divisions.

In the above-mentioned article, Gilmore discusses the term *campiña*, which in Monteros, as in Seville, means "a specific type of flat, treeless terrain devoted exclusively to large-scale dry-farming and perhaps olives" (Gilmore 1977, p. 438). In Monteros of course, most of the campiña is not treeless, but is devoted to olive cultivation. But, too, in Monteros the term *campo* is more all-embracing than is *campiña*, which is utilized more pointedly in opposition to the term *sierra*, or mountains. When distinguishing between the town itself and the countryside, the term *campo* is more likely to be articulated.

house with the expectation of encountering a myriad of friends and acquaintances, people who have taken to the street for business or relaxation. The only possible exception is the late afternoon siesta in summer; but during this season the outdoor bustle lasts until 11:30 P.M. or midnight, as if the townspeople were trying to compensate for lost hours of sociability earlier in the day. All this activity comprises the *ambiente*, the lively atmosphere, that the people of Monteros, like those elsewhere in Andalusia (Gilmore 1977, p. 448), cherish dearly and strive to preserve.

In the winter during the olive harvest the rhythm of activity in the *pueblo* completely changes. Families rise early, while it is still dark, and congregate at the edge of town, where trucks and vans pick them up to transport them to the fields. By eight, fires are lit in the groves as people gather round to eat the breakfasts they have brought with them. Work hours at the harvest are fixed by the national government: from 9:00 A.M. to 5:00 P.M. with an hour's break for lunch. During all this time, it is the *campo* that bursts with activity, while the *pueblo* is comparatively deserted. Most of the people who remain in town—shopkeepers, bureaucrats, and small schoolchildren—conduct their affairs indoors. The moribund at-

A Gypsy boy sings during a work break at the olive harvest.

Man wielding the vara.

mosphere perks up in the early evening as workers return in droves from the fields, but it soon dies down again. People are tired, the air is cold, and there is need to recuperate for the start of a new work-day in the morning.

Until about 1960, workers not only commuted to the fields dur-ing the olive harvest but sometimes actually slept and lived at the farms. Most of the groves are located far from the *pueblo*, some as much as ten or twelve miles away, requiring a one- or two-hour journey by foot in each direction. When there were few vehicles to transport workers, the men and women would sleep at the *cortijos* on straw mattresses in long communal rooms with fireplaces that could be used for cooking and heating. Traces of this system still exist. Throughout the countryside there are still *cortijos* that are temporarily inhabited by migrant workers who come to Monteros from poorer regions to participate in the harvest.

Overall, then, the workers' principal domain in winter is the *campo*. It is the large landowners who populate this domain in sum-mer, however. The wealthiest Monteros families maintain several residences, including a townhouse in Monteros itself, a manor house at the *cortijo*, and apartments or homes in one or more cities like Granada and Madrid. During the winter, hired estate ad-ministrators conduct most of the business, but should the owners themselves want to be on hand to witness the harvest in progress, they tend to stay in the comfort of their townhouses and make just an occasional jaunt to the *campo*. In summer, on the other hand, the manor houses become pleasant country homes where these elite families, usually attended by servants, can swim and relax and escape the stifling heat that most of Andalusia experiences during that part of the year. A quick automobile ride allows them the op-portunity to share in town social life whenever they wish.

Still, because these wealthy elite are few in number and the working class many, the dominant impression is that the town populace as a whole moves out to the *campo* in winter and returns to its normal urban milieu for the rest of the year. The olive harvest, in this respect, creates a reversal of ordinary spatial relations, a rever-sal that, as we shall soon see, influences the tempo of sexual life as well.

Let us now turn to some aspects of spatial relations during the harvest itself. Olives are collected by work teams, which vary in size but average perhaps six to eight people per tree. Men and women work side by side, but a strict division of labor by sex has been main-tained as long as anyone can remember. Men wield long poles called *varas*, which are about six or seven feet long and are used to knock and shake the branches so that the olives are disengaged from the tree and fall. To hit the lowest branches, the men simply stand on the ground, but to reach those above they have to climb the tree and wield the *vara* from there. Meanwhile, huge drop cloths (*mantones*), traditionally made of burlap but now more commonly of nylon, are placed underneath the tree to catch the olives. It has been found too impractical or expensive to cover the entire area, and so the thousands upon thousands of olives that escape the ground coverings have to be collected by hand. This is the job of the women, who throughout the long days of the harvest remain on hands and knees, picking up olives, placing them in baskets, and transferring them finally to large burlap sacks. Whether standing on the ground or sitting on the branch of an olive tree, men are invariably situated at a markedly higher level than women, who during most of the harvest remain crouched below.

What can be the justification for such a division of labor? With one exception, to be related presently, informants themselves cannot answer this question. Some people claim that men are better at wielding the *vara* than women, but most simply attribute the work

Women collecting olives.

methods to custom. Superior physical strength is certainly not at issue, for the goal is not to hit the branches as hard as possible; they have to be tapped with just the right amount of moderated force so that the olives will be disengaged from the tree without causing any permanent damage to it. Nor is skill, passed on from father to son or mother to daughter, at all involved. In a decade of studying rural life among Hispanic peoples, harvesting olives is the only major agricultural task I have ever witnessed that requires virtually no training. With a quarter of an hour's practice, any untutored individual can pick olives off the ground or wield the *vara* as well as most people who have been carrying out these tasks every winter for fifteen years. In fact, in the 1975 harvest there was such a serious labor shortage that for the first time in memory a few women had to take the poles. When I visited the one work team in which this occurred, the women seemed embarrassed and shy at their public performance of a traditionally male role. Yet everyone had to agree that they performed the task "as well as or better than" the men.

I have been unsuccessful at tracing the historical antecedents of this curious division of labor, and I imagine that no single cause is responsible for its emergence. However, I can relate a four-part explanation spontaneously offered by a sophisticated, well-educated young landowner, who sums up his opinion by tracing the system to Andalusia's Moorish past.[3] His testimony constitutes the closest I have come to what Victor Turner (1967, p. 50) would term the exegetical aspect of harvest symbolism.

First, this landowner claims that traditionally, when women never wore pants, rules of modesty prevented their being situated in the branches, where men could leer at them. This reasoning, to be sure, reveals my informant's preoccupations with female anatomy though it must be dismissed as inaccurate. Everybody else assures me that since well before the Civil War of 1936–39, women olive pickers wore trousers under their skirts, just as they do today.

His second explanation is that collecting olives off the ground is analagous to sweeping and housecleaning, which are purely a woman's domain. In fact, there are some women's household tasks

---

[3]Certainly, sex roles and relationships in Islamic society, both historically (see, e.g., Guichard 1976, pp. 105–240) and contemporaneously (Dwyer 1978; Mernissi 1975), bear close resemblance to those in Monteros and southern Europe generally. Without going into the matter fully, I wish merely to say that I find it difficult to attribute contemporary European male-female dynamics simply to prior contact with Arabic civilization.

in Monteros that men will engage in though, significantly, cleaning the floor is not one of them. At a party that my wife and I once hosted, I automatically bent down to remove an olive pit that I had just accidentally dropped to the floor. The men around me were aghast that I should deign to engage in such a feminine activity, and warned me against ever doing so in public again, lest my reputation be permanently damaged. With this type of strict enforcement of the norm, it is likely that there exists among most olive harvesters an unconscious association between picking olives off the ground and cleaning the floor of a house. Both activities are clearly more appropriate for women than for men.

The third notion is that women in Monteros are considered to be morally of a lower order than men and therefore are situated in the lower position during the harvest. In this town, as we saw in chapter 5, women are associated with the Devil, men with God. It is believed that women are potentially more disruptive of the social order than men and therefore must be kept under tight control. Their intrinsically reduced value as human beings also presumably determines that they should earn relatively meager wages. In 1924, a man was paid 1.5 *pesetas* a day for the olive harvest (the equivalent today of about two cents) in contrast to a woman's 1 *peseta*. From that time until 1975, when men got 435 *pesetas* a day as compared with 405 for women, there has always been unequal remuneration by sex. There *has* been a steady trend toward equal compensation since the 1920s, but this trend reflects developments at the national level (the government establishes rates of pay at the olive harvest) more than it does local conditions and ideology. Male economic dominance is consonant with the alleged moral superiority of men, and both principles find expression in the harvest division of labor.

Finally, my informant points to the fact that the harvesting activity is a metaphor for sexual intercourse. The *vara*, he says, is both shaped like the phallus and wielded by men. In addition, men hover over women at the harvest in a spatial relationship analogous to that which exists during what is considered to be the only normal, healthy way to carry out sexual activity. Men drop the olives, or seeds, down onto the women, who collect them and place them into hollow, rounded receptacles—*sacos*, or "bags"—thus fulfilling a similar role to the one they play in the childbearing process.

There is no direct evidence to confirm this fourth interpretation, though it is curious that the expression *tomar por saco* ("take [it] by the bag [or sack]") is used euphemistically to mean *tomar por culo* ("take [it] by the ass"), which are common expletives and insults. Apparently, bags and sacks are thought of metaphorically as sexual receptacles. In the collection of olives, agricultural technology mirrors sexual technique.

Sexual Norms at the Harvest

The analogy between the olive harvest and the sexual act does not seem quite as farfetched as it might at first if we consider that the harvest in Monteros is a period of intense sexual awareness, sensitivity, arousal, and frustration. It is without question the most sexually charged public occasion of the year, which is why one landowner calls it a *"vacación sexual"*—a "sexual vacation." When I asked one of the town intellectuals, a different man from the one cited above, why there should be such a heightened atmosphere of sexuality during the harvest, he answered automatically, as if he had already thought about the matter a good deal. "It is at this time," he said, "that people are close to the land; and the land is fecund. It is, after all, a harvest, and harvests have always been associated with Dionysian acts and fantasies. This is a strictly Jungian interpretation. Why don't you think about it?"

This is the closest that I have been able to come to what we might term a native or emic interpretation of the harvest, for even though this informant lives off his rents and does not himself participate in olive collection, he has resided in Monteros all his life and has been a long-term student of the town's history and culture. Certainly none of the olive collectors has been able to provide me with any alternative explanation.

Of course, the conditions under which the harvest is carried out are conducive to the production of sexual innuendoes and bawdy behavior. Townspeople are, as we have seen, uprooted from their normal spatial domain, the *pueblo*, within whose boundaries the rules of social intercourse are clearly delineated. These rules, among other things, prohibit all but the most cursory contact between unrelated adult men and women. Yet the olive harvest necessitates extensive and continuous interaction between people of the two sexes. The harvest places men and women who merely greet one another on the street with a courteous "Adios"—if that much—in close contact with one another. It thereby affords the opportunity for the open expression of sexual fantasies. Just as townspeople are uprooted from their usual *pueblo* milieu during the harvest, so too are the rules of interaction between men and women temporarily suspended.

The only reason the rules can be reversed is that members of each work team—called the *cuadrilla*—establish a small action set of their own that lasts for the two or three months that these men and women are thrust into one another's presence. *Cuadrillas* vary in size; a small one consists of fifteen or twenty workers, a large one of thirty or forty. These people accompany one another from morning until evening every day that the weather permits; there are no holidays or festivals during this economically critical segment of the year. Most of the workers find themselves separated from relatives, friends, and everyday work associates. *Cuadrilla* members, wrenched out of their usual *pueblo* context, find themselves relatively free from the pressures of the public eye.

Equally important, members of the *cuadrilla* are chosen arbitrarily, with no consideration for their personal attributes (other than their ability to do the job, which, as we have noted, is the greatest equalizer of all). They therefore have no permanent stake in developing ongoing relationships. The *cuadrilla* is a kind of safety valve. Its impermanence, and the total lack of long-range commitment between its members, ensures that its members can display extraordinary behavior without fear of serious threat to reputation or status within the *pueblo*.

Workers are reminded of the impermanence of the *cuadrilla* every day as they move across distinct spatial and temporal boundaries. Each morning, it is enough for men and women merely to mount the vans and trucks that transport them to the fields to assume an altered social identity as members of a work team. Literally, once their feet cease to touch *pueblo* territory, they become subject to a different, less sexually restrictive, set of rules. The normal constraints are severe enough, I might add, that this apparent haste and eagerness for escape are entirely understandable. By the same token, with the descent from the vehicles at the town's edge each evening, workers fall once again into ordinary social relationships; bawdy behavior and sexual innuendoes immediately cease, and men and women resume their usual social distance and formality. As one informant stated, "We can kid around (*gastar bromas*) at the olive harvest (*a la aceituna*). But just watch us in town! There's none of that. A simple 'Adios' and that's it." Just as the Big-Heads of chapter 2 serve as symbols of emotional abandon and release, so the olive harvest permits nonconformity to the usual social codes and becomes the arena for the expression of otherwise prohibited behavior. At the olive harvest, townspeople actually become partially transformed into Big-Heads. They not only observe a social drama but also participate in it.

Speech and Sex during the Harvest

Let us now examine some examples of the way people act during the olive harvest. This behavior can be divided into three categories: traditional exclamations and other spontaneous utterances spoken by a single individual; sexually provocative banter between a particular man and woman; and group-organized bawdy events, which are named, predictable features of the harvest. In all these instances, both actors and audience can be identified. Men and women participate in a social drama, knowing full well that they are being observed by coworkers who derive vicarious pleasure and release from the show.

Structurally the simplest category of behavior is the first one, the exclamations and casual utterances. The remarks themselves are not unusual; in fact, they can be heard daily within the *pueblo* during any season of the year. The notable thing about them, however, is that they emerge during the olive harvest in mixed company, among unrelated men and women, whereas ordinarily they would be confined to the family circle or to sex-exclusive groups. On one occasion, for example, a man climbing an olive tree had his hand pierced by a long sliver. Rather than controlling his response, as he certainly would have in the presence of women back in town, he shouted "*¡Me cago en la Madre! ¡Me cago en la Virgen!*" ("I shit on the Mother! I shit on the Virgin!") The usual restrictions on these common expletives are unenforced during the olive harvest.

For this reason, too, a Gypsy who had been ordered by his doctor to take pills daily at lunchtime could shout out, in mixed company, that the pills were *pastillas follarinas*—"fucking pills." The other men of the *cuadrilla*, taking this to mean that the pills were aphrodisiacs, every day would ask the Gypsy loudly in joking spirit to give them some of his "fucking pills." The language, and the ideas behind it, are ordinarily taboo when both men and women are present.

On one occasion, at 5:00 P.M. as the workers were waiting for the van to take them home, a thirty-nine-year-old married woman began wiggling her torso and shoulders provocatively and singing, "*Aquí lo tienes, aquí lo tienes*" ("Here you have it, here you have it"), and then immediately switched the movement to her hips, chanting "*Y dice el zagal, 'Ayí lo voy, ayí lo voy'* " ("And the young guy says, 'There I'm going for it, there I'm going for it' "). She began her singing in a hushed voice, as if merely to entertain herself and pass the time until the van showed up. Soon, however, she realized that she was diverting everyone standing nearby her as well, which was no doubt her original intention, and she began to repeat the song with louder voice and more vigorous movement. Two or three other women, seeing the favorable reaction of the group, joined in, so that the first woman's supposedly casual, unselfconscious attempt to divert herself turned into an intentional joking episode. For women to act this way in their own company is not unusual. To do so in front of men, and with no apparent negative reactions, is unheard of except at the olive harvest.

Virtually anyone at the harvest is likely to come out with these kinds of exclamations and casual utterances. Certainly, even if a person is too inhibited to speak in this manner in front of members of the opposite sex, he or she will still relish the act and become a willing part of the audience. Except under the specified circumstances discussed below, I never became aware of prudish criticism of this type of behavior or of withdrawal from the scene when confronted with bawdiness. The olive harvest, I would contend, exists as much to provide a release from inhibitions as it does to collect olives.

The second type of behavior, sexually provocative banter, occurs among fixed pairs of unrelated men and women who are obviously sexually attracted to one another and use the occasion of the olive harvest for the public expression of unfulfilled fantasies. The audience, that is, the coworkers who happen to be within listening distance, follow the verbal affair—which is the best way to describe it—closely, derive pleasure from it, and speculate among themselves in private as to where it might lead. Here is a typical interchange between a man and woman, both married and in their thirties, who early in the season established a joking relationship and maintained it for the duration of their *cuadrilla*'s existence.

Woman: What are you in the mood to eat?

Man: Watermelon.

Woman: (licking her lips) A watermelon opened up and juicy!

Man: And what are you in the mood to eat?

          (There is a thirty-second pause, while the woman thinks how to respond.)

Woman: A banana. As dessert!

Man: How do you prefer banana? To start a meal or as dessert?

Woman: I like it any way! To start a meal—as dessert—whenever!

It is impossible to believe that this conversation had any other than a sexual meaning. Immediately preceding it, the woman had been relating the tale of a man who chased after his neighbor's wife for months on end until she finally capitulated to his desires. When they got into bed, however, the man proved impotent and the neighbor's wife was furious. To this tale, the narrator's joking partner responded by saying, "No one has to worry about me, baby! I'm always ready!" In Monteros, as we have had ample occasion to demonstrate, sex is an everpresent object of concern, not to say obsession, and people employ liberal doses of genital symbolism along the Freudian model. The people in Monteros immediately understand why a woman should desire a banana and a man a watermelon. It is only under special circumstances such as the olive harvest, however, that this type of symbolism is used openly in mixed company.

Not only is this symbolism an expression of sexual fantasy but it is also employed consciously as a mechanism of arousal—a form of verbal rape, if you will. I have no information about the private thoughts of the women engaged in these joking relationships, but I know that the men harbor plans of secretly consummating their verbal affairs, and toward this end, try to inject a sexual meaning into even the most innocuous conversation so that their intention is clear. It even happens when a *cuadrilla* first forms that two men, both attracted to the same women, will compete to establish a joking relationship with her, with the ostensible goal of sexual union. The men vie with each other, boasting between themselves when out of earshot of the woman about their plans for sexual conquest. Within a few weeks one man emerges as clear victor, as evidenced by the woman's greater willingness to banter with him, and thereafter he has her to himself. I have never witnessed the inverse process—that is, several women competing for the sexual attentions of one man—at least in public as at the fields. True, the olive harvest entails a suspension of normal sex-role behavior. But there are always ways in which the ordinary rules impinge.

Before examining such impingement, however, let us turn to group-organized bawdy events that occur during the olive harvest. In the previous two categories of behavior—dropped remarks and sexually provocative banter—there is no exclusiveness by sex. Men probably engage in these speech forms more frequently then women, though people of both sexes are capable of making these utterances without fear of criticism. In the group-organized events, on the other hand, the actors are *either* men *or* women, depending on the type of event. Nonetheless, on all such occasions both men and women are present for the performance.

Women, for example, often chant in unison short, sexually charged verses (of the type known as *coplas* in Spanish) as they ride back and forth between town and the groves. Brunvand (1968, p. 52) would say that most of these verses are of a "pretended obscene" character, while Hullum (1972–73) would term them "catches"; in any event, they are designed in their initial lines to impart a sexual meaning, but conclude with disillusioning images that negate the original impression. One, for example, begins as follows:

Una vieja y un viejo van pa' Albacete,

An old woman and an old man are going to Albacete,

Por el medio del camino va y se la mete.

In the middle of the road he goes and puts it in her.

The next to the last word of the verse, the direct object *la*, is feminine in gender, as are the most common terms used in Monteros to refer to the penis (*chorra, polla, minda, pitusa,* and others). The unmistakable impression is that on the road to Albacete the old man sticks his penis into the old woman. But immediately following this verse, the chanting women add:

La manito en el bolso,

His hand in his pocket,

Le saca el billete.

And takes money out of it.

We are now informed that the direct object *la* in the original lines refers not to the old man's sexual organ, but to his hand, which he uses for the perfectly innocent purpose of taking money out of his pocket.

The same ruse is used in the following, shorter verse:

Una niña en un baile se la chupaba,

A girl at a dance sucked it for him,

Caramelos de menta que le gustaba.

Mint candies that she liked.

Again, as in the previous verse, the direct object *la* refers initially to the penis, but later to mints, a much more acceptable item for a girl to suck.

This is not to say that the chanting women always hide behind catches of this type. There are also verses in which obscenities are stated outright, among them the following:

1. *Cuando viaja Sancho Panza necesita dos cajones,*
   When Sancho Panza travels he needs two boxes,

   Uno para su equipaje y el otro para sus cojones.
   One for his luggage and the other for his balls.

2. *Cuando viaja Lola Flores necesita dos maletas*
   When Lola Flores travels she needs two suitcases

   Una para su equipaje y la otra para llevar las tetas.
   One for her luggage and the other to carry her tits.

3. *Las chicas de* [Monteros] *no se bañan en la piscina*
   The young girls of Monteros don't swim in the pool

   Porque dicen que allí hay unas pijas submarinas.
   Because they say that there they'll find underwater pricks.

It is interesting to note that verses 1 and 2 above both concern trips, and that it is actually while the women are traveling that these verses are chanted. At least from a structural point of view, we may thus assume that the women identify themselves with Lola Flores in verse 2, and the men in their midst with Sancho Panza in verse 1.

While traveling to and from the fields women chant these *coplas*, and similar ones over and over, giggling madly after each one as if it were the first time they had heard it. The scene demonstrates, among other things, that humor does not necessarily draw its power "from being new and rare," as Zijderveld contends (1968, p. 291). Men who are present also laugh and enjoy the *coplas*, but I have the impression that the women sing mainly for themselves and derive a sense of excitement and pleasure at being able, in the presence of men, openly to conjure otherwise forbidden images.

A much less common, though at least as highly charged, event is known as *hacer las facas del rey*, or "making the king's sabers." Workers use the expression without knowledge of its derivation or even of what the term *faca* ("saber") means.[4] Here, the participants

---

[4] As early as 1919, in the fifth edition of *The Interpretation of Dreams*, Freud expressed the idea that sabers and other similarly shaped tools can be employed unconsciously as phallic symbols (Freud 1965, p. 391). I have no doubt that the *faca* was

are male, though the audience is, as always at the olive harvest,
mixed. This event occurs sporadically and spontaneously, and so it is
impossible to plan on witnessing it; in fact I was absent from the
fields on the few occasions when I might have seen it carried out. It
is possible, however, that my presence would have altered the
nature of the event and that in any case I would have had to rely on
verbal testimony. I shall relate one incident in a *cuadrilla* of about
thirty workers that I followed closely and knew well.

It was about ten days before the termination of the olive harvest
at a particular estate. The time was about 1:45 P.M., nearing the end
of the hour-long lunch break when all the workers gather in small
groups to sit around the fire and eat. At that time it occurred to
Miguel, a thirty-nine-year-old married man, to *hacer las facas del
rey* on Federico, who is also married, in his early fifties, and happened to be officially appointed leader of the work team. *Hacer las
facas del rey* begins when one man spontaneously tries to humiliate
another. The goal is to pin the victim to the floor, remove his pants
and undershorts, and then toss water and dirt on his crotch so that it
turns into a unpleasant, muddy mess. The person who gets the idea
is usually aided by two or three other men sympathetic to his cause.

On this occasion, Miguel called out to Federico, "I'm going to
hacer las facas del rey on you!" to which Federico good-naturedly
replied, "Fine, come on and get me!" Miguel and two other men in
the group immediately ran over to him, tossed him on the ground,
and began to remove his pants. At this point, Federico panicked at
the thought of public humiliation and begged his attackers to leave
him alone. He cried out, according to reports, until he was nearly in
tears. Miguel and the others let him go, not because he protested,
they said; the protest is normal for all men under attack. Rather,
they released Federico because his daughter was present, working at
the olive harvest that day, and it would have been unseemly for her
to observe him naked. Even in the midst of siege, the men recognized the validity of Federico's appeal and let him go.

Miguel then immediately turned on a twenty-year-old unmarried Gypsy, whom he knew was without relatives in the fields on that
occasion. The two fought it out until Miguel pinned the young man
to the ground. (This is the usual course of events, I am told. The
challenger and his victim wrestle until one overcomes the other. The
loser, of course, is subjected to the full, humiliating treatment.)
Once Miguel had the Gypsy under control, he was again joined by

---

somehow linked in the popular mind with the penis and that therein lies the origin of
the term *hacer las facas del rey*, though I am afraid that speculation at this point as to
the precise nature of the conceptual link could only be farfetched. I repeat, most people in Monteros do not even know the meaning of the term *faca*.

several other men who helped him disrobe the Gypsy and cover him with mud.

Later, at the end of that workday, I am told, Miguel lay down to rest while waiting for the van and fell asleep. The young Gypsy wanted to take reprisal and do the same to Miguel, but it was pointed out that to *hacer las facas del rey* while a person is asleep is unfair. The Gypsy agreed to wait for another occasion, one that, fortunately for Miguel, did not arrive. The olive harvest ended and that *cuadrilla* disbanded before the young man worked up the courage to challenge him to a fight again.

We have here what is for several reasons an extraordinary event. First, in a society in which extreme modesty is the norm, there is a male genital display in mixed company. According to all reports, women do not attempt to hide their heads in embarrassment at the event, but are fully part of the audience, and laugh and join in with the excitement as wholeheartedly as do the men. Second, the sexual competition that—as we shall see—is such an important part of male relationships in Monteros receives on this occasion exaggerated expression. To *hacer las facas del rey* is literally to obliterate the genitals of one's masculine opponent by covering them with mud. The aggressor attacks not the whole person, only the genitals—the repository of maleness. To eliminate a man's genitals symbolically is to emasculate him and thereby to emphasize one's own comparative potency.

The event, from this perspective, can be seen as a performance of projected male wishes and concerns. At the same time, to *hacer las facas del rey* is actually to reveal male organs to women observers, something that the men can usually accomplish during the olive harvest only through verbal imagery. The performance thus reassures men of their own masculinity and impresses this quality upon the women without ever requiring the aggressors in the show to disrobe and violate norms of modesty. In fact, the only person who is disrobed becomes emasculated as the attackers proceed to cover his genital region with mud. For men who speak often about conquering women and who worry as well about the size of their sexual organs, the display must provide a good deal of temporary comfort and reassurance. It also undoubtedly operates as a safe means to express aggression against a symbolic male competitor.

The Impingement of Daily Norms

I have spoken until now as if behavior at the olive harvest represented a more or less complete break with behavior in town. This, of course, is an oversimplification in order to emphasize the truly extraordinary nature of speech and action within the *cuadrillas*. In reality, there is an interchange of influences, such that the norms of the wider society impinge on behavior in the fields, just as behavior in the fields inevitably has consequences for the way people treat one another back in town.

We have already seen how Federico panicked at the prospect of being disrobed in front of his daughter. Whenever children and parents of the opposite sex are present and within hearing distance in the fields, an attempt is usually made to avoid sexual topics of conversation lest these relatives be embarrassed and their usual distance and respect with regard to such matters be undermined. Women and their daughters can chant bawdy songs together as long as the men in their family are not present. With the husband or son on the scene, standards change abruptly; the atmosphere becomes much more proper and formal. One woman, in fact, was extremely upset because men were speculating in front of her son about an affair she might have been having with her olive harvest joking partner. This was an inexcusable breach of social rules, causing her deep humiliation. No matter what the occasion, family solidarity, morality, and reputation must be maintained at all costs, and this woman's casual, quite harmless behavior within the *cuadrilla* had threatened her position in her own family and, with it, her family's position in society at large.

Just as outside morality impinges on standards at the olive harvest, so too behavior at the olive harvest influences how people act toward one another within the *pueblo* context. Joking partners, for example, make more than the ordinary attempt to avoid one another back in town, lest their reputations be adversely affected. I know one couple who have maintained an ongoing joking relationship within the same *cuadrilla* for several consecutive years, and yet refuse to attend dances or social gatherings if the other is to be present or even to greet one another on the street. Wives and husbands of joking partners usually find out about the spouse's relationship; this causes husbands to threaten a fight with their competitors, and wives openly to chide their husbands about the new romance. Once joking partners realize that knowledge of their relationship has invaded the *pueblo* domain, they are usually forestalled from engaging in a clandestine affair that could only, with time, bring shame upon them and their families.

Always, then, the domain of the olive harvest and that of the *pueblo* come into at least limited contact, and standards and behavior appropriate to one arena influence those in the other. Nonetheless, the standards and social atmosphere in each domain

are sufficiently distinct that they can cause embarrassment and conflict whenever the domains overlap. The olive harvest, more than
any other major event, provides men and women who normally
have to be on their guard the opportunity for open expression of
mutual sexual fantasies and concerns. It is a time of release from the
ordinarily severe restrictions of daily life.

Skits and Society

9

Dramatic action and social action face each other like mirrors across a hall. The dramatic arts employ social realities to gain admittance to the kitchen of consciousness. Social arts use dramatic action to explore the perimeters of the possible.

> Henry Glassie,
> *All Silver and No Brass* (1975)

We have already observed through the analysis of Giants and Big-Heads as well as of speech that Monteros men are concerned about domination and control by individuals or events over which they have no influence. If we could isolate one fear common to all segments of Monteros society, it would be the fear of victimization, of being placed at the mercy and whim of others and thereby losing personal autonomy. There are, of course, any number of potential sources for the violation of personal autonomy, among them economic exploitation and political domination. The working people of Monteros are acutely aware of their economic and political impotence, an awareness based on the realities of forty years of oppressive dictatorship. What they instead concentrate on preserving is their personal pride and dignity. Any personal affront immediately transforms an individual into a victim. To be pitied or scorned or laughed at—these are the forms of domination that have to be avoided at all cost.

In Monteros, there are two basic mechanisms of self-protection against pity and ridicule. The first is never to reveal anything important. *"La última verdad nunca se dice a nadie"* ("You should never tell the ultimate truth to anybody"), cautions a well-known saying. Each person, it is believed, is composed of a central core of critical thoughts and experiences. To expose these to anyone, even to a close friend or spouse, is to lay oneself open to possible victimization by providing others with knowledge that can be exploited to their own personal advantage. *"A mal tiempo buena cara"* ("In bad times [keep a] good face"), instructs another common proverb. The good face should be maintained not, as we might think, merely out of a stoic ability to keep our worries to ourselves. Rather, it is a defensive device, a way to prevent people from discovering our problems, lest they use them against us or cite them in a celebration of our misfortune. Pride, dignity, and personal autonomy are therefore maintained in part through simulation and disguise. Everyone tries to present a favorable facade, and assumes that all others do likewise.

The second defensive mechanism is to attack rather than wait to be attacked, to victimize rather than allow oneself to be the victim. In the analysis of the olive harvest, we saw how one man can be overcome and publicly humiliated by others when they decide spontaneously to *hacer las facas del rey*. This act operates not only as a projection of unconscious sexual desires and concerns but also as an expression of the issue of domination and control in Monteros society. Here, as in other aspects of town culture, people who are acutely aware of their economic and political subordination easily adopt the role of aggressor when afforded the opportunity. In Monteros, to subordinate another is to elevate oneself. What occurs when men *hacer las facas del rey* is an extreme, but typical, example of the types of pranks through which people daily try to maintain and increase their personal autonomy and integrity. These same themes of domination, victimization, and personal control are nowhere better encapsulated than in the realm of folk drama, to which we turn in this chapter.

The Skits

In Monteros, as throughout Andalusia, festive occasions were traditionally accompanied by brief skits, known as *juegos de cortijo* ("farmhouse games") or simply, as in Monteros, *los juegos* ("the games"). These skits were performed exclusively by and for the poorly educated, working-class people of Monteros. Whenever there was a joyful gathering, whether for a baptism, a wedding, or the annual family pig slaughter, skits were spontaneously organized. Though never planned or rehearsed, they were nonetheless an in-

tegral, eagerly anticipated part of the event. They were also regularly performed on the final day of the olive harvest, when the
employer would provide food and drink for a celebration known as
the *botijuela*. With the recent steep rise in the cost of labor, olive
grove owners have stopped subsidizing the *botijuela*, so that by 1975
there was only one work team among whom this event was carried
out. With the demise of the *botijuela*, along with the increase in
worldliness and sophistication that comes from expanded outside
contacts, the skits have all but disappeared.

In fact, it is difficult to find out about the skits, because the
people who know them well and have acted them out are generally
embarrassed by them. When an informant is asked about these skits,
he will more likely than not deny knowledge of them, or else laugh
nervously and dismiss them as "idiocies," unworthy of consideration. "Men dressed up in ridiculous costumes and made fools of
themselves" is how one farm administrator put it to me. "That's all
there was to it." People say that television and radio destroyed their
appetite for the skits because these folk performances seemed so
nonsensical in comparison with contemporary drama. Nonetheless,
there are still a few men in Monteros who genuinely enjoy perform-
ing the skits and try to do so whenever they are together and the occasion seems appropriate. It is from them that I was able to learn
about these "games."

I should caution that my texts and analysis derive exclusively
from tape-recorded interviews. I first learned of these folk dramas
after a few of them were spontaneously performed at a Christmas
celebration that my wife attended. (I was busy observing the only
wedding to which I was invited during my entire year of fieldwork.)
We spent a year in Monteros without repetition of the dramas. The
actors were pleased to teach me all they could about the skits, but
they insisted that it would be difficult to enact a planned, rehearsed
performance; the lack of spontaneity and of audience participation
would inhibit their ability to improvise and would thereby deprive
the skits of authenticity. I thus satisfied myself with descriptions of
the performances. As we shall see, however, even these artificially
produced scripts are highly instructive.

It is significant that the skits are termed *juegos*, meaning
"games," for they, like all folk drama (Abrahams 1972, p. 352), may
best be viewed as a form of play. If we draw on Johan Huizinga's
penetrating conception of play (1955), we may well understand why
this is so. These skits, like all play forms, were performed voluntarily
within distinct spatial and temporal boundaries; they could, in
other words, be initiated or suspended at any time. They were

unserious in their goals, and in fact were meant to be humorous, and yet they were seriously executed. Like all play forms, too, the skits existed independent of the immediate satisfaction of biological wants or needs. They were not concerned with the moral issues of truth and falsehood, good and evil, or vice and virtue, but in their day they were enchanting, captivating, and absorbing, probably because they dramatized issues that were of immediate psychological and cultural concern to audience and actors alike. Despite their virtual disappearance, it is possible to see how they encapsulated the values, attitudes, and experiences that still persist among the adults in Monteros. If we consider that the skits were performed frequently until about the mid-1950s, we may also suppose that they had at least some role in generating contemporary cultural patterns, not merely reflecting them. We shall return to this socialization function later.

The closest American analogue to the Andalusian *juegos* would probably be the brief skits which are performed at children's summer camp and the parlor games that used to be played at children's birthday parties.[1] Unlike those in the United States, however, the Andalusian performers were exclusively adult men. Neither children nor women—two groups whom we see constantly associated in Monteros—were involved directly as actors, though as members of the audience they could be drawn unknowingly into the show. For as Arcadio de Larrea Palacín, a leading expert on Spanish folk drama, declares, "in our opinion, the distinctive thing about folk theater consists in its intention to convert the audience into actors, to make it participate in the action" (Larrea Palacín 1968, p. 352). In Monteros, as we shall shortly see, not only did the audience remain in ignorance of the potential role they would play in the skits, but also, on occasion, even some of the actors were carried along toward a denouement of which they were unaware. The Andalusian skits were temporally and spatially discrete, but in most of these "games" it would be difficult clearly to define who was actor and who audience.

The best we might do in this regard is to return to our original point that the skits were a dramatization of the elements of control, domination, and victimization in Monteros society. If we examine them from this point of view—only one of many that are possible—we can say that those in the show who controlled and dominated were the actors; the victims, in contrast, were drawn

---

[1]For children's folk drama, see Yates (1951), and Heck (1927, pp. 38–39), who reports on the skit known as "Mother, Mother, the Milk's Boiling Over."

from the audience, though from only particular segments of the audience, usually selected according to their sex roles. This is merely to confirm an observation made long ago by Montoto y Sedas that "many games [i.e., skits] have as their ultimate goal a hoax, a practical joke against one or more spectators, who are converted into actors . . . and that in some [skits] the whole audience is the object of these hoaxes" (quoted in Larrea Palacín 1968: 352). Let us examine a few skits in detail to illustrate these notions concretely.

The Opening Formula

For the analysis of the skits, I shall cautiously utilize the all-too-convenient ethnographic present tense. This usage seems justifiable, given the facts that the skits are still very occasionally performed and that most of the Monteros populace has at one time or another witnessed them. We should examine, first, the opening formula of the skits, a standardized formal prelude functioning in a fashion similar to the familiar "Once upon a time" of folktales. It sets the event apart as a discrete entity and places the audience in an appropriate frame of mind.

All skits begin when one of the players very rapidly and animatedly shouts the following:

Refuego:	1
[A nonsense word]	
El que no se quita le pego,	2
I'll hit the person who doesn't shut up,	
Y aquel que se ha quitado,	3
And (as for) the one who has already shut up,	
Es porque le he pegado.	4
It's (only) because I've hit him.	

Thus, the very prelude to the skit foreshadows the theme of domination and victimization. The call for the audience's attention is phrased as a show of force. Though destined to be humorous, this opener nonetheless expresses the idea that people will come to order only under the threat of corporal punishment. Interpreted literally, the statement is no innocuous plea for audience cooperation. It is a warning against potentially violent attack, and it operates to foreshadow the real attack, whether verbal or physical, that will occur during the course of the skit. To that extent, it is also a clever dramatic device, arousing aggressive feelings in the audience and building tension.

Next, depending on the skit, the person who narrates the opening formula calls for the assistance of one or several other actors who usually already know the plot. For instance, in the skit known as *La Zorra* ("The Fox"), the narrator, playing the role of the property-owner, says:

Quisiera encontrar un guarda guarducha,	1
I would like to find a guard,	
Para que me guarde media docena de gallinas.	2
To watch over half a dozen hens for me.	

The narrator in this manner summons a guard, a priest, a doctor, or whatever character is necessary for the particular drama.

Let us continue, however, with our example from "The Fox." When a potential guard steps forth, a humorous quarrel ensues between him and the property-owner.

Guard:	*Pá guarda yo soy bueno.*	1
	I'm a good guard.	
Owner:	*Usted tiene cara de lapaguero.*	2
	You have the face of a *lapaguero*.[2]	
Guard:	*Y usted de porquero.*	3
	And you of a filthy, nasty person.	
Owner:	*Usted con los labios en la esquina.*	4
	You with the lips in the corner.	
Guard:	*Y usted con el culo en la vagina.*	5
	And you with your ass in the vagina.	

[2]Shirley Arora (1979:9) of UCLA states that the pattern noun-*de*-noun is common in Spanish folk speech. My informants claim that *lapaguero* is a nonsense term devoid of semantic content. Neither Professor Arora (personal communication) nor I have been successful in tracing a meaning for the word.

Owner:	*¡Usted toma!* [i.e., *tome*] (offering money)	6
	Take this!	
Guard:	*¿Cuanto paga?*	7
	How much do you pay?	
Owner:	*Un duro.*	8
	A *duro* [five *pesetas*, the equivalent in 1975 of seven cents].	
Guard:	*Yo quiero veinte reales.*	9
	I want twenty *reales* [also worth five *pesetas*].	
Owner:	*No, yo le doy un duro.*	10
	No, I'll give you a *duro*.	
Guard:	*Veinte reales.*	11
	Twenty *reales*.	
Owner:	*No, un duro.*	12
	No, a *duro*.	
	[There is a few seconds' pause.]	
	Bueno. Toma [i.e., *Tome*] *usted veinte reales.*	13
	OK. Take twenty *reales*.	

And with that, the opening of the skit terminates and six men's caps are placed in a circle on the ground to represent the hens over which the guard is supposed to watch.

We can identify two more or less discrete segments of this humorous quarrel between the owner and the guard, each one revealing an important cultural message. The first segment (lines 1–5) consists merely of a series of insults that the players toss at each other in rapid sequence; we could term this segment simple verbal dueling; it is openly aggressive.[3] In this case, it pits two people against each other, each of whom tries simultaneously to defend himself against attack and yet destroy his opponent in the process. The theme of domination and victimization here, as in the formal

---

[3]Verbal dueling, as a folkloristic genre, is a widespread phenomenon. For an excellent list of relevant sources, consult Barbara Kirshenblatt-Gimblett's bibliographic survey (1976, pp. 205–6) and comprehensive bibliography (ibid., pp. 227–84).

prelude to the skits that was analyzed earlier, could not be more evident.

In the second segment of this quarrel (lines 6–12) there is a seemingly pointless argument about pay; each party insists on the same amount of money but couches his demand in a different monetary unit. My Monteros informant claims that it is the sheer "idiocy" of the quarrel that creates laughter among the audience, but I would claim that more is at work. For we have, in the *juego* of "The Fox," a classic confrontation between a propertied individual and a common worker. In preceding chapters, we have already examined the deep feelings of cultural inferiority among Monteros workers, and these sentiments are nowhere more hurtful than in the domain of speech. It is not surprising, then, that a working-class audience should find this quarrel sequence funny, for the sequence places the educated elite on an equal level with the illiterate commoners; the message is that all men, regardless of formal education, are foolish to the same degree. Lest the audience forget, however, that circumstances in the real world give these people a truly different social rank, the formal pronoun *usted* instead of *tu* is used between them. Despite the hurling of insults, these men could never treat each other on familiar terms.

It is significant that the property owner is the character who initiates the ridiculous argument by responding with an insult (line 2) to the guard's very straightforward offer of service. From the workers' point of view, property owners are indeed culprits. In the skit, however, the guard wins, insofar as that can be said to be possible, by indeed receiving the unit of payment that he requests. Here the skit demonstrates a reversal of the class system, and especially a freedom from domination by men of property. It is the cathartic, vicarious release from the normally stilted and restricted interaction between members of different social strata that more than anything causes these opening sequences in the skit to be humorous.

What I have called the opening formula to the skit and the verbal dueling sequence are lumped by Lafuente y Alcántara under the single rubric *entrada de juego* ("game opening"), a term I never heard in Monteros. Of this *entrada*, he says simply that the skits "begin . . . with a kind of introduction or preliminary scene, reduced to a brief dialogue, which has to terminate with some joke" (quoted in Larrea Palacín 1968, p. 351). He goes on to claim that this opener "generally has no connection with the action which has to be put on afterwards" (ibid., p. 351). If we think solely in terms of plot, Lafuente's estimation may be true. But if we delve into the mood and ambience that the opener creates, he could not be farther from the truth. In Monteros, at any rate, both the opening formula and the verbal duel incorporate the themes of control and victimization that arise not only in the skits themselves but also in life.

"The Fox"

Let us now examine the actual plot of *La Zorra*, and those of several other popular skits as well, to determine if and how they project dominant cultural concerns and patterns in Monteros. We should recall that at the termination of the verbal duel six men's caps are placed on the floor to represent hens. The owner then leaves the scene temporarily. The guard begins to watch over them but within a few seconds becomes distracted, looking in the other direction or closing his eyes as if to nap. At this point a man dressed as the fox—he wears traditional esparto-grass sandals (*alpargates* or *alpargatas*) on his ears and a long cord as a tail—enters and steals off with one of the caps. The owner immediately enters and asks the guard, "Where is my hen, Origá?" (All the hens are referred to by name in the actual performance.) "She's just laying eggs," responds the guard, and, satisfied for the time being, the owner goes away. The guard soon becomes distracted again, and the fox enters and successfully captures another hen. When the owner returns and asks about this one, the guard answers, "She was here just a moment ago. You went outside, and she's gone to lay eggs." With this, the owner cautions, "You'd better take good care of her. If not, the fox will get her!"

This action is repeated three more times; each time a hen is taken and the guard invents an excuse to explain the disappearance to the owner: the hen is "laying eggs," "in the nest," or whatever. When only one cap is left on the ground, the guard says loudly to himself, "Now I have to get that fox because she's carried away all the hens. What will I have left to show to the owner?" The fox then appears, the guard pretends to shoot her, and she falls to the ground. To terminate the skit, the guard announces, "*Va. La zorra está mata'o. El juego ha termina'o*"—"There. The fox is killed. The game [skit] has ended."[4]

There seem to be at least two distinct cultural messages being transmitted by this skit. First is the notion of attack, most obviously the fox's attacks on the hens and the guard's final vengeance on the fox herself. To the extent that people in the audience identify with either

---

[4]Newell's Game 102 (1963, pp. 155–58), "Hawk and Chickens," bears close resemblance to *La Zorra*.

of these victims, the hens or the fox, they can empathize with their fate and become apprehensive about their own precarious position.

In the matter of psychological identification, we can receive some assistance from symbolic associations in speech. In Monteros, the term *zorro*, in the masculine, is the usual generic term for fox. Significantly, however, the skit concerns the *zorra*, a female fox, which is also one of the most common colloquial ways to refer to a loose, sexually insatiable woman. Women, as we have already seen, derive enormous power from their role as repositories of family virtue. A man is obsessed with the possibility that his wife might deceive him because, as Julian Pitt-Rivers long ago pointed out, a wife's unfaithfulness "defiles his manliness. In a sense it testifies to his lack of manliness, since had he proved an adequate husband and kept proper authority over her she would not have deceived him" (Pitt-Rivers 1971, p. 116). The *zorra*, then, is the uncontrolled woman; when her husband is not observant, she attacks and threatens his claim to masculinity, which includes, among other things, his ability to protect and control.

If the fox represents the uncontrolled woman, what are the *gallinas* or hens? Not surprisingly, the term *gallina* in Monteros refers colloquially to a coward, as it does elsewhere in Spain. But in Monteros a *gallina* is also a man who does not rule the roost, as he is supposed to. He is a man, for example, whose wife regulates the couple's sexual life, particularly the frequency of intercourse. It was in this context, in fact, that the expression first came to my attention. One friend was criticizing another, behind his back of course, for allowing his wife to rule over their sexual life. The critic scorned such weakness as being characteristic of a *gallina:* "What do I care whether or not my wife wants to screw?" he asked bluntly. "All I care about is that *I* want to." To speak thus is to boast of one's nonhenlike male behavior. Or if a man enters into market negotiations and consequently backs out because the deal is not going his way, the opposing party might say, "Go ahead! Show yourself to be a *gallina!* I can't help it if your wife rules over you." In other words, the term *gallina* refers specifically to the quality of cross-sex relationships at home; if the man shows himself to be weak in other contexts, this character trait is perceived as an extension of his deficiencies in the sexual domain.

Examining "The Fox" from this point of view, we can see the skit as a sexual drama as well as a drama of rebellion against the class system. The hens, I believe, can be interpreted as weak men who are being destroyed by a dominant, powerful woman. In the end, the heretofore unvigilant guard, representing the defect of negligence, wins retribution by destroying the fox and resuming his rightful role as controller. For men who perform this skit, as well as for men in the audience, "The Fox" dramatizes their deepest fears and most profound wishes. No wonder it has always been the single most popular skit in the Monteros repertory.

But what about the skit's message for women and children, who are also in the audience? Here we must first recall that symbols usually have more than one meaning and that they may be interpreted differently by different people. Such is the case with the *zorra* and the *gallinas*. True, the term *gallina* refers to an emasculated man. But it also, of course, means hen, so that the *gallinas* may just as easily represent women. Viewing the skit from this perspective, we see it as a dramatization not only of male competition for the women, who are forcibly seized from their homes, but also of male domination over and destruction of women.

This interpretation receives support from the social context in which the skit is enacted. My informant says, "And the *zorra* does nothing more than come and take the *gallinas* away—nothing more than place itself in between the feet of the spectators; and the women, 'Ay! ay!' screeching and screaming. The audience all gather around to see what's going on in the skit as the *zorra* winds it way on hands and knees near the young girls and the women, and they all try to get away from it." The informant conveys the impression not only that the female onlookers are objects of attack for the *zorra*, but also that they are genuinely frightened and excited by the prospect of attack.

As for the children in the audience, the informant states the following: "While the *zorra* is robbing the *gallinas*, the guard distracts himself with whatever other thing he can think of, so the game can continue. And the little ones in the audience cry out, 'It's coming! it's coming! it's coming!' " Clearly, the children at this point in the skit identify with the weaker characters, the hens and the guard, rather than with the large, powerful *zorra*. There is evidence, then, that women and children, again pitted against the men, empathize with those they see as the victims of the play. In fact, when the *zorra* crawls among the young girls and women, there is not even any need for identification. They in reality are transformed into victims, under attack from a prowling, aggressive man. Under no other circumstances in Monteros, I am certain, could a man crawl near the feet of adult women in this manner. The women are converted into actual participants in the drama, so that what they perceive as a daily victimization by men receives concrete expression in the skit.

"The Robber" and "The Deal"

"The Fox" is not the only skit in which the women in the audience are drawn into the action as victims. In another, which is untitled but which we may call "The Robber," the plot begins with two men talking in an agitated tone of voice, with a third standing silently by their side.

Man A: *¡Este hombre me a robado a mí!*   1
          This guy has robbed me!

Man B: *¡Hombre! ¿Cómo qué te ha robado?*   2
          Man! What do you mean he robbed you?

Man A: *¡Sí, sí! A mí me ha robado no sé cuanto, no sé qué.*   3
          Yes, yes, he's robbed me of I don't know what all.

Man B: *Este hombre. Ya llego y lo mato.*   4
          This guy. I've arrived and I'm going to kill him.

At this point, the two men engage in a mock struggle to subdue the alleged robber, who tries to flee. They finally push him down on the floor, and the dialogue continues.

Man A: *Bueno. Este hombre ya está mata'o.*   5
          Fine. This guy is killed.

          *¿Y ahora qué vamos hacer? Si lo dejamos aquí todo
          el mundo lo ve y nos puede llamar la atención o nos
          [en]cierran.*
          And now what are we going to do? If we leave him
          here, everyone will see him and he'll draw attention
          to us or they'll lock us up.

          Total. Este hombre tenemos que desparecerlo.
          In short, we have to get rid of this guy.

Man B: *Bueno, pues. ¿Qué vamos hacer?*   6
          Well, OK. What are we going to do?

Man A: *Nada. Partirlo.*   7
          Nothing. Just cut him up.

Then one of the actors removes the victim's jacket while he is still lying on the floor and playing dead. The jacket is casually handed to an unsuspecting woman in the audience, who accepts it merely with the expectation of allowing the main plot, presumably involving only the three male actors, to develop. One of the men bends down and with his hand slices an imaginary line across the victim's body. The action is accompanied by the following interchange, which terminates the skit.

Man A:	*De aquí pa' arriba pa' mí.*	8
	From here and above is for me.	
Man B:	*¿Y de la bragueta?*	9
	And [what about the part of the body] with the trouser fly?	
Man A:	*¡Pa'el que tiene la chaqueta!*	10
	For the one who's holding the jacket!	

In most Andalusian skits, everything but the prelude is ad-libbed. Here, however, the comic effect relies largely on the rhyme between *bragueta* and *chaqueta* lines 9–10), so that the finale has to be said from memory.

Of course, the punchline receives its primary effect from the implication that it is the man's fly—or, really, what lies inside it—that belongs to the women who is holding his jacket. This statement, made publicly, causes the innocent female in the audience a good deal of embarrassment, which she good-naturedly deflects through laughter. The rest of the audience naturally howls with enjoyment at the unexpected sexual twist to the action, as well as at the fate of the woman with the jacket, who is transformed into the victim of verbal rape. Even on the surface, "The Robber" is essentially a drama of domination and victimization: one man is robbed by another, who is then himself overcome by force and murdered. But it is the woman spectator, at the last moment pulled against her will into the plot, who is the real object of all the male players' cunning deceit.

In yet another skit, commonly known as *El Trato*, or "The Deal," an unsuspecting female spectator again suffers at the hands of the male actors. A *trato* is, among other things, the occasion and verbal process in which two people, a buyer and a seller, bargain over the cost of an item. The word is generally reserved for the sale of relatively expensive items, like animals or land, rather than small ones, like clothing or food. In "The Deal," the price of a *burro*, or male donkey, is at stake.

As in "The Robber," in "The Deal" there are three male actors, two of whom speak and one of whom plays a mute role, that of the donkey. When the plot begins, the three players emerge from the audience: the donkey, the donkey owner, and a prospective buyer. The owner pulls his animal by a rope around his neck. The donkey crawls on his hands and knees, his entire body except his head covered by a blanket that drapes to the floor. He also wears a pair of esparto-grass sandals on his ears. "*¡Maestro!* (Good fellow!)" the buyer calls out. "Are you selling the donkey?" "Yes, I'll sell it," responds the other, who immediately adds as a public aside, "OK. The halter has to be held by a *señora* or *señorita* [married or unmarried woman]." The seller usually encounters some difficulty in finding a woman who is willing to accept the halter. We can well imagine that any woman familiar with Andalusian skits, even though she may not specifically know "The Deal," would be suspicious of the seller's motives. The seller simply approaches as many women as necessary until finally someone, wary though willing to go along for the fun of it, accepts the rope.

Then the buyer and seller begin to argue about price, only here, unlike the humorous quarrel sequence in "The Fox," the bargaining involves realistic sums. The actors raise and lower their offers for a few minutes until the interchange becomes tiresome and they reach an agreement. At this point, all three male actors simply walk away from the scene. As the donkey crawls out alongside his new owner, his blanket uncovers a bedpan, to which the rope that the woman spectator holds is directly attached. With this, it is revealed that the man playing the role of donkey had throughout the performance hidden the end of the rope so that the audience would not detect its termination point. Again, the woman is victimized; left foolishly holding onto a bedpan—which contains actual waste matter, at that—she is the butt of the spectators' laughter.[5]

All the actors in "The Deal," unlike those in "The Fox," have unambiguous male identities. The buyer and seller are men, and the donkey is specifically the male of the species. (Female donkeys are always distinguished from males in speech.) The donkey is presumably the figure held responsible for producing and leaving the excrement in the bedpan. Yet the donkey's owner must have also placed the bedpan there, so that he too is responsible for the embarrassing turn of events. In essence, the skit symbolizes that males in general leave dirt behind for women. Its message is that women

---

[5] "The Deal" is obviously a dramatic enactment of Aarne-Thompson Tale Type 1528, "Holding down the hat" (1961, pp. 436–37).

clean up after men. "The Deal," therefore, portrays more than victimization in the abstract; it dramatizes victimization of a highly
specific type, based on the reality of women's daily caretaker role in
Monteros.[6]

"The Blackbird" and "The Card Game"

Not all Monteros skits are designed to portray the victimization
of women. In some, unsuspecting men are the primary butts of the
action. In *El Avión*, or "The Blackbird," two men collaborate and
call on two more, ignorant of the plot, as volunteers. Again, since
the audience is well aware of the general character and theme of
these skits, male spectators are reluctant to offer their services. With
prodding, however, coupled with repeated assurances that no harm
will be done, players are always found to fill the necessary roles.

In "The Blackbird," the two original players extend their arms
in front of them and lock hands, so as to form a cradle. The first
volunteer, acting in the title role, rests his chest and arms in this
cradle, while his two feet are held up by the second volunteer. When
the blackbird is comfortably established in this position, the three
others call out, "Let's make a blackbird! Let's go flying!" At this
point, a group of other men emerge from the audience, unbutton the
blackbird's pants, and against his struggling motions, pull them all
the way down to his ankles. The victim, in the desperate but vain attempt to free himself, pulls his legs up under him and throws them
out, pulls them up again and throws them out, all to the vigorous
laughter of the audience. After a few minutes, when all have had
their fill, the man is released and the skit terminates.

Domination and control over an unwilling blackbird are clear
in this skit, but even more interesting is the way he vents his anger.
Though I have never myself witnessed "The Blackbird," one informant describes its ultimate humorous impact in the following way:
"And then the guy behind, since they took down the other guy's
pants, well, he gets the whole ass [*culo*] in his face. [Informant
laughs.] They give it to him there with all the smelly air. [Laughs
again.]" The final picture, then, is of a bound man, squirming his

---

[6]This skit provides an interesting reversal of the psychoanalytic notion that the
childhood concern with feces is eventually transformed into concern over wealth. In
"The Deal," wealth (in the form of money) precedes the revelation of feces. For
psychoanalytic research on the relation between money and excrement, read Brill
(1955, pp. 84–85, 137, 218), Freud (1963a), Ferenczi (1955, vol. 1, pp. 320–29; vol. 2,
pp. 248, 257, 362–65; vol. 3, p. 33), and Jones (1949, p. 129).

way to freedom by thrusting his malodorous buttocks in the face of his oppressor, who is also victimized.

We may presume that the spectators can identify with the bound victim and derive vicarious release from the manner in which he tries to free himself. The blackbird is a victim, but he also victimizes. For the audience, he can symbolize not only the struggle against external sources of control (i.e., the parents) but also against the internal mechanisms that force all of us to conform to requirements for the disposition of bodily waste. Surely it is significant that informants react to the specific form of rebellion rather than just to the struggle against authority itself.

I wish to discuss one final skit, which is untitled but which we may term "The Card Game." Here there are two men who enact prepared roles, one in full view of the audience, the other hidden among the spectators but ready to emerge at the appointed moment. A third man is the innocent and unsuspecting victim. The first player calls for a partner to help him out with a game of cards. When a volunteer emerges, the two cardplayers sit down on chairs facing each other, and the first tells the other that he has to repeat everything that is said. The following sequence, forming a short rhymed verse, ensues.

Player:	*¡Echa!*	1
	Throw out (a card)!	
Victim:	*¡Echa!*	2
	Throw!	
Player:	*Y vuelve echar.*	3
	And throw (it) out again.	
Victim:	*Y vuelve echar.*	4
	And throw (it) out again.	
Player:	*El que juega este juego.*	5
	He who performs in this skit, or He who plays in this card game	
Victim:	*El que juega este juego.*	6
	He who performs in this skit, or He who plays in this card game	
Player:	*No se puede enfadar.*	7
	Cannot get angry.	

Victim: *No se puede enfadar.*   8

          Cannot get angry.

With this, the verse terminates, and the first player casually remarks
that it has to be repeated. So the verse begins to be repeated.

Player: *¡Echa!*   9

          Throw!

Victim: *¡Echa!*   10

          Throw!

At this point the player who has been disguised as a spectator
emerges behind the victim and tosses a bucket of cold water over his
head. The verb *echar* is used flexibly in Spanish to refer to a variety
of activities, such as tossing out a card in a game or throwing a
bucket of water. When the victim, therefore, says, "*¡Echa!*" for the
second time, the other two feel justified in giving him a good dous-
ing. He is merely getting what he asked for, and further, what he
has already declared he cannot get angry about.

"The Card Game" is a commentary on life in that it manifests
at least one overriding theme of Monteros culture: illusion. An important message of this skit, as well as of others that we have analyzed, is that the world is unpredictable. Appearances belie reality.
Like the innocent man drawn into the card game, or the women
duped into holding a man's coat or a donkey's halter, we all must
beware of whatever is placed openly before us, for it certainly holds
some less innocuous motive or meaning.

Likewise, if we intend to remain our own masters, immune to
outside attack, we should adopt simulated facades. "The Fox,"
above all skits, perhaps embodies this idea most perfectly. The
guard cannot admit his neglectfulness to the owner. Time after
time, when the owner asks him to explain a chicken's disappearance,
he invents an excuse. This, to the young members of the audience,
can only operate to sanction deceit for the purpose of self-
preservation; later in life, this becomes an acceptable and openly
admitted reality.

No wonder it is said that "in [Monteros] there are no bad
horses." Why? If you own a horse, you never know when you might
want to sell him, so that it's wise to maintain his public image in the
best light despite any defects he may have. If your horse really has a
defect and you manage to fool a potential buyer by selling him at a
good price, the new owner must follow the same policy of lauding

the animal and the price at which he was purchased, should he himself ever hope to recoup the loss. Monteros skits incorporate a message of skepticism; they tell people to watch out for the supposedly fine horse that belongs to others, and yet they instruct them to present their own horse, no matter what its defects, as of high quality.

Andalusian skits are rarely performed nowadays; they have been all but eliminated by the widespread distribution of advanced systems of communication. Simple and unsophisticated on the surface, the skits nonetheless bear a deep relationship to the culture and society in which they once thrived. But it is also likely that in their day the skits provided an important socialization function. Children watching these performances could not help but be affected by them. The skits therefore operated not only as cultural metaphors but also as agents of instruction. They helped to communicate the values and lifestyle that, at least among most town adults, are still evident today. Their potential significance for and impact on contemporary Monteros should therefore not be underestimated.[7]

[7]The Segavecchia, central Italian male comic skits, briefly described by Sydel Silverman (1980), bear resemblance to the folk dramas analyzed in this chapter. The chapter, in slightly different form, appeared in volume 39 of *Western Folklore* (October 1979).

Religious Expressions of Masculinity

10

If religion has given birth to all that is essential in society, it is because the idea of society is the soul of religion.

Emile Durkheim,
Elementary Forms of the Religious Life
(1915)

Until the early 1970s, when Protestants were given the right to proselytize, Spain was a wholly Catholic country. Even today, when, of all the diverse sects, the Jehovah's Witnesses seem to be making some slight inroads, it would be false to characterize this nation as anything but Roman Catholic. Catholic churches, cathedrals, monasteries, and sanctuaries dominate the landscape. Catholic religious instruction is, and for most of the past half-century has been, an integral part of the public school curriculum. People mark the stages of their life with reference to Catholic ritual. No matter how irreligious or irreverent a Spanish person claims to be, it is unthinkable that his or her child should remain unbaptized or should reach puberty without taking First Communion. These are the rites that mark entry into the human community and that separate the civilized from the barbarian. To deprive an innocent boy or girl of these sacraments, which are necessary for survival and, ultimately, salvation, would be considered cruel.

Nonetheless, it would be false to state that the Spanish are uniformly religious. To put the matter in more measurable terms, longstanding evidence and experience show that the Spanish neither practice religion nor profess to be religious to equal degrees. At least two separate considerations come into play here: the popular image of religiosity and the actual practice of it. Popular stereotypes abound. The Basques, despite their political nonconformity and rebelliousness, are said to be deeply religious and to provide the Catholic hierarchy with a disproportionately large number of clerics. Andalusians, on the other hand, are said to be irreligious though superstitious; their churches are empty, though their reliance on amulets and other magical forms of devotion is well known. Throughout Spain, too, it is often stated that the wealthy practice religion regularly, albeit hypocritically; they support the Church without following its moral dicta. The poor, on the other hand, are thought to be morally principled while ignoring the outward manifestations of religiosity, particularly attendance at Mass. Everywhere, men are said to be less religious than women, just as city dwellers are considered less religious than those of the countryside.

Some of these popular stereotypes have their basis in reality. It is certain, for example, that over the course of centuries the Basques, with their impartible inheritance system, have provided for the future of many of their children by placing them within the Church. It is true, too, that on the whole a smaller proportion of people living in Andalusian agro-towns attend Mass than do those residing in the tiny corporate communities of Castile. Yet, as Juan Linz and José Cazorla have cogently demonstrated (1968–69), it is not true that urban Andalusians practice religion to a lesser degree than rural ones. Nor can we say, as I have elsewhere pointed out (1976), that when people cease attending Mass or participating in processions it necessarily means that their religious sentiments are diminishing and they are becoming secularized. The Church and its clerical representatives (see, e.g., Freeman 1968; Riegelhaupt 1973) may influence the religious behavior of the people in their charge.

All this is by way of pointing out, however briefly, that religion in Spain is a complex matter. Facile generalizations of whatever type are unwarranted and, moreover, dangerous, especially because religion has proved to be an everpresent concern in Spanish political life. The Civil War of 1936–39 was portrayed by the Franco forces as a war of the God-fearing against the Godless, of the forces of light against the forces of darkness. Yet in the 1970s the Church, which gave Franco its full support during the Civil War and after, could be said to have become as much a progressive as a conservative influence in Spanish social and political life. If, as Gerald Brenan says

(1964, pp. 37–56), the Church in the century before the war aligned itself with the bourgeois and wealthy against the poor, who could offer it little of the material support it needed, then in the 1970s it would be much more difficult to state that the Church invariably favors one class over another or that, correspondingly, it draws its adherents from one particular socio-economic group to the exclusion of others. Now, more than ever, religion must be understood in its local context, for the attitudes and motives that people express with regard to religion and the Church are a direct outgrowth of their own experiences and world view, and may not be easily transposed from one social situation to another.

With this word of caution, I wish to analyze four limited aspects of religious expression in Monteros: Mass and Communion; religious humor; lay brotherhoods, known throughout the Spanish-speaking world as *cofradías*; and processions. I confine myself to these four domains because, more than many of the multitudinous other aspects of religion and Catholicism, they can tell us something about what it means to be a man in this town. Religion, from my point of view, is a projective form like any other. Men, in their religious practices, beliefs, and attitudes, reflect the same dominant concerns as may be identified in their legends, riddles, and skits. And, as with these other modes of expression, religion also helps to resolve identity conflicts.

The Double Sex Standard

Any analysis of male religious attitudes and practices in Monteros must be prefaced with a few words about the double sex standard. Here I expand in particular on what has already been said in chapter 5 on the moral qualitites attributed to men and women. Traditional Monteros culture, to put the matter succinctly, rewards male expressions of sexuality while suppressing those of females. There is no better demonstration of this proposition than the emphasis on female virginity.

The ideal in Monteros, as throughout Mediterranean Europe, has been for a man to marry a virgin; a virgin bride is a precious treasure, embodying all the purity and virtue of the Mother of Christ. Barring marriage to a virgin, a man must at the very least marry a woman whom he himself has deflowered and one who he can be sure has had no sexual contact with any other man. Until the 1960s, in fact, this was the more common of the two preferred alternatives. Young couples who lacked the money necessary for a proper church ceremony and catered reception, or who encountered serious parental opposition to their match, would elope and live together in a consensual union for varying periods of time, sometimes waiting until the birth of two, three, or even four children before legitimizing their marriage. Even in these cases, it was more important that the woman should have given herself to no other man than that she be married in a regular church ceremony. And down to the present, widows are much less likely to remarry than are widowers, for a widow, having already experienced sexual relations with another man, is an intrinsically damaged commodity.

Men, in contrast, are accorded almost unlimited freedom in the pursuit of their sexual pleasures. Prior to marriage, men are expected to acquire sexual experience through engaging in as many affairs as possible. In fact, parents seem almost to revel in the fact that their young sons stay out late, having a good time with wine and women; daughters, at least until very recently, have been carefully guarded and have had to maintain a rigid curfew. Men are permitted to call out *"piropos"* or *"flores"* ("flowers")—traditional compliments to a woman's physical attributes—whenever moved to do so, while women themselves are expected to maintain a modest stance and underplay their sexuality and attraction for men. Once married, a man should protect the unity and reputation of his family by being faithful to his wife. But, unlike his wife, he may express his sexual fantasies openly whenever he sees an attractive woman. Should he occasionally stray, he will be forgiven by family and society alike for behaving in a way that might only be expected.

The emphasis on female virginity and purity in Mediterranean Europe has yet to receive adequate explanation. In a much-cited article, Jane Schneider (1971) has suggested that this cultural code originally arose to provide one very general basis for social organization in an otherwise atomistic society. But why, we may ask, does the code persist under much altered social, economic, and political conditions? And why was it this code, and not some other, that was devised to create an antidote to extreme individualism in this part of the world? In a subsequent work, Jane and Peter Schneider (1976, pp. 94–100) offer some alternative explanations. The Catholic Church, they claim, needed to combat all potentially competitive sources of allegiance and power while it was solidifying its own position in the Mediterranean. Among these potential competitors was the family; the double sex standard operated to pit men against women, and especially to ally women with the Church against men, such that the family as a social unit was no longer threatening. The Schneiders postulate, too, that the emphasis on virginity and on the seclusion of women operated as a brake on the expanding commercial empires from the East. If women could be secluded, and their sexuality suppressed, they would be less likely to purchase textiles, cosmetics, and other luxury items new to the market and essential for the consolidation of mercantile power. These hypotheses, however intriguing, have yet to be substantiated with concrete evidence. The Schneiders offer them to us in an extremely schematic fashion, as if simply to fill the present void in our understanding. Even if they could be demonstrated correct, we have yet to understand why the Mediterranean sexual code has persisted over so long a period.

The best I can do is to offer some ideas that the people in Monteros have actually articulated. One popular metaphor encapsulates vividly the male view of female sexuality. "Why," I once asked, "are you men so concerned about marrying a virgin? What difference could it possibly make if a man married a woman who was already deflowered?" My informant's response was immediate and simple. "Suppose you were thirsty and I put before you two glasses of water. And suppose, too, that I had already drunk out of one of them. Which would you choose?" I answered that I would of course choose the clean glass. "Then why should we not similarly prefer a virgin over a woman who has already been taken?" he retorted.

A deflowered woman, in short, is like a dirty glass of water, defiled, used, intrinsically polluted and polluting. Virginity, to put the matter in the words of another informant, represents *"lo intacto, la pureza máxima"* ("the intact [whole, undamaged, harmonious], the maximum purity"). Virginity is a symbol of the new, the pure, the good; it stands for *el colmo de la posibilidad*—"the height of potentiality and possibility." It therefore can be converted into a thousand beneficial things for the future. For this reason, "the act of deflowering in and of itself is bad, because it terminates the possibilities for the future; a whole series of potentialities that the virgin represents are lost." This is why the Virgin Mary herself is so important in Monteros, for she stands for permanent purity and permanent hope. It is inevitable that women should be deflowered, and in particular that one's wife will be; but the Virgin remains intact and undamaged forever.

But why should it be female virginity and not male that takes on such significance? Here we must call upon the different physical attributes of the two sexes for an explanation. A man when he loses his virginity remains physically unaltered; the dissemination of sperm inside a woman's body in no way changes his bodily composition. Puncturing a woman's hymen, in contrast, has a definite, ir-

reversible, and measurable physical effect. In fact, until a generation ago in Monteros, as elsewhere in Spain (Casas Gaspar 1947,
p. 296), a bride would have to show her bloodied bedsheets to her
husband's family in order to demonstrate her prior virginity.
Among Monteros Gypsies, this practice is still carried out. A
deflowered woman is therefore not only symbolically a damaged
commodity, but she is physically blemished as well. With the act of
intercourse, she loses her purity, her harmonious essence. This is yet
another reason, among those offered in chapter 5, why women, particularly women who are sexually experienced, are denigrated. The
potential for the future that the virgin woman embodies is, with her
deflowering, inevitably and irrevocably lost.

Mass and Communion

There are many possible means to measure religiosity, but certainly, in a country like Spain, attendance at Mass and participation
in the act of Communion are among the most critical criteria. It is
impossible to ascertain with any degree of certainty exactly what
proportion of the people in Monteros attend Mass either regularly or
intermittently. There are four Masses daily, held in two of the three
Monteros churches (the third church is utilized solely by an order of
nuns), and if a person chooses to claim falsely that he or she does attend, it would be difficult to disprove the statement. The town is
large enough and the number of Masses great enough that anony-
mity with respect to religious participation can be maintained. On
the other hand, it is evident that in attitudes as much as in actions,
women in the town are on the whole more religious than men. Even
when women only infrequently attend Mass or take Communion,
they are considerably less likely than are men to speak irreverently
of the Church or the clergy. If a woman misses Mass, she will usually
maintain a defensive stance, claiming that time doesn't permit her
this luxury. A man, on the other hand, is more likely to take an of-
fensive position, stating that anything in which the priests have a say
is inherently corrupt and should be avoided. Interestingly, these attitudes vary little from one social class to another. Upper-class
women, who are helped at home by servants and who are free from
the necessity of outside employment, surely attend Mass with
greater regularity than their working-class counterparts do. But
this, as I have said, can be attributed more to available time than to
anything else. Within all segments of society, men are the religious
skeptics, women the religious supporters.

I have no statistical figures to demonstrate that women attend

Mass more frequently than men, but certainly long-term residence in Monteros has provided me with more than enough impressionistic evidence to this effect. The two morning Masses held daily are over-whelmingly attended by women, along with a sprinkling of men. The noon Mass serves somewhat more men, but women are still in the vast majority. The evening Mass, held at 8:30 P.M., is more evenly distributed between the sexes, as are the noon and evening Masses on Sunday.

It might be claimed, from the above distribution, that men's work schedules prevent them from attending Mass with greater fre-quency. On life-cycle occasions, however, when work hours should not interfere, men demonstrate much less willingness to attend church than do women. With weddings, baptisms, First Com-munions, and funerals, the church is invariably packed to capacity. Nonetheless, on these critical occasions there is always a crowd of men standing in the Corredera outside the church; they have come to pay their respects to the celebrants but will not set foot inside the church door. Many men even refuse to attend the baptism and First Communion of their own children, claiming with an unmistakable tongue-in-cheek tone that work prevents them from doing so. The fact is that they obstinately refrain from participating in religious services. This causes serious disagreements and unhappiness at home, with wives at a loss to understand their husbands' behavior.

This is not to say that men do not attend church, for hundreds in the town do attend regularly, and many more participate in the life-cycle services. It is simply that there is an undeniable tendency for men to attend Mass in fewer numbers and with lesser frequency than women, and this tendency must be explained. We must realize, first, that for women the religious code supports and coincides with the cultural code, whereas for men these two codes are in diametric opposition to one another. According to Catholic religious teachings and ideals, we are all—men and women alike—imbued with sexual passions and desires. But at the same time, the Church teaches that these passions and desires are sinful and that we should therefore try to suppress our sexuality as much as possible. This, the Church tells us, holds as much for men as for women.

If we examine the cultural code, however, it is clear that men and women are taught to treat their sexuality in different ways. The double sex standard, as we have seen, demands that women suppress their sexual passions and desires whereas it encourages men to ex-press theirs. Women should remain virgins before marriage, men should acquire sexual experience; women should not flirt, men should flatter and seduce. Men, as they pass women in the street, stare and mentally undress them. Women, in contrast, must avert their eyes when passing men so as not to appear interested in them. Traditionally, women were not even supposed to greet a man without being first greeted by him, and this behavior still characterizes the elder generation.

Given these differences in cultural norms, we can well understand why women are more attracted to the Church than are men. When women go to Mass, they find support for the cultural ideals they are taught to follow. The Church helps them to control their sexuality and to bring themselves into line with accepted cultural rules. As one elderly woman from the town elite put it, the Church in Andalusia has always acted as a source of consolation to women who are caught between two evils: on the one hand, their husbands distrust them intensely and are forever jealous of them; on the other, strange men are forever chasing after them, eyeing them and watching for the opportunity to take advantage of them. The Church, in this case, not only helps women properly to suppress their sexuality but also provides them solace when control proves impossible.[1]

Men, in contrast, can only scorn or ridicule the priest's message. According to one male informant, men in Andalusia have always avoided the Church because they refuse to believe that their sexual escapades are sinful, or that they should place a strong brake on their sexuality. As we shall see in the next section, priests themselves are considered to be highly sexual beings who use their powerful position to exploit women sexually. That three Monteros priests have within the past decade left the clergy and married does nothing to counteract this image. Men refuse to obey a religious message that they say is meted out by hypocrites. Priests, the men of Monteros say, are like all male human beings; they need a sexual outlet. Moreover, from the male point of view, there is nothing intrinsically sinful or immoral about the pursuit of masculine pleasure. The masculine code, then, conflicts markedly with Church teachings, and the Mass, which is the most concrete expression of these teachings, becomes correspondingly devoid of significance. This is why many men who attend Church claim to do so only to maintain harmony within the home. Even they reject the main religious ideal. "Why is it," asks one male churchgoer, "that the only sin the priests care about is the sixth (i.e., the Sixth Commandment): fucking

---

[1]A sensitive analysis of male-female differentiation in religious practices has been carried out by Christian (1972, pp. 148–61), whose data for the Cantabrian region in northern Spain in many ways coincide with my own. He mainly emphasizes the female sense of impurity as a motivation for religious action.

(*follar*)?" If they cared more about the rest, he went on, they might win more support.

But there is more involved than the conflict or coincidence of religious and cultural codes to explain sexual differences in attitudes toward the Mass. We must understand as well that the church, as a physical and spiritual site, is a symbolic home. When people attend church, they find themselves in the company of the Holy Family: the Virgin Mother, God the Father, and the saints, who are like brothers and sisters. The very terminology of the Mass, in which the Virgin is referred to as "Mother," God as "Father," and so on, confirms this symbolic equivalence. But sometimes informants make the connection even more explicit, as when one woman confided to me that the Virgin was no longer paying attention to her prayers and requests because she had made so many demands that she had become like a nagging child.[2]

In Monteros, of course, a woman's place is in the home. Even a generation ago, when women, especially upper-class women, were severely secluded, they were permitted to attend church as frequently as they wanted. This not only provided them a source of diversion; it also was an expression of the fact that women were perceived as domestic beings. Today, as in the past, when women go to church they are leaving one domestic domain—that of their earthly family—for another—that of their Holy Family. Most Monteros men, in contrast, consider domesticity of whatever type to be inherently unmasculine. As men state regularly to me, the home is for sleeping or eating; otherwise, a man should be out working or spending time with his friends. No wonder, then, that overly persistent churchgoing men are accorded an aura of effeminacy, as if they were taking upon themselves more than the approriate share of domestic responsibilities.

The implication of effeminacy is especially strong for men who regularly participate in the sacrament of Communion. Even more than for the Mass as a whole, attitudes toward Communion vary between the sexes. On the basis of observations that I made during the summer of 1977, I can estimate that about one-fifth of the total number of those receiving Communion are males. And of these males, a good portion are boys under the age of ten or eleven who

---

[2]The analogy between the Holy Family and the earthly family has been discussed effectively by a number of scholars who have carried out research in the Roman Catholic world (Bushnell 1958; Christian 1972; Crumrine 1977; Wolf 1969). The Virgin Mary in her manifestations as bride and mother is treated fully by Warner (1976).

might easily have been pressured by their families into taking Communion. As one man put it, "Women take Communion more than men do because they are more easily swayed, because they are weaker, more feminine." To take Communion is unmistakably identified with being a woman or having a feminine character, and on these grounds alone, we can understand why men would be hesitant to participate in the sacrament.

But to understand more specifically why most men avoid Communion—and do so permanently—it is necessary to understand something about the form and essence of this sacrament. First, to take Communion requires being in a state of purity, which requires confessing to the priest and then atoning for one's sins according to his prescription. Priests in Monteros lament that their parishioners misunderstand the function of confession. The Church, they say, stipulates that a Catholic must confess and take Communion at least once a year. Apart from this annual requirement, however, a person is only forced to confess if he or she has committed what is know as a mortal sin, like robbery, murder, or adultery. For everything else, ranging from lewd dreams to nose-picking, no confession is necessary in order to take Communion. Despite these relatively minimal requirements, the priests claim that women persist in the belief that it is sinful ever to take Communion without confessing, and so the pettiest thoughts and deeds become the object of great concern and they spend literally hours confessing about matters of little consequence. Women are clearly more guilt-ridden than men, if we are to judge by confession, and are especially so when it comes to sex and the bodily functions in general.

Men, on the other hand, are taught by the culture to accept sexual desires and activities as a normal part of being a man. In fact, these desires and activities are an essential prerequisite to their masculinity. Men, consequently, perceive no need to purge themselves of sins which they believe themselves not to have committed. Moreover, the priest's celibacy itself becomes an impediment to confession. As one male informant put it, "I never confess because there is no way that a priest, a man who isn't married, can understand me. I love my wife. I love her sexually as well as emotionally. And I might be able to resist her one night or even two. But the time will come when I just can't turn my back on her. And this is something a priest can never understand." Of course, by the priest's assessment it would not be necessary to confess about having engaged in sexual relations with one's spouse in order to take Communion. But the belief persists that confession is an absolute requirement for Communion, and until it is dispelled men will resist participating in this sacrament.

Then, too, the act of confessing itself is repugnant to most men. As we have seen in chapter 9, men in Monteros cultivate a sense of discrete personal identity that requires that they never reveal a treasured core of thoughts and experiences. These thoughts and experiences are the essence of the individual; they are what makes him different from all other men. If they are not even to be revealed to one's spouse, how much less likely are they to be spilled out to a stranger, the priest, who is considered to have an interest in them only for his own self-aggrandizement, and not for any spiritual end. Priests, as we shall see in the following section, are thought to be interested in the personal secrets of their parishioners only in order to live vicariously through them; the priests' curiosity is considered morbid.

To justify their underlying distrust of the priests, the people of Monteros point out, as I have already mentioned, that within the past decade three of the priests who have served in this town have left the clergy and married. A fourth, who had enjoyed a long, respected station here, was arrested in a brawl in a discotheque in a nearby town. Women, in particular, fear that their confessors will within a few years be revealing the personal secrets of parishioners to their own brides, who will then spread the juicy news throughout the town. As a result, even women have begun to confess with less frequency than in the past. Nonetheless, a vast difference persists between the numbers of men and women receiving Communion, and it must be accounted for principally on the grounds of male notions of masculinity and personal identity.

But we may speculate, too, about some possible subsidiary factors involving the act of Communion itself, rather than the confession preceding it, that may account for this sexual differentiation. Communion is the culmination and most intensely sacred portion of the Mass. According to Catholic doctrine, the priest's act of consecration in the Mass transforms the wafer, or host (*hostia*), into the body of Christ. The wafer becomes transformed into the actual body of Christ, and is not a mere representation of it. During Communion, the priest first elevates the host and ingests it and the wine, which represents the blood of Christ. During this time the parishioners are all expected to kneel and bow their heads in adoration. Only after the priest has taken Communion do those parishioners who wish to receive Communion come forward and accept the wafer from the priest. Traditionally, and until relatively recently, parishioners receiving Communion would bend down on both knees before the priest on low benches located just in front of the altar. The priest would pronounce *"El cuerpo de Cristo"* ("The body of Christ"), at which the communicant would respond by saying "Amen," open his or her mouth, and have the wafer placed inside it. Nowadays, parishioners walk to the base of the altar and, standing, go through the same procedure. A small minority of communicants prefer to receive the wafer in their hands and place it in their mouths themselves, but the vast majority still have the priest do it for them.

There is at least one aspect of the traditional Communion procedure that might have been particularly distasteful to Monteros men: the requirement of kneeling at two points in the ceremony (when the priest takes Communion and when the communicant himself or herself participates in the act). We have already seen in analyzing the olive harvest that kneeling is regarded as an inherently feminine posture; it is a symbol of humility, inferiority, and subjugation in which no man likes to see himself. Women not only kneel when picking up olives but also when scrubbing the floor, an activity in which no self-respecting man would engage. Women, unlike men, also sometimes walk on their knees in processions to fulfill vows made to the saints. There is, in other words, a syndrome of traits in Monteros that presupposes that men, who are considered socially superior to women, should also remain physically at a higher level than women. Even within the church, no woman is ever allowed on the raised altar platform during a religious service, though between services, in order to clean the altar, and especially to scrub the floor, they are allowed to ascend to this sacred domain. Men, in contrast, often sit through Mass on the benches that line the altar platform, especially when the church is crowded.

I am suggesting that the act of kneeling is in itself a feminizing gesture, and that many men would unconsciously react against it by refusing Communion. This interpretation, in fact, is not solely mine. When I asked a woman of the Monteros elite how she might explain why fewer men than women receive Communion, she thought for a moment and then responded, "I don't know, but I've always thought that it would be hard for a man here to get down on his knees before another man. It's too debasing." Nowadays, of course, the reaction against kneeling would be insufficient to explain why so many men refuse to take Communion because all communicants receive the host while firmly on their feet. But it is still necessary to bend down while the priest himself takes Communion. I have been told that in the past, men, in a symbolic revolt against this portion of the Mass, would kneel only on their left knee, keeping their right leg bent to the chest with the foot on the ground. Even today this position can still be observed among some men during Mass, but never among women.

The Clerical Image through Jokes

If we had to identify the single dominant impediment to male religiosity in Monteros, it would be the attitude that men hold toward the clergy, especially priests. Most men believe that priests are just like other men. In particular, they think that priests are imbued with the same sexual desires and passions as other men, and that they hypocritically preach the repression of these natural impulses though they often become dominated by them. In addition, priests and the Church in general are accused of virtual robbery of a Machiavellian type. Through means both subtle and coercive, they persuade their parishioners to give donations of hard-earned money. Meanwhile the priests themselves live by fostering the impression that they are working, without in reality doing any work at all. That, in fact, is the basis for a common Monteros expression that states *"Eres más interesado que los de la iglesia"* ("You're more selfish than those of the Church"). Above all, it is the contradiction between what the priests say and what they do, or are at least reputed to do, that disturbs Monteros men and causes them to reject formal religion.

This underlying contradiction provides the overriding theme for religious humor in Monteros.[3] The great majority of religious jokes in this town may be divided into two types. The first is designed to mock the notion that priests, and the clergy in general, are motivated by the best interests of their parishioners. An informant told me the following popular story about nuns:

> Remember I told you that there was a time of hunger here in Spain? Well, it was in that time—about '43 or '44 [it was actually 1945]—when there was a convent of nuns who had nothing more to eat than bread and olive oil. For meals, they would take a piece of bread and pour olive oil on top of it. As they did so, they would quickly say, *"Kililisón"* (*Kyrie eleison*, "Lord, have mercy"). They were thanking God for the food they had. There was one nun, however, who would *chant* the word *"Kililisón"* thus: *"Ki . . . li . . . li . . . són."*

In narrating the joke, the word "Kililisón" is sung slowly, in drawn-out manner, as the narrator mimics the motion of pouring oil on top

---

[3]Anticlericalism through humor is given brief treatment by Silverman (1975, pp. 165–66) in her discussion of religious attitudes in central Italy.

of bread. The implication is that this was simply a trick enabling the nun to obtain more than her fair share of the oil.

Another joke suggests that priests inwardly have a coldly indifferent attitude toward the lives of their parishioners.

> A man lay on his bed dying, so a priest was called to give him the last rites. The priest said to him, "Don't worry, son, you'll go up there to heaven where it's beautiful and where you'll be through with all your suffering and where you'll have everlasting peace." And so on, went the priest, practically encouraging the sick man to kick off. The man responded to the priest, "That's OK, you go where *you* like. I'm staying right here! There's no place I like better than my own home!"

That is, the dying man indicates to the priest that any rational man—the priest included—would choose the certainty of a hard life on earth over the hypothetical luxuries of a heavenly afterlife. Religion, according to some Monteros workers, is a conscious clerical plot, designed to divert the masses from thinking about poverty and other worldly problems. This joke portrays an extreme version of the plot, in that a priest urges a mortally ill man to consider his very life of minor significance.

The sexual repression of the Church emerges in a number of other jokes. Here the conflict between Church norms and male cultural norms, discussed in the preceding section, is particularly evident.

> There was a man in confession who told the priest that he desired his neighbor's wife, that he just couldn't control himself, and that he wanted to sleep with her. The priest said [here the narrator assumes a stiff, stilted tone of voice], "You must not covet your neighbor's wife (*la del prójimo*), you must not covet you neighbor's wife." "I know that, Father," answered the man. "But the neighbors' wives are always better!"

This joke incorporates a common Monteros phrase—*la del prójimo*—that is used as a separate item of speech in everyday discourse. When a man sees a woman who catches his eye, he is likely to turn to his companions and refer to her by this very expression. Men in Monteros perceive nothing sinful in, and are certainly devoid of any sense of guilt at, enjoying the sight of a woman who attracts them. Nor, if they are in a relatively anonymous situation, as when they visit large cities and the family's reputation is not endangered, do they see anything wrong with actively pursuing such a woman. It is the Church, they claim, that places such unnatural restrictions on mankind.

The same message is incorporated within the following riddling joke:

> You know the foreigner's definition of a Spaniard? A small dark man with a moustache and a mean face (*una cara de mala leche*)—because the priests don't let him make love.

This joke, of course, is meant to be funny, but the thought behind it is serious: priests stifle the enjoyment of life and the expression of one's most necessary and intrinsic male inclinations.

In the second dominant type of religious joke, priests are revealed not as stiflers of sexuality, but rather as the fully sexual beings they are actually thought to be. The alleged hypocrisy of the clergy is nowhere better emphasized than in these stories. One concerns a woman who is trying to take Communion:

> A woman goes into a church dressed very provocatively with a low neckline. The priest therefore denies her Communion. She then goes to the priest's superior, the head of the parish, and complains, saying that *"por derecho divino"*—by divine right—she should be permitted to take Communion. The head priest replies, looking her up and down, "The left one, too!"

The priest's irresistible attraction for the woman caused him to misinterpret what she meant by "divine right." In Spanish the joke depends on the fact that the word *derecho*, when used as a noun to mean a "right" in the sense of a moral law, is masculine in gender. *Pecho*, the most common noun for a woman's breast, is also masculine, so that the priest could easily take the word *derecho* as a masculine-gender adjective, modifying that noun.

Finally, as the following joke shows, priests are considered no more worthy of salvation than are any other men:

> There was a bride and groom who were in a car driving to their wedding, when suddenly they had a disastrous accident and died. When they arrived in heaven, they told St. Peter, "We want to get married." Said St. Peter, "But that's impossible!" "Why?" asked the couple incredulously. "Because there aren't any priests here who can marry you!"

Monteros men say that priests are just as likely to go to hell as are prostitutes, bullfighters, and robbers, whose lifestyles all in some way contradict Church teachings. Priests are unworthy of special treatment, and therefore should receive none.

Religious Brotherhoods and Processions

Despite their relative anticlericalism and modest participation in formal Church activities, men in Monteros cannot be said to be unreligious. For one thing, almost all of them embrace some concept of a higher being, God, who created the world and is responsible for its daily operation. They are likely, too, as protection against illness or misfortune to wear religious medallions or crucifixes, either around their necks or attached to keychains. Even the most openly antireligious men show an occasional burst of deep religiosity by making vows (*promesas*) to the saints, to whom they pledge to pay homage if the saints help them by providing rain, curing an illness, or preventing them from overindulging in liquor or tobacco. Men, as much as women, are *devotos* (devoted admirers) of particular saints who have shown themselves to be especially miraculous in the achievement of individual or community goals. Nowhere is this devotion to the saints more clearly manifested than in religious brotherhoods and processions.

Lay brotherhoods, as George Foster has shown (1953), have long held an important place in Hispanic social and religious life. From recent studies, particularly those of Isidoro Moreno Navarro (1972, 1974), we may consider that the province of Seville is the epicenter of these voluntary organizations; here, without doubt, *cofradías*, or confraternities, as these brotherhoods are generally known, have their most widespread support and perform their most cirtical social and economic functions. But *cofradías* are important throughout the agro-towns of Andalusia, including Monteros, where, despite the fact that over the past half-century they have been reduced in number, they still maintain their vitality.

Currently, there are, and throughout the post–Civil War period there have been, three dominant *cofradías* in Monteros, each one organized around devotion to a particular saint: the Señor del Consuelo (Lord of Consolation), San José Obrero (St. Joseph the Worker), and the Virgen de la Cabeza (Virgin of the Head). Of these, the *cofradía* of the Señor del Consuelo, whose image is that of an enormous painting of a crucified Christ, copied from Velázquez, is undoubtedly the most important. Membership in this *cofradía* numbers in the thousands, and, indeed, is impossible to calculate ex-

*Men line up in procession for
St. Joseph the Worker.*

actly. Dues are minimal (ten *pesetas*, or about fifteen cents, per year), and many men, especially town emigrants, consider themselves to belong despite the fact that they never bother to pay the annual fee or attend the periodic meetings of the brotherhood. Traditionally, in the days before Social Security, this *cofradía*, like others, helped pay for the burial of deceased, needy members and also provided financial assistance to the widows of such members. Nowadays, its main function is to ensure the upkeep of the image of the Señor, to keep candles lit in the church in his honor throughout the year, and to organize the single most elaborate town event, the week-long Feria held in September in honor of the image and named after an important cattle fair, now nearly defunct, which coincided with the religious celebration.

The *cofradías* of San José Obrero and the Virgen de la Cabeza, with about 350 members each, are considerably less powerful, though they still play an important role in town life. San José Obrero is the youngest of the *cofradías*, dating only from the end of the Civil War when the Franco regime, in a probable attempt to coopt the socialist May Day celebrations, declared 1 May—the feast day of St. Joseph the Worker—to be a national holiday. Dues in this *cofradía* are a mere fifty *pesetas* (seventy-five cents) a year, and the money is used for the upkeep of the statue of San José, as well as for the annual breakfast and procession in his honor. The brotherhood of the Virgen de la Cabeza, a sculptured image guarded in a sanctuary high above the town, was traditionally a cattle breeders' association but nowadays incorporates a wider segment of the town populace. Its members likewise pay an annual fee of fifty *pesetas*; some members also temporarily lend the brotherhood heads of sheep whose lambs are sold at an annual auction to benefit the *cofradía*. The money is used for the upkeep of the shrine of the Virgin located high on a hilltop overlooking the town and to finance an annual *romería*, or pilgrimage, to the shrine on 15 April.

All these *cofradías* share two essential features: their membership is virtually limited to males, and, with one significant exception indicated below, membership is voluntary.[4] Why, we may then ask, do men who profess to be unreligious, and who practice formal religious duties to a much more restricted extent than do women, choose to belong to such brotherhoods and participate in their annual celebrations? Women, after all, have no comparable organizations through which they can express religious and social sentiments.

First, there is no doubt that membership is a symbolic means of defining and affirming social class affiliation. The *cofradía* of San José Obrero is the clearest case, for it is composed almost entirely of carpenters, masons, day laborers, mechanics, and other manual workers. A few storeowners also belong, but no one with social aspirations or pretensions, and certainly no *señoritos*, would consider joining. The *cofradía* of the Virgen de la Cabeza has a somewhat more widely distributed membership, including, besides the predominantly working-class brothers, many office employees and owners of commercial enterprises. There are also a handful of independent landowners, special devotees of the Virgin, who belong, but they are atypical.

In number of members and in class composition, the *cofradía* of the Señor del Consuelo has benefited from the fact that it is dedicated to the veneration of the single most holy image in town. Here there is no noticeable class restriction, for representatives of every occupational group and social position can be found on its membership list. On the other hand, this *cofradía* is considered to be a predominantly *señorito* body, not only because every male member

---

[4]There are a handful of women in the *cofradía* of the Virgen de la Cabeza. They take responsibility for cleaning and dressing the image before the annual *romaría* in her honor, but otherwise refrain from participation in *cofradía* affairs.

of the town elite belongs, but also because, in distinction to those from other classes, they all register their sons upon birth, often even before baptism, within the ranks of this brotherhood. While there are some men in Monteros who belong to no *cofradía*, every man of high social rank, and everyone who aspires to attain such a position, belongs to the *cofradía* of the Señor. Further, the *junta directiva*, or coordinating body of officers, of this *cofradía* is made up almost exclusively of men with money and high social rank, as it has been as far back as the Civil War. Though people without these attributes join the brotherhood, they can never hope to direct it.

It is clear that the *cofradía* of St. Joseph the Worker (the Virgin Mary's husband) has developed into a brotherhood of manual laborers because it is devoted to the veneration of a specifically working-class saint. Men from other occupational groups naturally find difficulty in identifying with or otherwise relating to such an image. But why should the *cofradía* of the Señor del Consuelo have achieved such importance for the town elite? For one thing, the elite, as the most educated, wealthy, and well-connected group in town, has since the Civil War been consistently in charge of important town affairs. If anything can be said to define Monteros as a unified community, it is, in addition to the fact that it comprises a single administrative-political unit, the common allegiance of its inhabitants to the Señor. The Señor is of such importance here that He can be said to represent the town itself. Not surprisingly, then, the elite has reserved for itself management of the most important annual town celebration, the Feria, which is devoted to the image of the Señor.

In addition, the Señor, in his own way, has come to represent law, order, stability, and historical continuity, all of which are highly valued by the Monteros elite. The *cofradía* of the Señor, unlike the others, has a special officer called the chronicler; the chronicler himself changes periodically, but he is always a highly literate individual with deep roots in Monteros who keeps a detailed record of brotherhood activities as well as of events of general interest within the town as a whole. There is a sense of historical mission in these records that is lacking in the other *cofradías*. This, as far as I can tell, has always been the case. When the old image of the Señor was destroyed by socialist workers during the Civil War, elite devotion to the image became even more solid than before. The image came to symbolize not only the town, but religion, political stability, and the predominance of the gifted, wealthy, and refined elements of society as well. This is why one *señorito* could say, "I don't believe in God, but I believe in the Señor del Consuelo." And

The Señor del Consuelo in procession.

this is also why he, like all those of his station, contributes a portion of his grain harvest each year to the support of the church in which the image of the Señor is kept. *Señorito* support of the Señor means self-preservation.

But we have yet to explain why men in general belong to *cofradías* and participate in their activities despite their relatively limited involvement in the more important Church functions of Mass and Communion. The best way to approach this issue is to analyze the single most important religious ritual in Monteros: the annual procession that takes place every year on 17 September in honor of the town's patron saint, El Señor del Consuelo, the Lord of Consolation. I have pointed out elsewhere (Brandes 1976) that processions throughout Spain are becoming greatly reduced in number, primarily because of recent Church reforms and the desire of most of the Spanish clergy to rationalize religion, in the sense of making it less mysterious and magical. Monteros is no exception, and many traditional processions, especially those of Holy Week, have since about 1965 been dropped from the town religious calendar. It is hardly surprising that in Monteros the processions over which the clergy had control were the first to go, while those in the hands of the *cofradías*—like that of El Señor del Consuelo—have survived.

*Affixing an offering to the back of
the image of the Señor del Consuelo.*

Processions, in this context, become an affirmation of popular religious sentiment against the formalism of the Church and its representatives. Above all, the procession of the Señor del Consuelo draws enormous attendance and support and is surrounded with deep emotional fervor. It therefore deserves our special consideration.

Preparations for the procession begin in the early afternoon when the painting of the Señor del Consuelo is removed from its position in the most elegant of the three Monteros churches and is bolted onto a heavy metal frame that has two parallel rails, thus enabling it to be carried. As the image rests on its frame on the church altar, barefoot devotees, the vast majority of them women, approach it, touch the feet of the crucified Christ with their right hand, then kiss their hand and make the sign of the cross. Other barefoot women crawl on their knees toward the image; as they slowly proceed up the center aisle, they occasionally catch the eye of people seated in the pews, at which point they squint and look upward in a sign of agony. A wooden box is placed in front of the image for donations, and during the afternoon it becomes filled with large bills. Other money is pinned onto the red cloth lining at the back of the painting, where little silver-colored bells, newly purchased in honor of the Señor, are placed as well.

At 5:30 P.M., young men in their late teens and early twenties take their places along the metal rails supporting the image. A half-hour later, with the church and nearby streets overflowing with crowds of devoted followers, the image is lifted from the altar and carried outside, where people cry out in unison, "¡Viva el Señor! ¡Viva el Señor del Consuelo! ¡Viva!" The street just outside the church is within minutes transformed from a mass of practically indistinguishable crushed bodies into two neat parallel lines stretching as far as the eye can see. Most of the many participants in the procession, who represent both sexes and all age groups, carry tall lighted candles.

For a total of three hours, the solemn procession winds its way through the narrow streets and ample plazas of Monteros. Three choirboys, two of them carrying large metal batons and one with the banner of the *cofradía* of the Señor, are in the lead. Toward the end of the procession comes the image, followed by the three Monteros priests and by lines of civil and military functionaries—the mayor and vice mayors, town councilmen, and Civil Guards. They are flanked on either side by two *maceros* ("mace-bearers"), town streetsweepers who are dressed for this occasion in elaborate Renaissance garb and who carry large wooden maces. Finally, there comes a band, playing somewhat incongruous Sousa-style marches, and women who are walking the entire route on their knees. Skyrockets set off by male spectators puncture the atmosphere with a thundering sound. When the image of the Señor pauses at the various town plazas, they burst at especially frequent intervals, creating an almost deafening noise. The only other stops are made when townspeople, leaning down from house balconies along the route, pin money on the back of the image. When, at about 9:00 P.M., the image reenters the church, it is replete with gifts, a testimony to the deep devotion of the people of Monteros and neighboring settlements to their Señor.

One can only describe the atmosphere during the procession as one of common humility, suffering, and abnegation. Turner would say (1969, pp. 94–108) that the event displays elements of *communitas*, because a spirit of sacredness, equality, and mystical love prevails. Notable in this respect is the participation of Gypsies alongside Castellanos—Gypsies never attend Mass—and the symbolic elevation of the streetsweepers to the level of town functionaries. Participants in the procession weep before the beauty and power of the image, and their public donations of money and

Women in procession.

displays of servility in honor of the image serve as a symbolic suspension of the worldly quest for wealth and prestige.

Yet, within all this humble ritual drama there is still evidence of the sex and status distinctions that pervade Monteros society. To walk on one's knees in procession, for example, is considered a specifically female, working-class mode of sacrifice. No man nor any woman of the elite would publicly display such a humiliating gesture. Similarly, fully a quarter to a third of all women in the procession go barefoot, but none of them—with the exception of one woman, who sees this act as a particularly great concession in honor of the Señor specifically because she *is* of the elite—are among the upper stratum of Monteros society. Of the men, there are barely a handful of the aged, accompanied by their wives, who walk barefoot in the procession. Once more, as in the olive harvest and the Mass, we are struck by the fact that women place themselves in a lower position than men. Men, on the other hand, are the only people who toss up skyrockets, and we should recall here that the expression *tirar un cohete*—"toss a skyrocket"—is among the most common euphemisms to describe seminal ejaculation. Even in religious processions, men assert their sexual role.

The skyrockets are expensive, however, and represent a monetary sacrifice in honor of the Señor. This mixture of suffering and sexual assertiveness is to be found in other aspects of the procession as well. There are thirty boys in all who carry the heavy image, fifteen on either rail. They are selected through competition and considerations of height; the boys who arrive first for the task get the job, and they have to be more or less of equal height so that the weight of the image is evenly distributed among them. Everyone in town considers it a great privilege to carry the image, and there is often fierce fighting to determine who gets the right to the limited spaces along the rail. Immediately, then, the boys who win the competition and are considered physically suited to the job have struck points in their favor. They are the victorious competitors; they, among all those in their age-group, have the opportunity to display corporal competence and strength.

Yet, as the procession winds its way through the Monteros streets, the boys agonize under the tremendous weight of the image, pausing whenever the opportunity permits to drink water offered them by those along the route. For the rest of their lives they will tell the tale of the tremendous battle with bodily fatigue that they underwent on that occasion. Suffering manifests itself in other ways. Men unabashedly attribute their hernias to the strain of having carried the image in their youth. And when one young man gave up his place along the rail to an emigrant who had come all the way from Switzerland especially to carry the image, it was considered by everyone in the community as an especially great sacrifice.

The combined power and suffering of the image-bearers mirror the same attributes in the Señor del Consuelo himself. The Señor, on the one hand, is a potent miracle-performer, equally capable of curing and inflicting illnesses. His great strength is recounted in numerous legends of the vengeance he inflicted during the Civil War. During the war, it is said, a man stole a gun from the *señoritos* and fired seven times into the painting. The next day, the man woke up mute and within a week he died. Another man is said to have defiled the image by poking out the Señor's eye. In the morning, he awoke, asked his wife to raise the shades, and discovered he was blind. Yet another sacrilegious man, who kicked the painting, wound up with permanently sore tumors running down his leg.

But the overbearing power of the Señor is matched by his suffering. One has only to look at the painting of the crucified Christ, his head hung pitifully sideways, his eyes downcast, blood streaming from his hands and chest, to recognize that he is a man who has sacrificed greatly. The dark, brooding landscape against which he is cast adds to this mood as well. There is no doubt that the boys who

Men with skyrockets.

carry the image, those who at once display power and suffering, identify closely with the Son of God, in whose Father's likeness they, too, are said to have been fashioned. Under such circumstances, it is unthinkable that women should ever be responsible for carrying the painting.

The procession of the Señor del Consuelo is critical for our understanding of town religion because it can teach us something about the conditions under which men are willing to display their religiosity publicly. The contrast with Mass and Communion is instructive. In Mass and Communion the priest, an actual male personage with whom every other man is presumed to be in competition, is in charge and on center stage. For reasons already described, the men of Monteros find this situation unacceptable. In the procession, on the other hand, leaders of the brotherhood of the Señor del Consuelo take complete control of the event. The town priests, along with a host of secular functionaries, accompany the image of the Señor. But they are in no way perceived to be in a position of authority. In fact, it could be said that the only true authority on this occasion is the Señor himself, and it is easy to bend to His power because it emanates from a supernatural being against whom all men are equally impotent.

It is significant, too, that the procession is an outdoor event. Mass and Communion occur not only in a conceptually feminine space, but also indoors where there is little opportunity for public display. If townspeople are asked why it is that men who never go to church are willing to participate in the procession of the Señor, the most common answers are the following: "They feel big and great"; "They can dress up and show off"; "It makes them feel important." In other words, the procession allows for the manifestation of an undeniable male narcissism, recognized by the people themselves. This narcissism is presumed to be particularly characteristic of the *cofradía* leaders and their male associates, all of whom adorn themselves during the procession with scapulars. To be seated anonymously on a bench listening to Mass in no way affords the same opportunity.

Finally, we must not overlook the fact that in honoring the Señor, men are essentially bowing to a self-portrait, a supernatural image of themselves. They are attracted to the Señor because He is invested with the coexistent qualities of power and weakness that they experience personally. If a figure as omnipotent as the Señor can be weak, so can they. This is one reason, I believe, that they are attracted to the procession: it permits them the opportunity to express debility openly, with no fear of social reprisal or embarrassment. Yet even on this occasion, and at practically all moments, expressions of dependency are matched by a show of strength. Consider just that the men who carry the image complain about being thirsty and request a water jug frequently. A manifestation of weakness, we would think, if we didn't know—as everyone present knows—that the water is spiked with gin. Under these conditions, the physical feat of the men who carry the heavy image becomes even more impressive than we might ordinarily realize.

I shall only mention briefly that my ideas about the procession are borne out by male participation in funerary ritual. In Monteros, as throughout most of Spain, cemetaries are considered to be dangerous and eerie because they are filled with spirits of the dead, whose corporal remains at night emit and cover the ground with a luminous substance known as *fuegos fatuos*—"fatuous fires." Consequently, cemetaries are located at a substantial distance from town. After a funeral Mass, which some men attend and more men wait through outside, the priest blesses the body of the deceased. From then on, it is the male relatives and friends of the deceased who take over. They vie for the honored and privileged, but also painfully tiring, experience of bearing the coffin on their shoulders to the cemetary. The vast majority of mourners, unable to secure a place at the coffin, march in procession through town and out to the cemetary. This act is perceived as a sacrifice of time, and perhaps of health as well, for they expose themselves at the cemetary to possible illness. But equally they demonstrate the courage and strength necessary to invade the dangerous territory that is on this occasion restricted to men. At this event, essentially the same conditions as in the procession of the Señor del Consuelo apply: men are free of priestly control and have the opportunity for open display of highly valued masculine attributes.

To understand the full symbolic impact of the procession, however, we must remember that it follows upon the parade of Giants and Big-Heads. We should recall that that parade is above all a public display of rebellion against authority and control. Young boys, fourteen to sixteen years of age, dress in costume and express their power by imposing fear and physical aggression on younger children. Here, in this procession, their immediate seniors enact the repentance. Humility before the Señor, being crushed under his image, is the means by which these young men express their submission to the ultimate and universal forces that dominate their lives.

Taken together, the parade and the procession encapsulate the primary experience of Monteros men. Men must assert themselves and display aggressiveness, even if only through humor. But they confront the world in a posture of self-defense, as if they might momentarily collapse under the impact of the powerful sex and status rivals against whom they wage constant, albeit symbolic, battle.

The Folklore of Dominance and Control

What makes itself felt in a human community
as a desire for freedom may be a revolt
against some existing injustice, and so may
prove favorable to a further development of
civilization; it may remain compatible with
civilization. But it may also spring from the
survival of primitive personality, which is still
untamed by civilization, and may thus become
the basis of hostility to civilization. The urge
for freedom, therefore, is directed against particular forms and demands of civilization or
against civilization altogether.

11

Sigmund Freud,
Civilization and Its Discontents (1930)

Throughout this volume I have examined a wide variety of folkloristic genres in order to show their relationship to the critically important themes of social status and sexual identity. It is obvious that masculine folklore in Monteros reveals a pervasive concern with social and sexual differentiation. In conclusion, however, I wish to make explicit that these two themes really address the same basic issue: dominance versus submission. Whether I am speaking of ritual or jokes, of nicknames or riddles, of slang or skits, the recurrent pattern is a preoccupation with power, domination, and control. Through their folklore, the men of Monteros not only express their images of the power hierarchies that constitute their universe, but also try to maximize their respective positions within those hierarchies.

There seem to be at least three modes, each of them represented in various folkloristic genres, through which men can express their concern with power and domination. The first is spatial. In the pageant of Giants and Big-Heads, there exists an implicit analogy between height and supremacy; parents and monarchs, the powerholders, are taller than children and subjects. Similarly, at the olive harvest, men, with their undeniable economic superiority and presumed moral preeminence, are situated at a markedly higher level than women. And in religious ritual of various sorts, activities like kneeling, barefootedness, and walking on one's knees all entail a submissive posture through reduction in height and characterize women more than they do men. In Monteros folklore there thus exists a largely unconscious yet undeniable relationship on the symbolic level between relative height and supremacy.

A second important mode for the expression of dominance-submission relationships is verbal. In everyday conversation, the nonreciprocal use of titles separates the economically and politically dominant segment of society from those with less power. The reciprocal use of the pronouns *tu* and *usted* also acts as a boundary-maintaining device, operating not only to divide the Monteros populace socially, but also to perpetuate the status divisions upon which the concentration of power ultimately rests. As for slang and colloquialisms, it is through these means that the men of Monteros demonstrate continual concern with their potential for being symbolically feminized, and express their fear of being reduced to the submissive posture that is supposed to characterize women in sexual intercourse. Clever repartees and riddles are additional verbal devices that actually elevate or reduce men, albeit temporarily, to dominant or subordinate positions.

The third mode for the expression of power relationships in Monteros is physical. In skits like "The Blackbird" and "The Card Game," for example, there occurs the actual physical domination of several actors over an unsuspecting colleague, just as female onlookers during a number of the other folk dramas are subject to humiliation and abuse by the men who control the show. When men *hacer las facas del rey* at the olive harvest, they force one of their number into an undeniably submissive posture and try to control him, just as they do in less dramatic and extreme form when men poke one another from behind and perpetrate other playful pranks. Finally, in the domain of ritual, we must not overlook the physical domination that Giants and Big-Heads try to impose on their youthful onlookers, nor the submissiveness that men who carry the image of the Señor del Consuelo experience as they suffer under its tremendous weight.

The prevalence of dominance and submission as a theme in male folklore in part merely reflects the severely unequal distribution of power among the opposing sex and status groups in society as a whole. However, the folklore we have examined—largely because it is so enormously varied and pervasive—actually may function to perpetuate social divisions as well. It has operated in this manner, first, by reinforcing negative stereotypes. Jokes that downgrade Gypsies implicitly justify Castellano political and economic domination. The same holds true for proverbs and jokes about women; these genres foster the impression that females, if given free reign, will undermine the social order, challenge the dominant position of men within that order, and ultimately destroy the emotional and physical security upon which the stability of any society rests.

By perpetuating negative stereotypes, the men of Monteros actually rationalize to themselves the suppression of female and Gypsy liberties. These groups are converted, through the folklore, into scapegoats whom men can conveniently blame for all sorts of ills ranging from the personal to the social. If men become sexually weak, it is their wives, rather than themselves, who can be held responsible. If status distinctions are more severe than people might wish, the women are held accountable, just as they are when town governmental matters, in the hands of a female mayor, are less smooth than desirable. Gypsies are considered a public nuisance and are said to drain society's wealth through their parasitism. Since they embody potentially invisible power, Gypsies must be held under tight and vigilant control. Male folklore thus justifies the social domination of Castellano men while at the same time absolving them of responsibility for the misfortunes that may result under their rule. For whenever social or personal failures become manifest, women and Gypsies can be declared the guilty parties.

Monteros male folklore further perpetuates systems of unequal power distribution through childhood socialization. Through daily exposure to slang, jokes, proverbs, and other verbal devices, children come to learn the predominant stereotypes of women and Gypsies and for the most part to accept the folkloristic portrayal of these oppressed groups. In observing skits, children in the not-too-distant past were presented with a graphic portrayal in microcosm of dominance-submission relationships, primarily as manifested between the sexes but also between status and age groups as well. The same is true, we should repeat, of the pageant of Giants and Big-Heads. Rituals and traditional performances of these types—as much as anything by the investment of time and energy that goes into them—implicitly legitimize in the minds of youthful spectators the relationships they portray.

There is no doubt, too, that the folklore perpetuates existing power relationships by providing a temporary sense of domination and control to men who normally lack it. Ritual is a good example.

Young men who play the role of Big-Heads are actually converted for the duration of the pageant into bullies whose unpredictable authoritarian demeanor is fully sanctioned. Similarly, during the performance of skits, grown men traditionally received social approval for seemingly irrational physical assaults on actors and audience alike. A different type of domination is manifested by the youths who carry the image of the Señor del Consuelo in procession; their personal sense of prestige and power emanates from community recognition of the supposedly remarkable physical feat in which they are engaged. In the same way, men who, because of educational deficiencies and economic vulnerability, are actually deprived of worldly control become temporarily dominant through riddling. It is reasonable to suppose that all of these situations by providing actual, albeit ephemeral, relief from social submissiveness ultimately stabilize the structurally critical and enduring distribution of power within Monteros society as a whole.

If the folklore we have analyzed perpetuates social divisions, we must not forget that it also helps on occasion to overcome them. Abrahams and Bauman (1978) have recently called our attention to the fact that festivals that ordinarily might be perceived as highlighting social differentiation may be viewed equally well as bringing distinctive and opposing segments of a community together. With regard to Carnival on the isle of St. Vincent and belsnickling (a type of mumming) in Nova Scotia, they write:

> Most of the time in the communities we have examined, the forces of order and disorder, respectability and license, do not confront one another. . . . On those occasions when these opposed segments of the community do come together, the result is characteristically confusion or embarrassment. In carnival and belsnickling, however, the two sets of elements, each clearly identifiable, participate together within a unified event productive of enjoyment and a sense of community. The picture is not one of hostility, but of harmony (Abrahams and Bauman 1978, p. 207).

This statement certainly applies to Monteros rituals, skits, and olive harvest behavior. To be sure, on these occasions the marked sex and status divisions that pervade the town receive overt expression. But at the same time these events, by bringing people together in an emotionally charged atmosphere, produce a temporarily heightened sense of social cohesion.

It is relatively simple to understand why the events function as sources of unification. At the olive harvest women and men who are normally uneasy in one another's presence have occasion to joke with one another in an otherwise tabooed, sexual manner. Overt sexuality is equally important in skits, during which members of the two sexes, ordinarily separated by a chasm of embarrassed self-consciousness, are brought together through the inevitably cohesive power of humor. The same can be said for the pageant of Giants and Big-Heads, where youth of all social strata are united through common observation of raucous activity. For a full understanding of all these events we must heed Glassie's reminder that in the traditional communities of rural Europe, "an occasional break for enjoyment is not a trivial matter" (1975, p. 125). Such breaks not only provide personal pleasure, but do so in a communal atmosphere that promotes a sense of shared enjoyment. In religious processions, of course, the experience is somber but similarly shared and evocative of deep emotions, and hence equally capable of temporarily obliterating ordinary social boundaries.

But folklore operates to bind people together on more than just special occasions. In Monteros, much of the folklore that emerges in daily interaction unites people who ordinarily confront one another in a competitive or otherwise adverse relationship. This is true of pranks, for example. They tend to place two or more men in unequal positions of power, but at the same time function, through permitted disrespect, to demonstrate the essential equality—and hence unity—among all parties involved. In the same fashion, nicknames, while separating social strata, provide people within the same stratum with a sense of equality that inevitably fosters emotional security and support. Nicknames also create a common identity among members of the same family. Thus, those folkloristic devices that seem to pull individuals apart from one another invariably unify people as well. In some cases broad segments of the community are brought together; in other instances unity takes place on a more limited scale. But in all instances we may observe in the folklore of Monteros the simultaneous exercise of both divisive and cohesive influences.

But male folklore, we must remember, addresses the issue of internal emotional control and domination, and not just the relationship among groups. As we have seen from the analysis of speech metaphors, men perceive themselves to be creatures of nature, governed by their special physical attributes, which occasionally impel them to act impulsively and contrary to normal role expectations. This perception, shared by society as a whole, implicitly sanctions male erratic behavior and provides a convenient explanation for socially irresponsible actions. The metaphors promote a conception of masculinity as acultural; men, to express their sexual identity, are compelled occasionally to burst out of routine social and cultural constraints. By submitting to their supposedly natural inclinations—or by speaking as if such submission is normal for any man—they can free themselves of guilt for otherwise deviant thoughts and actions. They thereby achieve a sense of personal autonomy, of freedom from socially as well as personally imposed rules, that they would deny to women.

The folklore also demonstrates that men, however attracted they might be to the unharnessed expression of individual will, are simultaneously frightened by the prospect of such rampant nonconformity. Gypsy jokes, more than any other genre, reveal the basic insecurities aroused by a group of individuals who are said to be governed by no laws and who are classified as existing totally outside Castellano society. The stereotypical libertarian quality of Gypsy life is both admired and scorned. We may suppose that men who narrate Gypsy jokes temporarily derive a sense of freedom from identifying with Gypsy protagonists who blithely ignore or controvert restrictive norms. But these protagonists simultaneously offer a frightening specter of the low cultural level to which Castellano society would sink if everybody conformed to the Gypsy model. For Monteros men, submission to social rules is ultimately necessary.

The same message is implied in the annual festival in honor of the Señor del Consuelo. On the first day children, disguised as Big-Heads, enact a humorous but nonetheless violent and unpredictable role that provides a concrete visual impression of, we might say, the absence of culture. Children are appropriate actors in this context because in actuality they are only partial cultural beings, still incompletely socialized. The following day the imposition of burdensome social guidelines is overt, as boys submit themselves, almost in self-punishment, to be crushed under the weighty image of an all-powerful authority. These youths, older than those who play the role of Big-Heads, have presumably matured to the point where they can be expected to conform; they are both capable of such behavior and cognizant of the benefits that it ultimately confers.

Men, through their folklore, thus come to struggle with feelings of self-control. The folklore not only teaches them the desirability of such control, but also sanctions and provides the culturally appropriate means for the occasional release from it. The temporary release may be direct and immediate, as it is for the men who enact roles in skits and in the Big-Head pageant. Or it may be vicarious, as occurs when men observe the Big-Heads in action, or when they narrate or listen to jokes. In any of these instances, liberation takes place on a humorous plane, where it produces no danger to the social order. Nor does this type of liberation threaten personal reputation, for the male actor or narrator or prankster fully conforms to approved masculine roles. In the competent performance of these roles, he can thus simultaneously earn prestige, acquire a temporary sense of transcendent power, and achieve freedom from social contraints. The impact of folkloristic performance on the individual, therefore, is to create a safety valve and prevent, or at least forestall, the eruption of truly hostile, divisive behavior.

Whenever we raise the image of hostility in Spain, we cannot help but recall the Franco regime, which, utilizing violence and repression itself, successfully squelched the political expression of large-scale social, economic, and regional divisions throughout the country. During forty years of dictatorial rule, these divisions festered below the surface without any legitimate means of release. General Francisco Franco died in November 1975 in the middle of my initial field stay, so that the present study was carried out at the tail end of that repressive political era. The year immediately following his death occasioned no relaxation of political rule. In fact, throughout a decade of research in rural Spain, I never experienced a greater political clampdown than that which occurred in the year following Franco's demise, when the turn of events and the allocation of power were still uncertain (Brandes 1977). Only subsequently did the democratic course upon which Spain has apparently successfully embarked manifest itself clearly.

Considering the political atmosphere in which the folklore I have analyzed here was observed and collected, it is reasonable to inquire briefly about the possible impact of the Spanish dictatorship on the folkloristic theme of domination and submission. Specifically, we may ask whether the policies of the Franco regime directly influenced the expression or exaggeration of this theme in folklore during the period of my study. My answer is perhaps oversimplified but, for lack of historical hindsight, still tentative. I would say that to the extent that the Franco dictatorship preserved traditional gender and status divisions in rural Andalusia it correspondingly fostered the social conditions under which this folklore has flourished. In other words, I believe that it is the social conditions rather than the regime per se that have mainly created the atmosphere in which male Monteros folklore can flourish. As these conditions disappear, so too will much of the folklore analyzed in this volume.

I state this opinion partly because of historical and distributional evidence. A number of the folkloristic phenomena we have described, including skits, the pageant of Giants and Big-Heads, and the behavior that accompanies the olive harvest, long predate the Franco era in Monteros, and owe their existence—as I have tried to demonstrate throughout—to circumstances much more fundamental than political policies, which change considerably from one decade to another, even in the case of a single dictatorial regime. As we have seen, the skits have all but disappeared along with the breakdown in conditions that sustained them; this occurred during the Franco period. At the olive harvest, too, women have begun to assume the traditionally male role in collecting the fruit, just another example of how changing economic circumstances under Franco have yielded alterations in behavior.

Then, too, there exist analogues to the folkloristic items described here for Monteros in other parts of the Mediterranean world as well as in European America. Many of the ethnic jokes, sexual jokes, and animal metaphors seized upon by the men of Monteros for their own social and psychological ends are also utilized by other peoples who find themselves in parallel circumstances. I predict that if we were carefully to trace the distribution and history of all these items, we would probably discover no necessary correlation between their existence and the particular political regimes under which they thrive. Certainly, pranks and riddles all over the world function in a roughly similar way to that which I have described in Monteros.

The matter boils down to the fact that much of Monteros male folklore ultimately owes its existence to severe cleavages in the social system, specifically to divisions between ethnic, gender, and status groups within Andalusia as a whole and within the town in particular. These cleavages are rapidly becoming less marked, and we may presume that with the advance of social equality a lot of the folklore that is designed to bolster unequal conditions, or to help men cope with their status anxieties, will disappear. Most scholars believe that the Franco regime severely retarded the march toward equality, and I agree with them. In that sort of indirect way, the regime has been responsible for perpetuating into the 1970s a good portion of the town folklore that existed earlier in this century.

On the other hand, we must recall that another huge element of Monteros male folklore refers to psychological concerns that transcend all political and economic circumstances. The childhood struggle to become socialized, to learn to control one's bodily functions and adjust to the authority of one's parents, is an obvious example, and this concern, as we have witnessed, emerges clearly in jokes and ritual. We might also argue that there is an inherently ambivalent quality to close male friendships wherever they are found, and that the ambivalence is overcome through teasing and prank-playing of one type or another, just as occurs in Monteros. And certainly the cross-sex banter that takes place at the olive harvest is not unique to Andalusian men and women.

Monteros male folklore, as I have analyzed it, thus assumes a particular configuration because of a combination of culturally specific and psychologically universal circumstances. There is every reason to believe that even as soon as five years from now the configuration will have changed. Many specific folkloristic items will have disappeared, and those that persist, like perhaps the pageant of Giants and Big-Heads, may by then have lost some of their current meaning and taken on a new symbolic significance. We may predict with certainty that a number of the pranks and riddles that I have observed will still exist a decade from now. They will always operate as a friendly means of expressing power and control, but may very well lose some of their implications for the definition of status groups. We can only guess at the direction this folkloristic evolution will take, but we can be sure that whatever happens will be instructive and worthy of study.

Of course, to the people of Monteros themselves the folklore seems a rather odd object of investigation. Throughout my field stay, people never ceased to be amazed that I should take the time and energy to record jokes and riddles, to uncover obsolete skits, and to attend the olive harvest and ritual functions. From the native point of view, neither folklore nor the genres of which it consists are objectively definable categories of experience. They are life itself, and like life, they are ends in themselves, not to be collected and analyzed, but to be enjoyed.

As a butcher friend of mine put it, "If they ask you in America why we have so many children, tell them it is because of our wine, our jokes, and our happiness." This statement, in effect, conveys a self-image of carefree joviality. Indeed, on the manifest level, Monteros men are nearly always jovial and high-spirited. They take pride in their verbal cleverness and state boastfully that "Here in Andalusia everything has two—even three—meanings." It is through folklore, which permits such oblique expression of sentiments, that men rise above the fear and antagonisms that otherwise would destroy them. And it is thus the folklore that ultimately enables them to lead fulfilled, stable lives in the company of family, friends, and community.

This stability, the force that binds, is as important a dimension of the male experience as are sex and status divisions. In Monteros, male folklore not only reflects simultaneous unity and separation but is the very medium through which these two tendencies are expressed. To a large extent, the folklore is much more than a mirror of the male world; in my judgment, it is that world, or at least that part of their world that they most enjoy and appreciate. To the men of Monteros, it is a never-ending source of sustenance, strength, and creativity.

References Cited

Aarne, Antti, and Thompson, Stith
  1961 *The types of the folktale: a classification and bibliography.* Second
        revision. Helsinki: Suomalainen Tiedeakatemia.

Abrahams, Roger D.
  1968 Introductory remarks to a rhetorical theory of folklore. *Journal of
        American Folklore* 81: 143–58.
  1972 Folk drama. In *Folklore and folklife: an introduction,* ed. Richard
        M. Dorson, pp. 351–62. Chicago: University of Chicago Press.
  1976 The complex relations of simple forms. In *Folklore genres,* ed.
        Dan Ben Amos, pp. 193–214. Austin and London: University of
        Texas Press.

Abrahams, Roger D., and Bauman, Richard
  1978 Ranges of festival behavior. In *The reversible world: symbolic in-
        version in art and society,* ed. Barbara A. Babcock, pp. 193–208.
        Ithaca, N.Y.: Cornell University Press.

Abrahams, Roger D., and Dundes, Alan
  1969 On elephantasy and elephanticide. *Psychoanalytic Review* 56:
        225–41.

Aceves, Joseph
  1971 *Social change in a Spanish village.* Cambridge, Mass.: Schenkman.

Almerich, Luis
  1944 *Tradiciones, fiestas y costumbres populares de Barcelona.* Barcelona: Librería Millá.
Anonymous
  1971 *The Celestina: a fifteenth-century Spanish novel in dialogue.* Trans. Lesley Byrd Simpson. Berkeley and Los Angeles: University of California Press.
Antoun, Richard T.
  1968 On the significance of names in an Arab village. *Ethnology* 7: 158–70.
Ariès, Philippe
  1962 *Centuries of childhood: a social history of family life.* Trans. Robert Baldick. New York: Vintage Books.
Arora, Shirley L.
  1977 *Proverbial Comparisons and Related Expressions in Spanish.* Berkeley: University of California Press. Folklore Studies number 29.

Barrett, Richard A.
  1978 Village modernization and changing nickname practices in northern Spain. *Journal of Anthropological Research* 34: 92–108.
Barrick, Mac E.
  1974 The newspaper riddle joke. *Journal of American Folklore* 87: 253–57.
Barron, M. L.
  1950 A content analysis of intergroup humor. *American Sociological Review* 15: 88–94.
Bauman, Richard
  1975 Verbal art as performance. *American Anthropologist* 77:290–312.
Beitl, Klaus
  1961 *Die Umgangsriesen.* Wien: Verlag Notring der Wissenschaftlichen Verbonde.
Berlyne, D. E.
  1968 Laughter, humor and play. In *Handbook of social psychology*, ed. G. Lindsey and E. Aronson, vol. 3: 795–852. 2d ed. Cambridge, Mass.: Addison-Wesley.
Bernard, H. Russell
  1968–1969 Paratsoukli: institutionalized nicknaming in rural Greece. *Ethnología Europaea* 2: 65–74.
Berreman, Gerald D.
  1962 *Behind many masks: ethnography and impression management in a Himalayan village.* Monograph No. 4. Ithaca, N.Y.: Society for Applied Anthropology.
Blum, Richard, and Blum, Eva
  1965 *Health and healing in rural Greece: a study of three communities.* Stanford: Stanford University Press.
  1970 *The dangerous hour: the lore and culture of crisis and mystery in rural Greece.* London: Chatto and Windus.

Bouissac, Paul
  1976 *Circus and culture: a semiotic approach.* Bloomington, Ind.: University of Indiana Press.
Bourke, John G.
  1891 *Scatalogic rites of all nations.* Washington, D.C.: W. H. Lowdermilk.
Brandes, Stanley
  1974 Crianza infantil y comportamiento relativo a roles familiares en México. *Ethnica* 8: 33–47.
  1975a *Migration, kinship, and community: tradition and transition in a Spanish village.* New York: Academic Press.
  1975b The selection process in proverb use: a Spanish example. *Southern Folklore Quarterly* 38: 167–86.
  1975c The structural and demographic implications of nicknames in Navanogal, Spain. *American Ethnologist* 2: 139–48.
  1976 The priest as agent of secularization in rural Spain. In *Economic transformation and steady-state values: essays in the ethnography of Spain,* ed. Edward C. Hansen, Joseph B. Aceves, and Gloria Levitas, pp. 22–29. Queens College Publications in Anthropology, No. 2. New York: Queens College Press.
  1977 Peaceful protest: Spanish political humor in a time of crisis. *Western Folklore* 36: 331–46.
Brenan, Gerald
  1964 *The Spanish labyrinth: an account of the social and political background of the Spanish Civil War.* Cambridge: Cambridge University Press.
Brill, A. A.
  1955 *Lectures on psychoanalytic psychiatry.* New York: Vintage Books.
Brunvand, Jan Harold
  1968 *American folklore: an introduction.* New York: W. W. Norton.
Burma, John H.
  1946 Humor as a technique in race conflict. *American Sociological Review* 11: 710–15.
Bushnell, John
  1958 La Virgen de Guadalupe as surrogate mother in San Juan Atzingo. *American Anthropologist* 60: 261–65.

Campbell, J. K.
  1964 *Honour, family and patronage: a study of institutions and moral values in a Greek mountain community.* Oxford: Clarendon Press.
Caro Baroja, Julio
  1964 *The world of the witches.* Trans. Nigel Glendinning. London: Weidenfeld and Nicolson.
  1965 *El Carnaval: análisis histórico-cultural.* Madrid: Taurus.
Casas Gaspar, Enrique
  1947 *Costumbres españolas de nacimiento, noviazgo, casamiento y muerte.* Madrid.
Cátedra Tomás, María

1976   Notas sobre la "envidia": los "ojos malos"—entre los "Vaqueiros de Alzada." In *Temas de antropología española*, ed. Carmelo Lisón Tolosana, pp. 9–48. Madrid: AKAL.

Child, Francis J.
1898   *The English and Scottish popular ballads*. Vol. 5. Boston: Houghton Mifflin.

Christensen, James Boyd
1963   Utani: joking, sexual licence, and social obligation among the Luguru. *American Anthropologist* 65: 1314–27.

Christian, William A.
1972   *Person and God in a Spanish valley*. New York: Seminar Press.

Clebert, Jean
1967   *The Gypsies*. Baltimore: Penguin Books.

Cohen, Eugene N.
1977   Nicknames, social boundaries, and community in an Italian village. *International Journal of Contemporary Sociology* 14(1 and 2): 102–13.

Cohen, Percy S.
1980   Psychoanalysis and cultural symbolism. In *Symbol as Sense*, ed. Mary LeCron Foster and Stanley Brandes. New York: Academic Press. In press.

Colson, Elizabeth
1962   Joking relationships among the Plateau Tonga of Northern Rhodesia. In *The Plateau Tonga of Northern Rhodesia*, pp. 66–83. Manchester: Manchester University Press.

Costa, Joaquín
1967   *Oligarquía y caciquismo, colectivismo agrario, y otros escritos*. Madrid: Alianza. (Originally published 1902.)

Cothran, Kay L.
1974   Talking trash in the Okefenokee Swamp Rim, Georgia. *Journal of American Folklore* 87: 340–56.

Crumrine, N. Ross
1977   *The Mayo Indians of Sonora: a people who refuse to die*. Tucson: University of Arizona Press.

Currier, Richard L.
1974   Themes of interaction in an Aegean Island village. Unpublished Ph.D. dissertation, Department of Anthropology, University of California, Berkeley.

Cutileiro, José
1971   *A Portuguese rural society*. Oxford: Clarendon Press.

Davidson, Levette
1943   Moron stories. *Southern Folklore Quarterly* 7: 101–4.

Davis, Natalie Zemon
1975   *Society and culture in early modern France*. Stanford: Stanford University Press.

Delaney, Janice; Lupton, Mary Jane and Toth, Emily
  1976   *The curse: a cultural history of menstruation.* New York: Dutton.
Dorian, Nancy C.
  1970   A substitute name system in the Scottish Highlands. *American Anthropologist* 72: 303–19.
Douglas, Mary
  1966   *Purity and danger: an analysis of concepts of pollution and taboo.* London: Routledge and Kegan Paul.
  1973   *Natural symbols: explorations in cosmology.* New York: Vintage Books.
Dundes, Alan
  1976   Projection in folklore: a plea for psychoanalytic semiotics. *Modern Language Notes* 91: 1530–33.
Dundes, Alan, and Falassi, Alessandro
  1975   *La terra in piazza: an interpretation of the Palio of Siena.* Berkeley and Los Angeles: University of California Press.
Dundes, Alan; Leach, Jerry W.; and Ozkok, Bora
  1970   The strategy of Turkish boys' verbal dueling rhymes. *Journal of American Folklore* 83: 225–49.
Dwyer, Daily Hilse
  1978   *Images and self-images: male and female in Morocco.* New York: Columbia University Press.

Elworthy, F. T.
  1958   *The evil eye.* New York: Julian Press.
Emerson, John Paret
  1969   Negotiating the serious import of humor. *Sociometry* 32: 169–81.

Farrer, Claire R.
  1975   Women and folklore: images and genres. *Journal of American Folklore* 88: v–xv.
Ferenczi, Sandor
  1955   *Final contributions to the problems and methods of psychoanalysis.* 3 Vols. New York: Basic Books.
Ferguson, George
  1954   *Signs and symbols in Christian art.* London and Oxford: Oxford University Press.
Fernandez, James W.
  1974   The mission of metaphor in expressive culture. *Current Anthropology* 15: 119–33.
  1976   Reflections on looking into mirrors. Paper read at the 75th annual meeting of the American Anthropological Association, November, Washington, D.C.
Firth, Raymond
  1973   *Symbols: public and private.* Ithaca, N.Y.: Cornell University Press.
Foster, George M.

1953   Cofradía and compadrazgo in Spain and Spanish America. *South-western Journal of Anthropology* 9: 1–28.

1955   The fire walkers of San Pedro Manrique, Soria, Spain. *Journal of American Folklore* 68: 325–32.

1964   Speech forms and the perception of social distance in a Spanish-speaking Mexican village. *Southwestern Journal of Anthropology* 20: 107–22.

1967   Peasant society and the image of limited good. In *Peasant society: a reader*, ed. Jack M. Potter, May N. Diaz, and George M. Foster, pp. 300–23. Boston: Little, Brown.

1972   The anatomy of envy: a study in symbolic behavior. *Current Anthropology* 13: 165–202.

Foster, Mary LeCron, and Brandes, Stanley, eds.

1980   *Symbol as sense: new approaches to the analysis of meaning.* New York: Academic Press. In press.

Freeman, Susan T.

1968   Religious aspects of the social organization of a Castilian village. *American Anthropologist* 70: 34–49.

1970   *Neighbors: the social contract in a Castilian hamlet.* Chicago: University of Chicago Press.

Freud, Sigmund

1925   Analysis of a phobia in a five year old boy. In *Collected Papers of Sigmund Freud*. Trans. Alix and James Strachey. Vol. 3: 149–289. London: Hogarth Press Ltd. (Originally published 1909.)

1950   *The interpretation of dreams.* Trans. A. A. Brill. New York: Modern Library. (Originally published 1900.)

1960   *Jokes and their relation to the unconscious.* Trans. and ed. James Strachey. New York: W. W. Norton. (Originally published 1905.)

1963a   Character and anal eroticism. In *Character and culture*. Trans. R. C. McWatters. Pp. 27–33. New York: Collier Books. (Originally published 1908.)

1963b   Humour. In *Character and culture*. Trans. R. C. McWatters. Pp. 263–69. New York: Collier Books. (Originally published 1928.)

Friedl, Ernestine

1964   Lagging emulation in post-peasant society. *American Anthropologist* 66: 569–86.

Fry, William F., Jr.

1968   *Sweet madness: a study of humor.* Palo Alto, Calif.: Pacific Books.

García Lorca, Federico

1974a   *La casa de Bernarda Alba.* In *Obras Completas*, 18th ed., pp. 787–882. Madrid: Aguilar. (Originally published 1936.)

1974b   *Yerma.* In *Obras Completas*. 18th ed., pp. 617–96. Madrid: Aguilar. (Originally published 1934.)

Geertz, Clifford

1973   Deep play: notes on the Balinese cockfight. In *The interpretation of cultures*, pp. 412–53. New York: Basic Books.

Gennep, Arnold van
1935 *Le folklore de la Flandre et du Hainaut Français (department du Nord).* Two volumes. Paris: Maisonneuve.

Gifford, Edward S., Jr.
1958 *The evil eye: studies in the folklore of vision.* New York: Macmillan.

Gilmore, David
1975 *Carnaval* in Fuenmayor: class conflict and social cohesion in an Andalusian town. *Journal of Anthropological Research* 31: 331–49.
1976 Class, culture, and community size in Spain: the relevance of models. *Anthropological Quarterly* 49: 89–106.
1977 The social organization of space: class, cognition, and space in a Spanish town. *American Ethnologist* 4: 437–51.

Gilmore, Margaret M. and Gilmore, David D.
1979 'Machismo': a psychodynamic approach (Spain). *Journal of Psychological Anthropology* 2:281–99.

Glassie, Henry
1975 *All silver and no brass: an Irish Christmas mumming.* Bloomington, Ind.: Indiana University Press.

Glazier, Jack, and Glazier, Phyllis Gorfain
1976 Ambiguity and exchange: the double dimension of Mbeere riddles. *Journal of American Folklore* 89: 189–238.

Gómez-Tabanera, José Manuel
1968a El Curso de la vida humana en el folklore español. In *El folklore español*, ed. José Manuel Gómez-Tabanera, pp. 67–128. Madrid: Instituto Español de la Antropología Aplicada.
1968b Fiestas populares y festejos tradicionales. In *El folklore español*, ed. José Manuel Gómez-Tabanera, pp. 149–216. Madrid: Instituto Español de La Antropología Aplicada.

Guichard, Pierre
1976 *Al-Andalus: estructura antropológica de una sociedad Islámica en Occidente.* Trans. Nico Ancochea. Barcelona: Barral Editores.

Hammond, Peter B.
1964 Mossi joking. *Ethnology* 3: 259–67.

Heck, Jean Olive
1927 Folk poetry and folk criticism as illustrated by Cincinnati children in their singing games and in their thoughts about these games. *Journal of American Folklore* 40: 1–77.

Herr, Richard
1974 *An historical essay on modern Spain.* Berkeley and Los Angeles: University of California Press.

Higueras Arnal, Antonio
1961 *El Alto Guadalquivir: estudio geográfico.* Serie regional, 12. Número general, 29. Zaragoza: Departamento de Geografía Aplicada del Instituto Juan Sebastían Elcano.

Howell, Richard W.

1973   *Teasing relationships.* Addison-Wesley Module in Anthropology, No. 46. Reading, Mass.: Addison-Wesley.

Huizinga, Johan
1955   *Homo ludens: a study of the play element in culture.* Boston: Beacon Press.

Hullum, Jan
1972–73   The "catch" riddle: perspectives from Goffman and Meta-folklore. *Folklore Annual of the University Folklore Association,* Nos. 4 and 5: 52–59.

Instituto Nacional de Estadística
1972   *Censo agrario de España.* Serie A, Primeros resultados. Madrid.

Johnson, Robbie Davis
1973   Folklore and women: a social interactional analysis of the folklore of a Texas madam. *Journal of American Folklore* 86: 211–24.

Jones, Ernest
1949   *Papers on psychoanalysis.* 5th ed. Baltimore: Williams and Wilkins.

Kenny, Michael
1966   *A Spanish tapestry: town and country in Castile.* New York: Harper and Row.

Kirshenblatt-Gimblett, Barbara, ed.
1976   *Speech play: research and resources for the study of linguistic creativity.* Philadelphia: University of Pennsylvania Press.

Koestler, Arthur
1964   *The act of creation: a study of the conscious and unconscious in science and art.* New York: Dell.

LaBarre, Weston
1962   *They shall take up serpents: psychology of the Southern snake-handling cult.* Minneapolis: University of Minnesota Press.

Larrea Palacín, Arcadio de
1968   El teatro popular en España. In *El Folklore español,* ed. José Manuel Gómez-Tabanera, pp. 339–52. Madrid: Instituto Español de Antropología Aplicada.

Legman, Gershon
1971   *Rationale of the dirty joke: an analysis of sexual humor.* 1st ser. New York: Grove Press.
1975   *No laughing matter: rationale of the dirty joke.* 2d ser. New York: Breaking Point Press.

Linz, Juan, and Cazorla, José
1968–1969   Religiosidad y estructura social en Andalucía: la práctica religiosa. *Anales de sociología* 4: 75–96.

Lisón Tolosana, Carmelo
1971   *Antropología social en España.* Madrid: Siglo Veintiuno de España.

Lope de Vega
1969 *Fuente Ovejuna.* William E. Colford, ed. Woodbury, N.Y.: Barron's Educational Series. (Originally published 1619.)

López Ontiveros, Antonio
1974 *Emigración, propiedad y paisaje agrario en la campiña de Córdoba.* Barcelona: Editorial Ariel.

McDowell, Bart
1970 *Gypsies: wanderers of the world.* Washington, D.C.: National Geographic Society.

Maloney, Clarence, ed.
1976 *The evil eye.* New York: Columbia University Press.

Maranda, Elli Köngäs
1971 Theory and practice of riddle analysis. *Journal of American Folklore* 84: 51–61.

Maranda, Elli Köngäs, ed.
1976 *Riddles and riddling. Journal of American Folklore* 89. (A special issue.)

Marinus, Albert
1951 *Le folklore Belge.* 3 vols. Bruxelles: Les Editions Historiques.

Meerloo, Joost A. M.
1971 *Intuition and the evil eye: the natural history of a superstition.* Wassenaar, The Netherlands: Servire.

Mernissi, Fatima
1975 *Beyond the veil: male-female dynamics in a modern Muslim society.* Cambridge, Mass.: Schenkman.

Meurant, René
1960 Géants et monstres d'osier. *Bulletin de la Societé Royale Belge d'Anthropologie et de Préhistoire* 71: 120–55.
1967 Contribution a l'étude des géants processionnels et de cortège dans le nord de la France, la Belgique et les Pays-Bas. *Arts et Traditions Populaires* 15: 119–60.
1969 Morphologie, montage et mode d'animation des géants d'Ath. *Revista de Etnografía* (Lima) 12: 41–58.

Mitchell, Carol A.
1977 The sexual perspective in the appreciation and interpretation of jokes. *Western Folklore* 36: 303–29.

Moreno Navarro, Isidoro
1972 *Propiedad, clases sociales y hermandades en la Baja Andalucía.* Madrid: Siglo Veintiuno.
1974 *Las hermandades Andaluzas: una aproximación desde la antropología.* Seville: University of Seville.

Mt. Pleasant, Myrna
1955 Moron jokes. *New York Folklore Quarterly* 11: 211–12.

Newell, William Wells
1963 *Games and songs of American children.* New York: Dover Publications. (Republication of the edition of 1883.)

Ortega y Gasset, José
1944   *Teoría de Andalucía y otros ensayos.* Madrid: Revista de Occidente.
Ortner, Sherry B.
1973   On key symbols. *American Anthropologist* 75: 1338–46.

Peréz-Díaz, Víctor
1969   *Estructura social del campo y éxodo rural: estudio de un pueblo de Castilla.* Madrid: Editorial Tecnos.
Pitt-Rivers, Julian A.
1971   The people of the Sierra. 2d ed. Chicago: University of Chicago Press.
1977   *The fate of Shechem, or the politics of sex: essays in the anthropology of the Mediterranean.* Cambridge; Cambridge University Press.
Plá Cargol, Joaquín
1947   *Tradiciones, santuarios, y tipismo de las comarcas gerundenses.* Gerona and Madrid: Dalmáu Carles, Pla.

Quintana, Bertha, and Floyd, Louis Gray
1972   *¡Qué Gitano! the Gypsies of southern Spain.* New York: Holt, Rinehart, and Winston.
1976   ¡Que Gitano! Gypsies, tourism, and the new Spanish economy. In *Economic transformation and steady-state values: essays in the ethnography of Spain,* ed. Joseph B. Aceves, Edward C. Hansen, and Gloria Levitas, pp. 9–13. Queens College Publications in Anthropology, No. 2. Flushing, N.Y.: Queens College Press.

Radcliffe-Brown, A. R.
1965   On joking relationships. In *Structure and function in primitive society,* pp. 90–104. New York: Free Press. (Originally published 1940.)
Real Academia Española
1956   *Diccionario de la lengua Española.* 18th ed. Madrid.
Riegelhaupt, Joyce
1973   Festas and padres: the organization of religious action in a Portuguese parish. *American Anthropologist* 75: 835–52.
Rigby, Peter
1968   Joking relationships, kin categories, and clanship among the GoGo. *Africa* 38: 133–55.
Rodríguez Becerra, Salvador
1973   *Etnografía de la vivienda: el aljarafe de Sevilla.* Seville: University of Seville.
Roheim, Geza
1924   Totemism and the fight with the dragon. *International Journal of Psychoanalysis* 5: 407–8.

Rosaldo, Renato I.
  1968 Metaphors of hierarchy in a Mayan ritual. *American Anthropologist* 70: 524–36.
Rowland, Beryl
  1973 *Animals with human faces: a guide to animal symbolism*. Knoxville: University of Tennessee Press.

Sacks, Harvey
  1974 An analysis of the course of a joke's telling in conversation. In *Explorations in the ethnography of speaking*, ed. Richard Bauman and Joel Sherzer, pp. 337–53. London and New York: Cambridge University Press.
Salamone, Frank
  1976 Religion as play: Bori, a friendly "witchdoctor." In *The anthropological study of play: problems and prospects*, ed. David F. Lancy and B. Allen Tindall, pp. 147–56. Cornwall, N.Y.: Leisure Press.
San Román, Teresa
  1975 Kinship, marriage, law and leadership in two urban Gypsy settlements in Spain. In *Gypsies, tinkers and other travellers*, ed. Farnham Rehfisch, pp. 169–99. New York: Academic Press.
  1976 Los dos mundos del Gitano: gitanos y payos. In *Expresiones actuales de la cultura del pueblo*, ed. Carmelo Lisón Tolosana, pp. 142–53. Madrid: Centro de Estudios Sociales del Valle de los Caidos.
Sapir, J. David, and Crocker, J. Christopher, eds.
  1977 *The social use of metaphor: essays on the anthropology of rhetoric*. Philadelphia: University of Pennsylvania Press.
Schieffelin, Edward L.
  1976 *The sorrow of the lonely and the burning of the dancers*. New York: St. Martin's Press.
Schneider, Jane
  1971 Of vigilance and virgins: honor, shame, and access to resources in Mediterranean societies. *Ethnology* 10: 1–24.
Schneider, Jane, and Schneider, Peter
  1976 *Culture and political economy in western Sicily*. New York: Academic Press.
Schwarz, Henry F.
  1976 Modelos dualísticos en la cultura de una comunidad tradicional española. In *Expresiones actuales de la cultura del pueblo*, ed. Carmelo Lisón-Tolosana, pp. 115–40. Madrid: Centro de Estudios del Valle de los Caidos.
Seidenberg, Robert
  1952 The sexual basis of social prejudice. *Psychoanalytic Review* 39: 90–95.
Silverman, Sydel
  1975 *Three bells of civilization: the life of an Italian hill town*. New York: Columbia University Press.

1980   Rituals of inequality: stratification and symbol in Central Italy. In *Social Inequality: Comparative and Developmental Approaches*, ed. Gerald D. Berreman. New York: Academic Press. In press.

Slater, Philip E.
1971   *The glory of Hera: Greek mythology and the Greek family*. Boston: Beacon Press

Sutton-Smith, Brian
1976   A developmental structural account of riddles. In *Speech play: research and resources for the study of linguistic creativity*, ed. Barbara Kirschenblatt-Gimblett, pp. 111–19. Philadelphia: University of Pennsylvania Press.

Thompson, Stith
1957   *Motif-index of folk-literature*. Vol. 4. Bloomington, Ind.: Indiana University Press.

Turner, Victor W.
1967   *The forest of symbols: aspects of Ndembu ritual*. Ithaca: Cornell University Press.
1969   *The ritual process: structure and anti-structure*. Chicago: Aldine.

Vicens Vives, Jaime
1970   *Approaches to the history of Spain*. Trans. Joan Connelly Ullman. Berkeley and Los Angeles: University of California Press.

Warner, Marina
1976   *Alone of all her sex: the myth and cult of the Virgin Mary*. New York: Knopf.

Weigle, Marta
1978   Women as verbal artists: reclaiming the sisters of Enheduanna. *Frontiers: A Journal of Women's Studies* 3: 1–9.

Wiley, Lulu Runsey
1957   *Bible animals: mammals of the Bible*. New York: Vantage Press.

Willeford, William
1969   *The fool and his scepter: a study in clowns and jesters and their audience*. Evanston, Ill.: Northwestern University Press.

Williams, Thomas Rhys
1963   The form and function of Tambunan Dusun riddles. *Journal of American Folklore* 76: 95–110.

Wolf, Eric R.
1969   Society and symbols in Latin Europe and in the Islamic Near East: some comparisons. *Anthropological Quarterly* 42: 287–301.

Wolfenstein, Martha
1954   *Children's humor*. Glencoe, Ill.: Free Press.

Yates, Norris
  1951 Children's folk plays in western Oregon. *Western Folklore* 10:
        55–62.

Zenner, Walter P.
  1970 Jokes and ethnic stereotyping. *Anthropological Quarterly* 43:
        93–113.
Zijderveld, Anton C.
  1968 Jokes and their relation to social reality. *Social Research* 35:
        286–311.

Publications of the American Folklore Society
New Series
General Editor, Marta Weigle